Applying Moral Theories

FIFTH EDITION

Applying Moral Theories

C. E. Harris, Jr.
Texas A & M University

WADSWORTH
CENGAGE Learning™

Australia • Brazil • Japan • Korea • Mexico • Singapore • Spain • United Kingdom • United States

WADSWORTH
CENGAGE Learning·

**Applying Moral Theories,
Fifth Edition**
C. E. Harris

Philosophy Editor: Steve
  Wainwright

Assistant Editor: Lee McCracken

Editorial Assistant: Gina Kessler

Marketing Manager: Worth
  Hawes

Marketing Assistant: Alexandra
  Tran

Project Manager, Editorial
  Production: Rita Jaramillo

Creative Director: Rob Hugel

Art Director: Maria Epes

Print Buyer: Barbara Britton

Permissions Editor: Kiely Sisk

Production Service: ITC, Deepa
  Ghosh

Copy Editor: Kevin Broccoli

Cover Designer: Matt
  Lagomarsino

Compositor: International
  Typesetting and Composition

© 2007 Wadsworth, Cengage Learning

For product information and
technology assistance, contact us at **Cengage Learning
Customer & Sales Support, 1-800-354-9706**

For permission to use material from this text or product,
submit all requests online at **www.cengage.com/permissions**
Further permissions questions can be emailed to
permissionrequest@cengage.com

Library of Congress Control Number: 2005938477

ISBN-13: 978-0-495-00705-0

ISBN-10: 0-495-00705-6

Wadsworth
20 Davis Drive
Belmont, CA 94002
USA

Cengage Learning is a leading provider of customized learning solutions with office locations around the globe, including Singapore, the United Kingdom, Australia, Mexico, Brazil, and Japan. Locate your local office at **www.cengage.com/global**

Cengage Learning products are represented in Canada by Nelson Education, Ltd.

To learn more about Wadsworth, visit
www.cengage.com/wadsworth

Purchase any of our products at your local college store or at our preferred online store **www.cengagebrain.com**

Printed in the United States of America
2 3 4 5 6   19 18 17 16 15

Contents

v

Chapter 3
Moral Theories   38

Chapter 4
The Ethics of Self-Interest   63

Chapter 5

The Ethics of Natural Law 88

Chapter 6
The Ethics of Utilitarianism   120

Chapter 7
The Ethics of Respect for Persons   153

Chapter 8

Virtue Ethics   192

Preface

The premise of *Applying Moral Theories* is that, despite the increasing interest in applied ethics, relatively little has been done to make ethical theory more accessible to students and more easily applicable to moral problems. This text was envisioned as a unique attempt to remedy this defect. Some of the special features that aid in this attempt are the following:

1. A common outline format is used to present each theory, facilitating comparisons.
2. Concept summaries are provided at the end of the shorter chapters and at crucial junctures in the longer chapters.
3. A checklist provides specific directions for applying each theory to moral problems.
4. Examples are used throughout the text, and the checklists are followed in applying each theory to several cases.
5. The same criteria of evaluation are applied to every theory, again facilitating comparison.
6. Appendix II provides 33 cases for classroom discussion and student analysis.

The most important improvement to *Applying Moral Theories* in the fifth edition is a thoroughly revised and considerably expanded chapter on virtue ethics. This is essentially a new chapter and it includes new sections on the ethics of Aristotle and feminist ethics. I have also added 11 new cases in the appendix and eliminated some of the cases from the fourth edition. In addition, I have combined the two chapters on metaethics into one chapter and eliminated material, which some reviewers said, was tedious to students. In another change, I have added a section on common morality at the beginning of the chapter on moral theory and argued that the various moral theories are simply vantage points from which to view that amorphous and complex stock of ideas that we call common morality. I stress in this chapter and in Appendix I, that no theory fully succeeds in adequately capturing all of common morality and that there is no need to adopt one single theory to resolve all moral problems. Sometimes one theory is more useful and sometimes another, and sometimes it is useful to look at a difficult moral issue from the standpoint of several theories.

The reader should keep several considerations in mind. First, this book is on moral theory, albeit oriented toward application. The discussions of particular cases are not intended to be full-scale treatments but, rather, short examples showing how the theories can be applied and illustrating some of the problems encountered in application. Their primary purpose is to illustrate methodological problems rather than definitively resolve difficult moral issues. Students should be encouraged to look at the case analyses critically and to identify factual, conceptual, and moral assumptions that might lead them to different conclusions.

Second, the chapter on egoism differs in some ways from the usual treatment of egoism. I present a version of egoism in which pursuit of self-interest is bounded by moral constraints. I believe this version of egoism has several advantages. One advantage is that it is a form of egoism that moral philosophers are probably more willing to call a genuinely "moral" position, because its adherent would more than likely be willing to universalize this form of egoism. Another advantage is that this version of egoism is probably a more plausible position for students and others who are attracted to the ethics of self-interest. I have often been impressed by the implausible nature of many standard philosophical versions of egoism. Few of us would be willing to pursue self-interest at any cost, but many people seem to be attracted to the idea that self-interest should be the most important positive motivating force in their lives. Lest the reader be tempted to say that this is not "really" egoism, it is worth keeping in mind that even this morally constrained version of egoism excludes many other-regarding actions that many of us would consider obligatory.

Third, the chapter on the ethics of respect for persons should not be taken as a strict version of Kantian moral theory. Many scholars would say that my use of what Kant would call the "contradiction in conception" test is not Kant's, and I do not use Kant's "contradiction in the will" test at all. My interpretation of the means-ends principle owes as much to Alan Gewirth as to Kant. I nevertheless believe that the chapter gives a reasonably clear presentation of a deontological position that still owes much to Kant.

Fourth, the book is more sympathetic to newer trends in applied ethics than might be immediately apparent. Some philosophers believe that there is no place for the standard moral theories in "applied" or "practical" ethics. If they are rule ethicists at all, they believe that applied ethics should be concerned with applying moral rules and principles to practical problems, without attempting to trace the rules and principles back to more fundamental theories. I still believe that appeal to more general theories and to moral standards is useful in applied ethics, but I am also sympathetic to the claim that such an appeal is often not necessary for resolving many moral problems. I have addressed some of the problems in applying lower-level moral principles in the section, Problems in Applying Moral Principles, in Chapter 3. I and my co-authors have given a treatment of casuistry, one of the most popular of the non-theory approaches, in *Engineering Ethics: Concepts and Cases*, also published by Wadsworth.*

I want to thank all of those who have encouraged and assisted me in the five editions of this book. For the fifth edition, in addition to the reviewers, special thanks goes to Mr. David Wiens, who researched and prepared most of the new cases.

C. E. Harris, Jr.

---

*Charles E. Harris, Jr., Michael S. Pritchard, & Michael J. Rabins, *Engineering Ethics: Concepts and Cases*, 3rd ed. Belmont, CA: Wadsworth, 2005.

Applying Moral Theories

WHAT IS ETHICS?

Patrick Thomas was in a quandary. A major customer of his company, Maine-based Bath Iron Works, had asked the boat builder to participate in a secret investigation of one of its suppliers. Thomas, the purchasing manager, knew that the customer was important to Bath's survival, but he still was not sure how to handle the request. So he went to the company's ethics officer, who discussed the problem with the chief executive. Within 12 hours, Bath had decided it would not participate in the investigation unless the supplier was informed of it. The customer eventually accepted Bath's decision.[1]

This story illustrates the way many firms are introducing ethics into their corporate culture. According to a 1994 survey by the Washington-based Ethics Resource Center, 60 percent of the firms surveyed have codes of ethics, 33 percent have training in business conduct, and 33 percent have an ethics office where employees can receive advice or report questionable business activities.

Observers cite several reasons for the trend. One reason is that some executives believe a common core of values can keep companies together. Global business and the diversity of backgrounds, even within our own country, increase the need to agree on company values. Another reason is that federal sentencing guidelines now require federal judges to take into account whether firms have strong ethics programs, when issuing sentences for corporate wrongdoing.

In business, government, the professions, and private life, ethics is "in." It is now more acceptable to talk about ethics than it was a few years ago. Many people, however, still find it difficult to think clearly about ethical issues. They consider ethical discussions "soft" or "ambiguous" or

---

[1] "'Business Ethics' Is Not an Oxymoron at Some Companies," *Salt Lake Tribune*, April 16, 1995.

"nebulous"—lacking in clarity and rigor. Here is the paradox: Ethics is enormously important but difficult to think about clearly and responsibly.

This book should help you overcome this paradox. When you have finished reading it, you should be able to think more clearly and responsibly about ethical questions. In the first four chapters, we shall discuss the nature and validity of ethics and the structure and evaluation of a moral theory. Then we will consider five moral philosophies that are especially influential in our society. These philosophies are (1) *egoism,* the theory that everyone should do what is in his or her self-interest; (2) *natural law,* the theory that one should do what is in accord with human nature; (3) *utilitarianism,* the theory that one should do what leads to the greatest overall human welfare; (4) *the ethics of respect for persons,* the theory that one should act in a way that respects the equal dignity of all human beings; and (5) *virtue ethics,* the theory that what is right is what a virtuous person would do in the circumstances. You will see how these philosophies are applied to particular examples, and you will receive guidelines for applying them to new situations.

This first chapter is devoted to clarifying concepts. In applying ethical theory to moral problems, it is important to think as precisely as possible. Our discussion will move from broader issues to more specific ones. First, we shall differentiate the three major issues in a moral problem: factual issues, conceptual issues, and moral issues. Then we shall focus on moral statements and distinguish them from other types of statements that express value judgments. Finally, we shall narrow the focus still further to consider some distinctions and concepts within the realm of moral discourse. We shall conclude with an example to which the concepts we have discussed can be applied.

THREE TYPES OF CLAIMS MADE IN MORAL ARGUMENTS

On January 17, 1912, Captain Robert Falcon Scott and his four companions reached the South Pole. Then, hauling their sleigh, they began the 800-mile walk back to their base camp on McMurdo Sound. They died 100 miles short of their destination, and Captain Scott's diary, found with their bodies the following spring, tells a story of heroism that still fires the imagination.

One of the men in the party, Capt. L. E. G. Oates, became frostbitten. He suffered terribly for weeks and realized he was slowing the party's march, thereby increasing their peril. On March 10, Oates asked the physician in the party, Dr. Wilson, whether he had a chance to survive. The physician said he did not know, but Captain Scott says in his diary that, in fact, Oates had no chance of surviving the march. Scott remarks that he doubts whether the party could make it to safety in any event, but he concluded that they might have "a dog's chance" if Oates were not present.

A few days later Captain Oates said he could not go on and proposed that they leave him in his sleeping bag. The party refused and finally induced him to come on the afternoon march. He struggled a few miles, and that night he was still worse. Captain Scott gives this account of Oates's death:

> This was the end. He slept through the night before last, hoping not to wake; but he woke in the morning-yesterday. It was blowing a blizzard. He said, "I am just going outside and may be some time." He went out into the blizzard and we have not seen him since.

Scott remarks a few lines later:

> We knew that poor Oates was walking to his death, but though we tried to dissuade him, we knew it was the act of a brave man and an Englishman.[2]

One of the members of the party, Edgar Evans, had already died at the foot of Beardmore Glacier. The other three members of the party, Scott, Wilson, and Bowers, died in their tent of cold and starvation, prevented by the blizzard from struggling the last 11 miles to One Ton Depot, where they would have found food and fuel.

In determining whether Captain Oates's action was morally right, you must consider three kinds of issues: factual, conceptual, and moral. They are the same types of issues that come up in most moral discussions.

Factual Issues

Some questions of fact are relevant to the case. One question is whether Oates's removal from the party would have made a significant difference in the others' chances for survival. Scott thought Oates's absence might increase the chances of survival a little, but not very much. Perhaps Oates thought that, because the party's chances for survival were virtually nil with him along, this difference was important. Another question has to do with Oates's true motives. Was his action motivated primarily by the desire to give Scott, Wilson, and Bowers a better chance at survival, or was it primarily motivated by the desire to end his own suffering? Given the strong sense of loyalty that the members of the party had to one another, we can probably say that the primary motive was the former.

---

[2]See Ann Savors (ed.), *Scott's Last Voyage* (New York: Praeger, 1975), p. 155.

Almost every moral problem raises some unanswered questions of fact that are relevant to the resolution of the problem. To decide on the morality of capital punishment, we need to know whether it deters crime. To decide on the proper distribution of wealth in our country, we must know the current distribution of wealth. We also must know how many people are poor and to what extent a policy of wealth redistribution would affect the incentive to produce wealth. To decide whether restrictions should be placed on advertising to children, we must find out whether children can distinguish between advertising "hype" or "puffery" and genuine factual claims. To decide on the morality of premarital sex, we must know whether the widespread practice of sex outside of marriage would lead to better or worse sexual adjustment and to what extent it would contribute to unwanted pregnancies and the spread of AIDS and other sexually transmitted infections.

Sometimes the major issue in what we would ordinarily call a "moral" debate is really a controversy over the facts. Two people may agree on the relevant moral principles but still reach different conclusions because they hold different beliefs about the relevant facts. For example, you and I might agree on the moral principle that reverse discrimination is justifiable if it is the only way to end the effects of past discrimination. You might believe, however, that no other method will eliminate the effects of past discrimination on women and minorities, and I might believe that an immediate end to discriminatory practices is sufficient. In this case, you and I would disagree about whether to adopt a policy of reverse discrimination, even though we agreed on moral principles.

It is important to keep in mind that disputes over the facts can be just as interminable and difficult to settle as any dispute over moral principles. One of the problems we face in determining our obligations to future generations with respect to the use of nonrenewable natural resources such as oil is that we cannot predict what the needs of future generations will be. Perhaps sources of energy yet to be discovered will drastically reduce the need for oil, but, of course, it is impossible to know the future. Similarly, we cannot know for sure what the long-term effects of the widespread practice of sex outside marriage would be. Insofar as moral judgments depend on factual premises that cannot be known with certainty, these judgments cannot be known with certainty.

Conceptual Issues

Was Captain Oates's act an instance of suicide? The answer depends on our definition of suicide. We might propose to label suicide as any action in which a person does something he knows will end his own life. But this definition is implausible because it would mean that a religious martyr who chooses to die rather than renounce her faith is a suicide, and we do not usually call martyrs suicides. Rather, we say that they held to their faith in the face of persecution and that death was an unfortunate, undesired consequence of their steadfast faith.

Can something similar be said of Captain Oates? Was his action primarily intended to increase the chances of survival of his companions, or was his death only an unfortunate and unintended (even if foreknown) consequence of his action? The answers depend on the extent to which Captain Oates's action was motivated by the desire to end his own suffering. The fact that he proposed ending his life only when he could not travel further strongly suggests that his motive was not self-interest.

The question about the definition of suicide is a typical conceptual issue. Conceptual issues have to do with (1) the meaning of a concept and (2) whether the concept applies or "fits" in a particular situation. We might consider them to be issues involving a definition and its application. Conceptual issues are important in many, but not all, moral debates.

Conceptual issues differ from factual and moral issues; they cannot be settled by an appeal to facts or moral standards. However, one can argue that one definition is better than another and whether the concept, so defined, fits a particular situation. This type of argument can appeal to many considerations, such as our intuitive sense of how a word or concept should be used or the convenience of using one definition rather than another. Sometimes factual and moral considerations are also relevant in arguments about definitions.

Conceptual issues are sometimes crucial in a moral debate. The debate over abortion is probably the best example. Is the fetus a person? The answer depends on how we define *person* and whether the fetus fits this definition. The issue cannot be decided by an appeal to medical facts or moral principles alone, but the answer is nevertheless crucial to the abortion debate.

When we consider the morality of bombing civilian populations in wartime, we encounter another conceptual issue. Many moralists believe it is wrong to kill innocent people directly, but this raises the question whether civilian populations are innocent. Are people innocent as long as they are not in uniform or not directly connected with the war effort? Does it make any difference whether the civilians live in a democracy, where they have some voice in governmental actions, or in a totalitarian state, where they do not?

Conceptual issues are often prominent in business ethics. We can certainly hold individual managers responsible for their actions, but does it make sense to say that a corporation is a morally responsible agent? Corporations are like human beings in some important ways: they pay taxes, they have general policies that guide their action, and they have procedures for arriving at those policies. Yet they are also unlike individuals in that they have an indefinite life, and they can only carry out their policies through the actions of individual human beings. Are they enough like human beings to be held morally accountable for their actions?

Another issue in business ethics that involves a conceptual issue is the scope of the concept of bribery. American law sometimes allows U.S. corporations to pay extortion, when it is necessary, for example, to buy "protection" of corporate property in a foreign country. But bribery is illegal and usually considered immoral. Where does extortion end and bribery begin? When an American company pays a fee so that its products will be considered for purchase (but not necessarily chosen) by a foreign government official, this behavior is often thought of as bribery, but a good case can be made that it should be regarded as payment of extortion. Again, paying a fee to a foreign official to expedite the consideration of one's application to do business might be considered bribery, but perhaps it should be considered an extortion payment instead.

Finally, recent advances in medical technology have brought forward the need for a redefinition of death. Formerly, permanent cessation of vital signs was a sufficiently reliable criterion for death. Modern technology, however, has made it possible for people to be kept "alive" in the sense that their vital organs are functioning, even though they are not conscious. What should be done with "permanently vegetative" patients depends to a considerable extent on whether we consider them "dead." A conceptual issue is thus at the center of the controversy.

Moral Issues

Some issues in a moral problem involve genuine disagreements over moral principles. If Captain Oates's action was a genuine suicide, was it morally right? Captain Scott records in his diary that Dr. Wilson had morphine in his medical supplies and that the members of the party debated whether they should end their lives with morphine or wait to die naturally. Would it have been morally wrong to have taken the morphine? The Judeo-Christian tradition has held that genuine suicide is immoral, although many acts that will almost certainly end in one's death are morally per-missible. One of the traditional grounds for this belief is that life is a gift of the Creator and that a human being should not take his or her life before the Creator takes it. By contrast, some existentialist philosophers argue that the ability to take one's life is the supreme manifestation of personal freedom. What other considerations are relevant to the morality of suicide? How would you decide the issue?

Moral questions are, of course, the most characteristic feature of moral debates. You can probably easily call to mind some of the moral issues suggested by the other examples. If the fetus is considered a person, is an abortion still sometimes permissible? If civilians are believed to be innocent, is killing them permissible if greater numbers of innocent people can thereby be saved? Does the state have a right to prohibit people from smoking marijuana, even if it is harmful, as long as they know what they are doing? Here we have arrived at the very heart of a moral discussion.

The first step in facing a moral problem is to distinguish the factual, conceptual, and moral issues. You will often find that, in a discussion of a moral problem, people are not sufficiently aware of the differences among these three kinds of issues. Thus, they are also not aware of the important differences among the methods for resolving them. Factual issues are resolved—when they can be resolved—by empirical investigation. Conceptual issues are resolved by determining the meaning and applicability of a concept. Moral issues are resolved by appealing to moral principles or standards. Now we shall look more closely at the nature of moral principles as they are embodied in moral statements.

THE NATURE OF MORAL STATEMENTS

We all have some intuitive knowledge of what ethics is. We make ethical statements every day. We may, however, still find ourselves unable to describe ethics successfully. We shall focus on the nature of ethics by looking at the nature of ethical statements. We begin by considering a class of statements to which moral statements belong—namely, normative statements.

Normative versus Factual Statements

To understand the nature of ethical statements, we must first distinguish between normative statements and factual statements. A *normative statement* expresses a value judgment of some kind, and its correctness is determined by reference to a norm or standard. Here are some examples of normative statements and the standards used to determine their correctness:

Normative Statement	Type of Confirmation
"Picasso is a great painter."	Aesthetic standard
"Do not use a singular subject with a plural verb."	Grammatical standard
"It is illegal to omit this item from your tax statement."	Legal standard
"You should not lie to your father like that."	Moral standard
"Stand when a lady comes into the room."	Standard of etiquette

In contrast to normative statements, *factual statements* make claims that can be confirmed or disconfirmed by experiment, observation, or research. In the following list, factual statements are paired with the type of experiment, observation, or research that could confirm them:

Factual Statement	Type of Confirmation
"George Washington was the first president of the United States."	Historical research
"The sun is shining."	Observation
"Water is composed of two parts hydrogen and one part oxygen."	Scientific research
"The law you are violating in omitting this income from your statement was passed by Congress in 1978."	Legal research

The distinction between the way normative statements are confirmed (by appeal to a standard) and the way factual statements are confirmed (by appeal to experiment, observation, or research) is of great significance. Indeed, the distinction leads to an important question about the justification of moral statements. Most of us feel more comfortable with factual statements because we are better able to determine whether they are true or false. But how do we confirm normative statements?

An Important Corollary

We shall adopt the rule that normative statements, including moral statements, cannot be confirmed by appeal to factual statements alone. A normative statement must always be assumed along with the factual statement to produce the normative statement we are trying to confirm.

Let us take a simple example to illustrate this claim. We shall use the type of normative statements in which we are most interested—namely, ethical statements. Consider the following argument:

The wealth of the United States is at present unevenly distributed among its citizens.

Therefore, the present distribution of wealth in the United States is morally wrong.

The first sentence is a simple statement of fact. An economist could determine whether it is true by scientific means. The second sentence is an ethical statement. Most moral philosophers believe you cannot derive the second statement from the first without assuming a moral statement. So let us add the statement:

An uneven distribution of wealth in a country is wrong.

You may or may not agree with this moral statement; in fact, most people would probably not agree with it. The important point is that the statement must be presupposed for the argument to work, so the complete argument now is as follows:

The wealth of the United States is at present unevenly distributed among its citizens.

An uneven distribution of wealth in a country is wrong.

Therefore, the present distribution of wealth in the United States is morally wrong.

Moral philosophers have different ideas about the relationship of moral statements to factual statements, and what we have given here is an illustration rather than a proof. Nevertheless, we shall assume hereafter that a moral statement cannot be derived from a factual statement.

This assumption has important implications for ethical argumentation. You cannot justify an ethical claim by an appeal to facts alone. Therefore, if you attempt to support an ethical claim exclusively by reference to facts, something will be missing, even if the facts are relevant to the argument. You should examine your argument to find the ethical assumptions implicit in what you say. Then you should state these assumptions clearly and show why you think they are justified.

Some philosophers, primarily those endorsing *ethical naturalism*, hold that moral statements can be derived from factual statements alone, thereby apparently denying our rule. For example, we shall see shortly that advocates of natural law moral philosophy hold that the "natural inclinations" of human beings to engage in certain types of behavior, such as procreation, provide the basis for moral statements. These claims, however, are controversial and introduce confusion in an elementary discussion of moral reasoning. So we shall assume that there must always be a moral statement in an argument that has a moral conclusion. In the case of natural law, we shall say that an argument from a natural inclination, such as the tendency of humans to procreate, yields the conclusion that pro-creation is good only if we assume a principle such as, "The natural inclinations of human beings provide moral guides for conduct."

Characteristics of Ethical Statements

Now that we have distinguished normative statements from factual statements and drawn an important corollary from this distinction, we must focus more closely on moral statements. How do they differ from other normative statements, such as those in aesthetics or etiquette? How do they differ from nonnormative statements with which they have some similarities, such as those in religion? Moral philosophers have not been able to find any single characteristic that is unique to moral statements, but they have identified several characteristics that, when taken together, give a good description of moral statements.

Prescription of Conduct   Moral statements prescribe conduct. This criterion distinguishes moral statements from aesthetic statements. The statement that Picasso was a great painter does not explicitly give direction to behavior, whereas the statement that we should not lie to our parents does—but this criterion is not enough to distinguish moral statements from all others. For example, the statement that we should knock before entering a room also prescribes a certain type of conduct, although we would not classify it as a moral statement.

Impartiality   Moral or ethical statements are based on impartial con-siderations. Philosophers sometimes say that moral standards are based on the reasons that an "ideal observer" or an "impartial spectator" would accept. If we want to make a genuine ethical claim, we must not allow our personal needs to dictate what we call right or wrong. Moral statements are not supposed to advance the interests of one person or group exclu-sively but rather to take a universal view in which each person's interests count the same. The implied impartiality of moral statements accounts at least in part for their power. If a moral statement were a mere expression of my own interest, others would have no reason to pay any special attention to it. After all, my interests and yours might not be the same. But, if a moral judgment is genuinely impartial, it stands to reason that you should pay attention to what I say, because you should make the same judgment in the same circumstances.

　　Keep in mind that some apparent exceptions to this point are not really exceptions when they are properly understood. For example, a request to be treated in a certain way does not necessarily violate the requirement of impartiality. Suppose I am a clerk in a bank that is being robbed. I say to the robber who is holding a gun in my face, "You should not kill me. I don't deserve to die." Although I am making a statement about killing that applies directly only to me, I am implicitly saying that no one else should be killed in similar circumstances either. Thus, the requirement of impartiality has not been violated. Similarly, if I say, "It is wrong for you to have done that to me," I intend to convey the idea that even you would consider your action wrong if you looked at it impartially. But impartiality alone does not distinguish moral statements from most other normative statements. The rules of etiquette and grammar should be applied impartially. Therefore, we must look for other characteristics.

Overriding Importance   Moral statements are generally thought to have a particularly serious or overriding importance. Compare the moral statement "You should not lie to your father" with the other normative statements given earlier. A violation of the moral rule against lying is more important than a violation of a rule of etiquette or the rules of grammar. Similarly, a moral judgment is more important than an aesthetic judgment, and ultimately moral statements are more important than statements about law.

Most moral and political philosophers in the Western tradition have argued that laws must be evaluated by moral standards. Something is not right simply because it is the law. The belief that laws can be immoral and that moral considerations override legal ones is the foundation of the tradition of civil disobedience. But some people say that religious statements, especially the direct commands of God, override even ethical statements. When Abraham in the Hebrew Bible was told to sacrifice his son, he believed that this command superseded even ethical prohibitions against killing the innocent. Thus, some people do not see overriding importance as a unique characteristic of moral statements.

Independence of Arbitrary Authority   Moral statements cannot be established or changed by the decisions of authoritative bodies, nor can their truth be established by a mere appeal to consensus or tradition. That it is impolite to enter a room without knocking is a matter of tradition and consensus, as are the rules of grammar to some extent. But we can always question majority opinion or tradition in a matter of ethics. We can concede to the French Academy the right to determine proper French usage, but we have more difficulty imagining an institution that determines moral propriety. Even religious institutions do not claim to determine morality by decree but rather to interpret divine law, which exists independently of the institutions. But again this characteristic is not unique to morality. The validity of factual statements is also independent of arbitrary decrees. In addition, many philosophers and artists claim that it is possible to argue rationally about aesthetic judgments, so these judgments are not arbitrary either.

Thus, we see that none of the four characteristics is unique to moral statements. Taken together, however, they give a good description of the nature of ethical or moral statements or of the moral standards from which these statements are derived. We shall refer to these characteristics from time to time in the following chapters, especially in our evaluation of a moral theory. The failure of a moral theory to do justice to one of these four criteria must be taken as a mark against the theory.

CONCEPTS IN ETHICAL DISCOURSE

Before we consider additional examples, we should focus on some concepts and distinctions within ethical discourse itself. Two pairs of terms are of special importance. First, many ethical theorists see an important distinction between consequentialist and nonconsequentialist theories. These theorists believe that all moral philosophies can be classified into one of these categories and that this distinction is vitally important in understanding the nature of ethical theories.

In *consequentialist moral theories,* actions, persons, or motives are morally judged solely according to the nature of their consequences, particularly for the production of some good. The two consequentialist theories that we shall consider are egoism and utilitarianism. Roughly, *egoism,* at least in its most common version, holds that actions are to be judged by the extent to which they promote a person's self-interest. *Utilitarianism* states that actions are to be judged by the extent to which they promote the welfare of humanity in general. Thus, in the case of egoism, the good is self-interest; in the case of utilitarianism, the good is the welfare of humanity in general.

Nonconsequentialist theories of ethics, at least in their more common versions, hold that actions, persons, or motives are to be judged not directly by their consequences but by their conformity to moral rules. Of course, the consequences of actions are important here too, but only as these consequences conform to certain moral rules. What these rules are depends on the particular nonconsequentialist moral theory in question. The two nonconsequentialist theories that we shall consider are natural law and the ethics of respect for persons.

In *natural law,* the supreme moral rule or standard might be stated as "Act in a way that conforms to the natural inclinations of human beings."

As we shall see, these natural inclinations include the tendency to preserve one's life, produce children, be a part of a social group, and develop one's uniquely human intellectual faculties.

In the *ethics of respect for persons*, the supreme rule or standard might be stated as "Act in a way that respects equally the dignity of every human being." Respecting the equal dignity of human beings requires that actions should be judged by whether they treat human beings as free moral agents who can order their lives by their own purposes and values.

Most of us are naturally inclined to look to consequences as a way of determining the moral acceptability of an action. "What better way," we might say, "do we have of determining what we ought to do than by looking at the consequences of various alternatives?" Nevertheless, we shall see that the consequentialist approach has severe problems. Furthermore, Hebrew-Christian morality is basically nonconsequentialist, so that consequentialism is contrary to the most influential Western tradition in morality. The controversy between consequentialist and nonconsequentialist moralities is one of the most important issues in contemporary ethics.

The second pair of terms we shall define is *right* and *good*, probably the most commonly used ethical words. Two contrasts between these words are worth noting:

1. Goodness can be thought of in degrees, but rightness cannot. Something is either right or not right, whereas an action can be good, better, or the very best thing to do in the circumstances. The word *good* can denote anything from merely morally acceptable to highly morally praiseworthy.
2. *Good* refers to a wider range of phenomena than *right* does. *Good* refers to actions and the motives of actions, but it can also describe persons or things. *Right*, on the other hand, refers primarily to actions. We can speak of good people and good things, as well as good actions and good intentions, but we cannot substitute "He is a right man" for "He is a good man." Nor can we say that knowledge or courage is *right*, although we can say either is *good*.

Moral philosophers have long debated the meaning of *right* and *good*. Following one influential tradition in contemporary moral philosophy, we shall use the word *good* as a general term of moral commendation. Thus, to say that a person or an action is *good* is to commend morally the person or action.

Right, as we have seen, usually has the more restricted meaning of "morally obligatory" or at least "morally permissible," as applied to actions.

Because *right* does have special reference to actions, we shall use *right* in the formulation of moral standards, the fundamental criteria for determining what is morally permissible and impermissible for any given moral philosophy. Thus, the moral standard will usually read "Those actions are right that . . ."

We have distinguished moral statements from factual statements and from other types of normative statements. We have also defined some important concepts within the sphere of ethical discourse itself. Now let us look at a case that uses the concepts we have discussed. Remember that we are concerned with identifying the issues in the case, not with resolving them.

A Burn Victim's Desire to Die

In July 1973, an unmarried 26-year-old man, whom we shall call James, was severely burned when he and his father set off an explosion from a leaky propane gas pipeline.[3] The father died before reaching the hospital, and James sustained second- and third-degree burns over two-thirds of his body. He is now blind in both eyes, although he might possibly be able to recover sight in one eye. After nine months of treatment, the tips of his fingers have been amputated, his hands are useless, he cannot get out of bed by himself, and the burns are still not healed. To keep the open burns from becoming infected, James must be immersed daily in a bath of antiseptic solution. The baths are preceded by injections that make James unconscious, but the dressing of the burns after his bath is still quite painful.

James is an intelligent and articulate young man. He has persistently pleaded to be allowed to leave the hospital and go home to die. He says that he will not wait to die a natural death from the infection that would begin in the open burns but would take measures to end his own life. He has recently refused permission for further surgery on his hands.

The physicians called in a consulting psychiatrist to have James declared incompetent, but the psychiatrist has concluded that James is rational. James's argument for wanting to end his life is that he can no longer do what he most enjoys, so his life will no longer be meaningful. He has been an active person, participating in sports and other outdoor activities. He does not find enough value in living blind and as a cripple to make it worthwhile to

---

[3]Adapted from Robert B. White, "A Demand to Die," *Hastings Center Report* 5 (June 1975), pp. 9–10. See also videotape, "Please Let Me Die," by Robert B. White. Used with permission.

endure the painful treatments and the problems of adjusting to a new life-style. James has asked the psychiatrist to help him get out of the hospital, so he can go home and die. Should the psychiatrist honor James's request? Let us apply the concepts discussed in this chapter.

Factual Issues

The psychiatrist must answer a number of factual questions before she can make a decision. One of the questions is whether James could adjust to his new lifestyle. James says he would never find life worth living as a person with disabilities, but the psychiatrist has access to histories of other victims of catastrophes and will want to determine on his own James's prospects for future happiness. The psychiatrist will also want to know the law governing these situations. What can she do legally without incurring unacceptable liabilities for herself or the hospital? You may think of other factual issues that are important in the case.

Conceptual Issues

Two important conceptual issues arise in the case. The first is whether this proposed action should be called *suicide.* Because James wants to end his life by some direct means and out of concern for his own well-being, most people would consider his action to be suicide.

The second question, which is more difficult, has to do with the concept of rationality. Is James rational enough to make such a serious decision about his own future? The psychiatrist has to have a clear concept of what she means by *rationality* before she can answer this question. Of course, factual issues can be raised here as well. The psychiatrist might have a clear concept of what it means to act rationally but still be puzzled about whether James's behavior falls under the definition. If she defines *rationality* as involving, among other things, making decisions on the grounds of all available evidence, she might still wonder whether James fully understands the degree to which he will be able to manage his own affairs at home. Nevertheless, having a clear concept of rationality is an important first step in determining whether James is rational.

Moral Issues

This case has two important moral issues. One is the morality of killing oneself. This question is especially interesting because James is not dying. Given sufficient time, the burns will heal and James will be sent home. He should be able to live out his normal life span, even though he will be handicapped. The second issue has to do with the obligations and pre-rogatives of the psychiatrist. Does the psychiatrist have an obligation to help James get out of the hospital? Does she have an obligation to help James end his life if she is asked to assist? Does she have the right to try to keep James in the hospital if she thinks James is not rational? Does she have the right to try to keep James in the hospital if she disagrees with James's decision to end his life, even if she believes James is rational?

Moral and Factual Statements

Recall that moral conclusions do not follow directly from the facts of the case. For example, the fact that James will recover and can eventually be sent home does not necessarily mean that taking his own life would be wrong, although this consideration is relevant to the issue. The fact that the psychiatrist is prevented by law from directly administering a lethal injection to James at his request does not settle the question of whether she should morally be allowed to do so. The fact that the psychiatrist may be opposed to all forms of suicide does not necessarily mean that she should act to prevent James from killing himself.

Characteristics of Moral Statements

The moral questions at stake seem to exhibit the four characteristics of moral statements. First, the answers given to the moral questions at issue prescribe the conduct that James and his psychiatrist should follow. The statement that it is wrong for James to commit suicide implies that James should not take any measures to end his own life. The conclusion that the psychiatrist has an obligation to help James get out of the hospital implies that she should take steps to achieve the goal.

Second, the moral statements made about this case are ordinarily made from an impersonal standpoint. If we are making judgments about the case from an observer's perspective, this impersonal standpoint can be assumed. But, even if we take the psychiatrist's standpoint, we would presumably ask what should be done based on her moral and professional obligation. Self-interest is not a legitimate consideration unless it would apply to any other psychiatrist in the same situation. If injecting James with a lethal drug would result in the psychiatrist's incarceration, that consideration would appropriately carry some moral weight. But it would carry moral weight with any other psychiatrist in the same situation.

Third, the moral issues have a serious and overriding importance. The moral issues are more important than issues of medical etiquette or the aesthetic questions regarding James's burns. They are even more important than the legal issues in the case, because we might conclude that the laws should be changed to accommodate our moral beliefs about what should be done.

Fourth, the issues cannot be settled merely by an appeal to authority, consensus, or tradition. Deciding whether it is wrong for James to take his own life or whether the psychiatrist should help James take his life involves more than taking a vote or determining how the issue would have been decided in the past.

Concepts in Moral Philosophy

We can look at this problem from either a consequentialist or a nonconsequentialist perspective. An egoist would ask about the consequences of the alternatives for James's or the psychiatrist's self-interest. A utilitarian would ask about the consequences for the general human welfare. Nonconsequentialists, such as natural law theorists and advocates of the ethics of respect for persons, would approach the issues differently. They would ask whether James's or his psychiatrist's actions were in accordance with human nature or the respect due human individuals. We shall leave the steps of this determination for another time; the important point is that the consequences of alternative actions are not the decisive point. For example, by the standards of natural law, James should not kill himself, even if the remainder of his life produces no benefit for him or anyone else.

Finally, in a discussion of the case, we would use the terms *good* or *bad*, intending thereby to commend or condemn the actions, motives, or people involved. We would also refer to the actions of the people involved as right or wrong, intending thereby to classify them as morally obligatory, merely morally permissible, or morally impermissible. The concepts and distinctions we have discussed in this first chapter, then, are an important part of a clear analysis of moral problems.

CONCEPT SUMMARY

An important part of ethics is making distinctions. When analyzing a moral problem, you should first distinguish between questions of fact, questions involving the definitions and applications of concepts, and questions that directly appeal to moral principles.

Moral statements themselves are a type of normative statement, as are statements in such areas as aesthetics, etiquette, law, and grammar.

Normative statements differ from factual statements in that normative statements make value judgments that appeal to norms. Most moral philosophers believe that moral statements cannot be derived from factual statements. An important corollary of this belief is that moral statements cannot be justified by an appeal to facts. This point is important in moral arguments.

Several characteristics, taken together, give a good description of moral statements. Moral statements prescribe conduct, they are based on impartial considerations, they have overriding importance, and they cannot be established by a mere appeal to consensus or tradition.

To understand a moral theory, you must know whether it is a consequentialist theory (one that judges actions, persons, or motives according to their consequences) or a nonconsequentialist theory (one that judges actions, persons, or motives by their conformity to moral rules). Egoism and utilitarianism are consequentialist theories, and natural law and the ethics of respect for persons are nonconsequentialist theories. We shall use the word *good* as a general term of moral commendation and the word *right* to mean "morally obligatory."

MORALITY: RELATIVE OR OBJECTIVE?

For 18 months, Del Monte Corporation tried to buy a 55,000-acre banana plantation in Guatemala, but the government refused to allow the sale. Del Monte officials made inquiries and asked for meetings, but nothing happened. Then they hired a business consultant for $500,000. The consultant was a wealthy businessman who frequently contributed to political parties in Guatemala.

The businessman feared that disclosure of a relationship with a large U.S. company would diminish his influence in Guatemala and perhaps even provoke left-wing threats against his life. So he demanded and received company assurances of anonymity. To further protect him, Del Monte paid him outside the country. It charged his fee to general and administrative expenses on the books of several Panamanian shipping subsidiaries. His fee was entirely dependent on his ability to get the Guatemalan government to allow the sale of the plantation.

Suddenly the Guatemalan government reversed itself and permitted the sale. Now Del Monte owns the profitable banana plantation, for which it paid $20.5 million, and the "business consultant" is considerably richer.[1]

In many parts of the world, some forms of bribery or payoff are a common and accepted practice. The practice even has names: in Arabic countries it is called *baksheesh,* and in Latin American countries it is called *la mordida.* Everything from large transactions requiring government approval, such as Del Monte's purchase of the plantation, to getting a small-business license or renting an apartment may require it. Many of the government officials who accept the payoffs are poorly paid, and payoffs are a legal and accepted way of augmenting their salaries. Yet, in the United States and most industrialized countries, such practices are regarded as unethical and are usually illegal.

---

[1] Jerry Landauer and Kenneth Bacon, "Del Monte Corp. Finds a Foreign Consultant Can Help a Great Deal," *Wall Street Journal,* July 14, 1975, p. 1.

Are such practices morally acceptable? Many people—including many college students—would justify them by making statements such as "Morality is relative" or "When in Rome, do as the Romans do." It was entirely proper, they might say, for the Del Monte officials to employ the business consultant because this is the way business is conducted in Guatemala, and morals are always relative to a particular culture.

All of these responses convey the same idea: that morality is in some sense relative to the individual or the culture. Unlike science, ethics does not convey truth about the world that is independent of what human beings think. Others believe that ethics has a more objective component. It is not simply a reflection of individual opinion, nor is it simply the reflection of the views of a certain group or society.

These questions about the basis of ethics are covered in the branch of ethics called metaethics. *Metaethics* deals with questions about the nature and justification of ethical claims. This is contrasted with *normative ethics*, which focuses on actual questions of right and wrong and on the moral standards for determining right or wrong. This chapter will focus on questions in metaethics. The rest of the book will be concerned with normative ethical theories.

In this chapter we shall consider two versions of moral relativism, Then we shall look at the most common form of the idea that morality is objective, namely the view that morality is based on religion. Finally, we shall consider the idea that the important notion about morality is not the question whether morality is "true," but rather the question whether our moral beliefs are rational. According to this account, a simple objective/relative dichotomy is inadequate.

CLASSICAL MORAL RELATIVISM

Moral relativism holds that "moral appraisals are essentially dependent upon the standards that define a particular moral code, the practices and norms accepted by a social group at a specific place and time."[2] As a consequence, no single moral code has universal validity. This means that the truth of moral beliefs is dependent on human beings.

Let us begin by considering what we shall call *classical moral relativism*, which holds that no moral views have validity except relative to the culture in which they are endorsed and that we should never attempt to impose our views on those who hold differing moral beliefs. Classical moral

---

[2] *The Oxford Companion to Philosophy* (Oxford: Oxford University Press, 1995), p. 758.

relativism is composed of three theses: the Diversity Thesis, the Relativity Thesis, and the Toleration Thesis.

The Diversity Thesis

The argument for classical moral relativism begins with what we shall call the *Diversity Thesis*, namely the empirical or factual claim that moral beliefs vary from culture to culture and even in the same culture over time. Most people in our culture find infanticide morally unacceptable, but the Roman writer Seneca wrote, "We destroy monstrous births, and we also drown our children if they are born weakly and unnaturally formed."[3] Attitudes of various cultures toward the suffering of animals are also surprisingly different. In Latin America, a chicken is plucked alive with the thought that it will taste more succulent. The Hopi Indians do not object in the least to their children's playing with a bird by tying a string to its legs, even though this play often results in broken legs, wings being pulled off, and usually the death of the animal. As one Hopi put it, "Sometimes they get tired and die."[4] Cultures exhibit vast differences in attitudes toward adultery, premarital sex, property ownership, violence, the expression of hostility, and many other issues.

These examples illustrate the diversity of moral beliefs in various cultures and in what we might consider different moral traditions, but even the same moral tradition varies over time. For example, the Western religious tradition has undergone some remarkable changes. Attitudes toward divorce, once prohibited except for marital infidelity, are now much more tolerant. Historian John Noonan shows that the Christian Church has completely reversed itself on the moral permissibility of usury, the taking of interest for money.[5] In the Hebrew Bible, usury is strongly condemned as exploitation of the poor. The Christian Church encouraged this attitude until the 16 century and the rise of modern commercial civilization. Now taking interest on money is accepted by almost all Christians. The attitude of many religious groups toward many other moral issues, such as sexuality and the proper sphere of activity for women, has also changed or is in the process of changing.

The Diversity Thesis is complicated by the fact that much of the apparent diversity in moral beliefs can be traced to differences in non-moral beliefs. Thus, appearances to the contrary, the difference may not

---

[3] Seneca, De ira, I, 15, quoted in Edward A. Westermarck, *Christianity and Morals* (London: Kegan Paul, Trench, Trubner, 1939), p. 239.

[4] Richard Brandt, *Ethical Theory* (Upper Saddle River, NJ: Prentice Hall, 1959), p. 103.

[5] John Noonan, *The Scholastic Analysis of Usury* (Cambridge, MA: Harvard University Press, 1957).

represent a genuine *moral* difference. For example, some indigenous people routinely kill their parents before the parents become senile. Most of us would be inclined to call this behavior cruel and barbaric. But suppose you believed, as they do, that a person spends the afterlife in the condition in which he or she dies. Then ask yourself whether you would rather live forever in the prime of life or in a senile, decrepit condition. If you held the same beliefs about the afterlife as these people do, would you not also be inclined to kill your parents while they are in the prime of life? Perhaps both you and these people share a common moral commitment that might be stated as "Act so as to benefit your parents." The apparent moral difference dissolves into a difference in nonmoral beliefs.

Other differences in moral beliefs can be traced to differences in circumstances rather than to nonmoral beliefs. Consider the change in the Christian attitude toward usury. In a subsistence culture, charging your neighbor interest on a loan when his crops have failed may drive him into poverty. And if the economy is not inflationary, there may be no justification for charging interest on the grounds that it is necessary to ensure that the amount returned is equivalent in purchasing power to the amount loaned. Charging interest in these circumstances becomes a form of exploitation. In a commercial civilization, on the other hand, borrowed money is used to earn money, and inflation is a fact of life. Further, a creditor, in making a loan, forgoes the opportunity to make any other investment, so that interest takes on a very different moral character. One might even say that forbidding a creditor to charge interest would mean that he or she is exploited, not the borrower. Different circumstances mean that the same moral beliefs ("One should not exploit others") have very different implications.

Even though much of the supposed diversity in moral beliefs can be explained through differences in the circumstances in which people live and in the nonmoral beliefs that they hold, probably not all apparent moral diversity can be explained in this way. Businesspeople in Guatemala, for example, may well believe that their way of doing business is morally superior to practices in the United States, being more sociable and more conducive to genuine human relationships than the mechanical, impersonal American way. Many scholars believe that there are genuine differences in moral beliefs embodied in the varying attitudes toward the proper treatment of animals and the conditions under which the killing of human beings is permissible.

The Relativity Thesis

From the fact of moral diversity, classical moral relativists attempt to derive the *Relativity Thesis*, namely the view that moral beliefs are true or valid only relative to some group. The Relativity Thesis could be called *metaethical moral relativism,* because it is a claim about the justification of ethical statements.

An important point to keep in mind is that relativists always maintain that there are valid moral beliefs and that there is such a thing as truth in morality. However, validity or truth in moral beliefs is not absolute in the sense of being universally applicable to all human beings. Instead, moral beliefs are true *in relation* to some group. Relativists do not believe that there is no truth in ethics but rather that there are many truths. Even if no absolute and universal moral truth is objectively the same for everyone, people do make moral judgments that distinguish right from wrong. Relativists believe that it is unreasonable to say that people are wrong in making such judgments. Each individual or each society should find its own moral truth and live by that truth.

Probably the most common argument for the Relativity Thesis, however, is a combination of the Diversity Thesis and moral skepticism (the belief that there is no way to establish which moral beliefs are correct). The argument goes like this:

> Human cultures reveal a variety of moral beliefs (the Diversity Thesis) and there is no way to establish which beliefs are correct (moral skepticism). Therefore, moral beliefs are relative to a given culture.

But the fact that moral beliefs differ might only show that some of them—or perhaps all of them—are false. And the fact that we have so far found no way to establish which moral beliefs are correct in a way that is conclusive and universally convincing does not show that no such method exists. It only shows that we have not yet discovered the method. Even if there is no such method, this does not establish the Relativity Thesis.

Consider an analogy from science. Suppose a controversy arises over whether there is life on Mars. And suppose further that people in the United States generally believe that there is life on Mars, while people in Russia generally believe there is not. This disagreement in belief does not show that both views are equally true, relative to their own culture. The beliefs of either most Russians or most Americans may simply be wrong. Or the nature of life on Mars may be so different from life on Earth (perhaps based on an element other than carbon) that it is not clear whether either view is right or wrong. Suppose further that there is no way, at least at present, to establish which belief is correct. Few of us would be tempted to say that this demonstrates that the beliefs of the Americans or Russians are true relative to their own cultures. We would be more inclined to say that we just do not know which beliefs are true.

The most obvious response to this statement is to say that there are still important differences between science and ethics. For example, we can at least imagine what experiences might confirm the truth or falsehood of the statement that there is life on Mars. We could imagine a spaceship traveling to Mars carrying human beings or scientific instruments capable of detecting life. Even though we may not be able to perform this experiment, we know what it would take to show that the statement "There is life on Mars" is either true or false. No equivalent experiment or experience is possible that would verify or disconfirm the moral validity of the Hopi practice of playing with birds or the Roman practice of allowing fathers to have life-and-death power over their children.

This reply, however, is unsatisfactory. First, although we can imagine how some scientific beliefs might be confirmed or disconfirmed, this does not hold true for others. According to one account, when Einstein first proposed his ideas on relativity, he had no idea how they could be validated or refuted. Second, even if we cannot imagine confirming or disconfirming experiences, it is not clear that this should be a decisive consideration. How could one go about establishing the claim that the only ideas that should be considered true or false are those that could be at least conceivably confirmed or disconfirmed by experience? Can this claim itself be confirmed or disconfirmed by experience? So unless the analogy between ethics and science can be more conclusively dismissed, we can say it strongly suggests that the fact of moral diversity does not establish the truth of moral relativism.

The Toleration Thesis

People who advocate moral relativism often say that one of its advantages is that it supports the *Toleration Thesis*, which in its strongest form holds that we should not pass judgment on or attempt to forcibly change the moral beliefs of other cultures. In some versions of the Toleration Thesis, a person from one culture may attempt to persuade members of other cultures to adopt his or her own moral beliefs. In any case, the Toleration Thesis is a version of *normative moral relativism*, because it is a view about what we should do (or not do), rather than what we should believe about the nature of moral beliefs. It is important to see, however, that the Toleration Thesis does not necessarily follow from the Diversity Thesis and the Relativity Thesis. If our culture has a principle of toleration, we may be obligated, according to the relativist, to be tolerant. But if our culture does not have such a principle, no such obligation follows. Or if a principle of toleration is not a part of the moral beliefs of another culture, the members of that culture have no moral obligation to practice tolerance toward us, even if we believe in toleration. So, even though many people associate moral toleration with moral rela-tivism, no logical relationship exists between the two.

Evaluating Classical Moral Relativism

We have already seen some reasons for doubting the validity of classical moral relativism, but there are others.

First, defining the society or culture to which a moral judgment is relative poses a problem. Suppose Bertha and Barbara disagree over abortion. Bertha may be a devout Roman Catholic and Barbara an atheist. Are we to say that they are members of different cultures, even though they are neighbors? Do all Americans belong to the same culture? Do all members of cultures strongly influenced by European civilization represent the same culture? Until we have a better understanding of how to define the limits of a culture, we cannot have a conception of the community to which moral judgments are relative.

A second problem with classical relativism is that it seems to make moral decision making either too easy or impossibly difficult. Consider the case of abortion again. If the Relativity Thesis were correct and a given society (however it is defined) enjoyed a high degree of consensus on the issue, majority opinion would tell all members of the society whether abortion is right or wrong. Yet arriving at a decision on the abortion issue seems more difficult than this. If, on the other hand, no consensus existed on the issue, there would be no way to determine the truth on the abortion issue for that society.

A third difficulty with classical relativism is that it makes the notion of moral progress difficult to understand, much less accept. For example, our society once tolerated slavery, but people in most contemporary societies would probably find it morally unacceptable and even morally repugnant. Many people would even say that society's change of attitude toward slavery represents moral progress. But if the Relativity Thesis is correct, it is hard to make sense of this idea. All we can say is that at one time our society found slavery morally acceptable—and therefore it was morally valid—and now we do not find it morally acceptable—so it is no longer morally valid. But this conclusion seems unsatisfactory. Most of us probably want to say that the idea that slavery is wrong is better, morally speaking, than the idea that slavery is morally right. And even if we do not believe in moral progress, most of us find the notion at least meaningful.

A fourth problem with classical moral relativism is that it seems to imply that moral reformers are always wrong. Martin Luther King, Jr., acted contrary to the beliefs of most people in the South when he led public protests against segregation. If the truth of a moral view is determined in relation to the moral standard of one's culture and we consider the South to be a culture, then King acted against the truth. Yet many of us would say that King's actions were morally right, a view that is impossible to maintain from the standpoint of classical moral relativism.

A fifth problem is that moral relativism implies that if it is true, people from different societies and cultures are not really contradicting one another when they make incompatible judgments. Suppose we believe that the conduct of Hopi children who play with birds until the birds are dead is wrong. We might express this belief by the statement, "The Hopi children are wrong when they play with birds until they are dead." If the moral relativist is correct, however, all this remark really means is, "According to my moral beliefs, the Hopi children are wrong when they play with birds until they are dead." Similarly, if the moral relativist is correct, all the Hopi would be saying in reply is "According to our moral beliefs, our children are not wrong when they play with birds until they are dead." These two statements are not incompatible with one another. Indeed, according to the relativist, we cannot say the Hopi are simply wrong, for we are always implicitly saying that they are wrong *according to our moral beliefs*, and people can be wrong by one set of moral beliefs and not wrong by another. So moral relativism does not agree with our usual way of understanding morality whenever some moral beliefs are incompatible with others.

Many people are comfortable holding onto relativism on some issues. They might say, for example, that it is right for Guatemalans to accept bribes but that it is not right for citizens of the United States. But most of us would find it hard to carry out this position consistently. We have already mentioned the practice of the Hopi in playing with birds. Even more difficult to accept would be the practice of cannibals in killing and eating human beings. Or what about the Nazis' practice of torturing innocent human beings?

An important assumption in our thinking and speaking about morality is that moral judgments can be genuinely opposed to one another. Many college students say that they are moral relativists, but they are uncomfortable with saying that Hitler was not wrong when he ordered the execution of Jews or that Mother Theresa was really not more morally admirable than Joseph Stalin. Yet if moral relativism is correct, the Nazi who says Hitler was a good man and the Jew who says Hitler was a moral monster are not contradicting one another. Each is expressing a moral judgment that is true or valid in relation to his or her group, which is all that can be said about the truth of the two moral judgments.

Sixth, many critics have argued that relativism is incompatible with the *universalization principle*, which says that if something is right for you, it is also right for me, provided the circumstances are the same. This principle, closely related to the criterion of impartiality discussed in Chapter 1, is widely endorsed by moral philosophers. Relativism, however, seems to deny the principle, for if our moral principles are different, something can be right for you and wrong for me, even though the circumstances are the same. One possible answer to the problem is that moral principles form part of the circumstances themselves, so that the universalization principle does not apply when two people have differing moral principles. If, therefore, my principles are egoistic and yours are altruistic, the universalization principle would have binding force *within* a group that adheres to the same moral principles, such as a group of egoists, but not *outside* it.

Our ordinary use of the universalization principle, however, seems to be broader than this. The point becomes especially obvious when we recall that anyone could declare himself or herself a member of a different culture and thereby escape the requirements of the universalization principle. Our neighbor could simply decide that he is a member of a different culture and is therefore not subject to the same moral requirements as we are. Moral relativism thus seems to provide a way of subverting the legitimate requirements of the universalization principle.

Finally, classical relativism does not provide a basis for resolving intercultural conflicts. Consider the case presented at the beginning of the chapter. Although bribery is not accepted in North American society, let us assume for the sake of argument that it is accepted in Guatemalan society. Classical relativism says that the statement "People may accept bribes" is true for the Guatemalan businessperson and not for the North American businessperson. Why, then, should either the Guatemalans or the North Americans change, since they are each acting correctly by their own cultural values? How can the standpoint of classical relativism even supply any motivation for either side to accommodate the other?

LIMITED MORAL RELATIVISM

Philosopher David Wong has formulated a version of relativism that we shall call *limited relativism*. It is still a form of relativism because it holds that there is no single correct or true morality. It is a limited relativism because it holds that, even though there is no single correct or true morality, there are limits on what can count as a true morality. Limited relativism requires modification of the Relativity Thesis, because it holds that not just any moral code could count as a legitimate morality. It requires modification of the Toleration Thesis, because it holds that there are standards for criticizing, and in some cases rejecting, a moral code. Not all moral beliefs should be tolerated. Wong summarizes his version of relativism by saying that "the universal limits on adequate moralities do not narrow the range of such moralities to just one."[6]

We can summarize Wong's limited relativism by considering his views about the diversity of morality and the limits of that diversity.

The Diversity of Morality

Citing Thomas Nagel's classification, Wong holds that there are five different sources of value. First, there are specific obligations to other people or institutions, which depend on some special relation that we may have to those people or institutions. For example, parents and children have special obligations to each other, and professionals have special obligations to their clients. Employees have special obligations to their employing institution, and citizens have special obligations to their country. Second, there are constraints on action deriving from general rights that everyone has, such as rights to freedom of speech and freedom from assault or coercion. Third, utility or the general public welfare is a source of value. Fourth, there are what Nagel calls "perfectionist ends or values, such as the intrinsic value of scientific or artistic achievements and creations. . ."[7] Finally, there is commitment to one's own projects or goals, such as building a business or promoting a social or political cause.

These values can and do conflict, and it is not possible for a single culture or person to embody all of them fully. For example, people in the modern West emphasize individual rights over the network of special relationships of families and other social groups. Traditional cultures in Africa, China, Japan, and India place greater importance on this network of relationships.[8] Confucianism, for example, places central importance on loyalty to the family and kinship groups, and more indirectly on loyalties to legitimate leaders. Moralities centered on such values are significantly different from those that focus on individual rights, such as the rights to liberty of expression. One of the differences is that in traditional cultures, there will be more restriction of individual freedom.

It is important to see that Western cultures do not fail totally to value loyalties to family and other groups, or the communal harmony that results

---

[6] David B. Wong, "Pluralistic Relativism," *Midwest Studies in Philosophy*, Vol. XX (1995), p. 386. Wong refers to his relativism as "pluralistic relativism," but I find the term "limited relativism" more appropriately descriptive.

[7] Wong, "Pluralistic Relativism," p. 379.

[8] David B. Wong, *Moral Relativity* (Berkeley: University of California Press, 1984), ch. 9. See also David B. Wong, "Relativism," in Peter Singer (ed.), *A Companion to Ethics* (Oxford: Blackwell, 1991), pp. 445–446.

from these tight-knit loyalties. Nor is it the case that non-Western cultures fail to place any value on individual freedom. In cultural conflicts, we do not typically see one set of values confronting another totally different set. Rather, it is a matter of the relative weight placed on one value (for example, individual freedom) as opposed to another value (for example, a network of loyalties). Furthermore, two cultures may hold some values in roughly equal esteem. Most cultures value courage, love for children and parents, and loyalty, for example.

There may not be any way to arbitrate some value conflicts between cultures, and even some moral conflicts within our own culture. Can we show that the Western emphasis on individual freedom is better than the non-Western emphasis on a network of loyalties? How do we arbitrate the conflict between our general loyalty to human welfare (for example, to feed the hungry on the other side of the world) and our loyalties to our own children? Or how do we settle a conflict between an artist's desire to promote her artistic excellence and her obligations to her family? Wong believes that there is no criterion that enables us to adjudicate these value conflicts in a decisive and objective way. Value pluralism leads to a degree of moral relativity.

Limits to Moral Diversity

According to Wong, there are, however, limits to moral diversity. Not every moral belief is legitimate, simply because it is held by members of a culture. There are criteria by which we evaluate a moral code, so that not all differences between cultures are equally justified. The first of these ways is internal criticism: an argument that a system of moral values is incoherent or internally inconsistent. In traditional Chinese culture, for example, rigid gender roles result in a subordination of women to men that prohibits women from making their full contribution to society, but this subordination can be criticized as being inconsistent with core Confucian values themselves. It is, Wong believes, inconsistent with the Confucian tradition of community and "filiality," or the relationship of children to their parents. These values imply, Wong believes, that every person should be allowed to realize those values by making his or her full contribution to the community.[9] One does not have to step outside Chinese culture itself to argue that gender subordination is wrong.

A second way that the values of a culture can be criticized is through external criticism: the values of a culture can be criticized by arguing that a moral code does not measure up to universal criteria for any adequate morality.

---

[9] Wong, *Pluralistic Relativism*, pp. 386 and 394.

These criteria are derived from considerations of the function of morality. Morality is partly a system of rules to help humans to live together with some measure of harmony. "It regulates conflicts of interest between people, and it regulates conflicts of interest within the individual born of different desires and drives that cannot all be satisfied at the same time."[10] Any human society develops ways of dealing with such conflicts, and significantly different moralities may be able to regulate conflicts equally well. When this is the case, we may say that different moral beliefs are true for their culture of origin.

Sometimes we find, however, that a culture's way of dealing with conflicting interests may not be very successful. Here, we should not be content with saying that the less successful moral beliefs are true for the culture in question. For example, many cultures exhibit a greater toleration of bribery than is common in the contemporary West. An argument can be made that the acceptance of bribery, however, is not an effective way of harmonizing conflicting interests between people. Bribery allows economic conflicts to be resolved by money, instead of by open economic competition, based on providing the best service at the best price. Subverting above-board economic competition stifles ambition and produces a resignation and cynicism that is incompatible with economic development. Thus, bribery is not an appropriate part of any moral code. Wong also believes that the torture of political dissidents cannot be a part of an adequate morality, although he does not explain his belief.[11]

Because it makes less sweeping claims about moral relativism than classical relativism does, limited relativism becomes more plausible. "A moral relativism," Wong asserts, "that would allow for this kind of constraint on what could be a true or most justified morality might not fit the stereotype of relativism, but would be a reasonable position to hold."[12]

According to limited relativism, we may pass judgment on others with differing moral beliefs if they fail to meet either the internal or external criterion, but what we are entitled to do depends on the particular situation. In most situations, there are reasons both for tolerating the differing views and reasons for intervening and attempting to change them. These reasons must be weighed against each other in particular cases. We might intervene to prevent human sacrifice, but not to prevent a

---

[10] David B. Wong, "Relativism," in Peter Singer (ed.), *A Companion to Ethics* (Oxford: Blackwell, 1991), p. 446.

[11] Wong, "Pluralistic Relativism," p. 392.

[12] Wong, "Relativism," p. 447.

violation of freedom of the press. Exposure to another culture may lead us to accept some of its differing moral beliefs as true or valid for that culture, but not to accept others. Each disagreement between cultures must be assessed on its own merits. Philosopher Simon Blackburn, another writer with views in some ways similar to Wong's, says, "there are [only] particular problems of when to tolerate and when to oppose."[13]

Evaluating Limited Moral Relativism

The limited moral relativist can answer some of the criticisms of classical relativism. Limited relativism does not give a simplistic answer to conflicts between cultures. We need not either reject opposing views because they are not ours, or tolerate them because they are true relative to another culture. Each conflict must be examined on its own terms. We can make sense of moral progress, because human moral codes might gradually become more adequate, as measured by the two criteria Wong proposes. Moral reformers need not always be wrong, for we can evaluate them by whether they propose changes in a society's morality that enables it to better meet the two criteria. Although some moral differences may be equally valid, we might want to say of others that they do "contradict" each other, for their implicit claim to meet the test of resolving conflicting interests might not be equally valid. Limited moral relativism may also be able to partially meet the requirements of the universalization principle, for at least some moral beliefs may be universally valid. Finally, with its criteria for a successful morality, limited moral relativism does provide suggestions for resolving intercultural conflicts.

Wong's limited moral relativism is still open to criticism, however. It shares with classical relativism the problem that it does not provide any criteria for defining the limits of a culture, although such criteria might in principle be provided. Another problem is with what we have called Wong's "external" criterion for arbitrating conflicts between moral codes, namely the ability of the moral code to resolve conflicting interests. Although arbitrating conflicting interests is surely an important function of any moral code, it might not be the sole—or even the most important— criterion for evaluating moral codes. Other criteria might be proposed: harmonizing humans with nature, creating wealth, or simply conformity with the "truth" in some more absolute sense.

Another problem is that applying either the internal or external criteria to specific conflicts between moralities could be controversial.

---

[13] Simon Blackburn, "Relativism" in Hugh LaFollette, *Ethical Theory* (Oxford: Blackwell, 2000), p. 43. For another exposition of his views, see *Ruling Passions* (Oxford: Clarendon, 1998), pp. 279–310.

With regard to the internal criterion, can we always be sure that a morality is incoherent? Traditionalists might argue, for example, that assigning a subordinate place to women is not really inconsistent with traditional Confucian values. With respect to the external criterion, it is not always easy to determine how successfully a moral code resolves conflicting interests. Perhaps traditional cultures, with their emphasis on social harmony and kinship loyalties, more effectively resolve conflicting interests than do Western cultures, with their emphasis on individual rights.

Despite these problems, limited moral relativism shows promise of providing a middle way between extreme relativism and extreme objectivist views, such as the one presented next in the divine command theory.

CONCEPT SUMMARY

Perhaps the most popular foundation for subjectivism in ethics is moral relativism. Classical moral relativism can be thought of as consisting of three theses. The Diversity Thesis is an empirical claim that there are genuine moral differences between cultures. Although there are differences in moral beliefs, identifying them is more difficult than one might suppose. The Relativity Thesis holds that moral beliefs are true or valid relative to a culture. This thesis does not follow necessarily from the Diversity Thesis. In its strongest form, the Toleration Thesis holds that we should not pass judgment on, or attempt to change, the moral beliefs of other cultures. This is a normative judgment that does not follow necessarily from the Relativity Thesis.

In answer to the various objections to classical moral relativism, some philosophers have proposed a limited version of relativism. The limited version holds that we can judge a moral belief by whether it is internally coherent and agrees with universal criteria for a legitimate morality. In applying these criteria, we must approach cultural differences individually, neither holding necessarily that there is a single correct moral belief on the topic, nor holding that differing moral beliefs are always equally valid.

THE DIVINE COMMAND THEORY

The best-known version of the claim that morality is objective is the claim that religion is the basis of ethics. When panels of experts are formed in hospitals or by governmental agencies to render opinions on ethical questions, religious figures are almost always included and are often dominant.

Showing that moral judgments have their foundations in the commands of God would, for many people, provide a sufficient answer to our quest for objectivity in ethics. What could be more objective than the commands of God? Not surprisingly, this idea has been elaborated into a theory of the objectivity of ethics known as the *divine command theory*.

We must be careful to distinguish several different senses in which ethics can be based on the commands of God. One sense is psychological: the fact that God commands something could motivate either positively or negatively. As a positive motivation, the hope of reward in the afterlife or some other manifestation of divine favor can lead to morally praiseworthy action. As a negative motivation, the fear of punishment in the afterlife or some other manifestation of divine disfavor can be powerful deterrents to certain types of behavior.

It would be hard to deny that the use of religious motivation to produce ethical conduct is an important influence in many people's lives. But the psychological account of religious motivation does not answer the question about the objectivity of morality. After all, people can be motivated to do what is wrong as well as what is right. A tyrant can motivate his subjects to act in accordance with his will, but this capability would not convince us that his commands are objectively right. Or a father who is a harsh disciplinarian may be able to bend his children to his will, even if his will is often morally perverse. Children may be motivated to many actions by the desire for parental approval, but this does not show that the actions carrying parental approval are objectively right.

To find the possible religious basis of moral objectivism, we must turn to the logical sense in which ethics is based on religion. Here three positions are possible. First, one can say that God, being omniscient, always knows what is right and wrong and, being perfectly good, always commands us to do what is right and not to do what is wrong. God commands us not to commit rape and murder because they are wrong and to love others because it is right.

Now it is certainly true that knowing the commands of God would be enormously helpful to an ethically concerned person in determining what is right. If God's knowledge in other areas is infallible, His knowledge of moral truth should also be infallible. But two questions must be asked: (1) How do we know God's commands, and (2) where does God get his ethical knowledge?

Let us consider the first question. In learning about God's commands, do we look to the Bible, the Koran, or some other religious document? The religions of the world differ significantly on some moral issues, such as the legitimacy of the use of violence and the proper treatment of animals. After we decide on a source of revelation about God's commands, how do we decide on its proper interpretation? Consider how even Christian authorities disagree over the morality of such issues as war, abortion, sterilization, and birth control. If religious authorities cannot agree on what God's commands are, how much confidence can we have in them as a guide for moral conduct?

The second question serves to point out that, according to the first version of the divine command theory, God serves only as a reliable conveyor of ethical truth but not the ultimate source of ethical truth. This view shows that the version of the divine command theory cannot provide a satisfactory answer to the question about the justification of moral truth. Appealing to God as an omniscient knower of ethical truth is not the same thing as appealing to God as the *ultimate ground of moral truth*.

A second version of the divine command theory addresses the issue of the ultimate ground of moral truth by holding that God's commands make certain actions right and others wrong. What makes right actions right is that God has commanded them, and what makes wrong actions wrong is that God has prohibited them. It is, in other words, God's commands that justify our moral beliefs. On this account, we do not need to ask about the ultimate origin of ethical truth, for God's command is the ultimate origin. Though this version of the divine command theory may answer the objection to the first version, it has serious problems of its own.

One objection that is sometimes made to this version is that, if we derive our moral beliefs from divine commands, we give up moral autonomy or independence. We base our morality on superior power rather than on moral conviction. Acting as a genuine moral agent involves being self-directed; a person behaves in a certain way because he or she believes that way is right. Subservience to divine commands requires replacing autonomy with mere obedience, which is morally wrong.[14]

At this point, a defender of the divine command theory could reply that we often think it is reasonable to take things on authority. When we go to the physician, we usually accept his or her directions. The scientist accepts the authority of reports of experimental work that he or she has not verified. Yet we do not think the patient and the scientist have surrendered their autonomy in an unacceptable way. But there is an important difference between accepting an authority on a truth that is independent of that authority and accepting an authority that establishes the truth. The second version of the divine command theory holds that God establishes moral truth, and so the analogy does not apply.

---

[14] This argument has been challenged recently. See Philip Quinn, *Divine Commands and Moral Requirements* (Oxford: Clarendon, 1978), ch. 1.

A more serious problem is that the claim that divine commands justify moral judgments seems to lead to moral arbitrariness. If God's command is sufficient to justify any action as good, then God could command me to make it my chief end in life to inflict suffering on other human beings. And it would be morally proper for me to do this. If no moral criterion is independent of God's will, He could command us to commit rape or murder, and it would be right for us to do so.

We could reply, "But God would never do this, for He is a loving God." This response is the basis of the modification of the divine command theory proposed by philosopher Robert M. Adams. The fact that something is contrary to God's commands means that it is wrong, Adams maintains, only if we assume that God has the character of a loving being. If God were really to command us to make cruelty our goal, then He would not have that character of loving us, and I would not say it would be wrong to disobey Him.[15] However, if a divine command must be consistent with love to be ethically binding, then love is the most important moral criterion, or at least equally as important as the fact that something is commanded by God. The criterion of love is then independent of God, and the second position becomes equivalent to the first one. Therefore, many philosophers have concluded that the second version of the divine command theory must also be rejected.

A third version of the divine command theory holds that the statement "X is good (or bad)" means the same thing as "X is commanded (or prohibited) by God." In this version, the divine command theory is established by definition. But again severe problems arise. First, many people do not mean (or at least do not think they mean) the same thing by "X is good" and "X is commanded by God." The divine command theory does not appear to give a definition that is plausible for many people.

A more important objection, however, is that the claim that something is good *means* that God commands it seems incompatible with the language that religious believers themselves often use. Suppose I say, "Praise the Lord, for He is good." If whatever God commands is good, then I am really saying, "Praise the Lord, for He acts according to His commands." This sounds very strange indeed! We might as well praise the standard meterstick for being one meter long! This objection suggests that the word *good* does not mean the same thing as being in accord with God's commands.

---

[15] Robert M. Adams, "A Modified Divine Command Theory of Ethical Wrongness," in Gene Outka and John P. Reeder (eds.), *Religion and Morality: A Collection of Essays* (New York: Anchor Books, 1973), p. 527.

It is important to see that the rejection of the divine command theory is not the same as the rejection of belief in God. Many believers are willing to recognize that logic and mathematics are valid independently of God's commands. The fact that one and one are two does not depend on God's commands. Why should the situation be any different with morality? Many major figures in the Jewish and Christian traditions would agree in rejecting the position that the validity of ethical beliefs depends on the commands of God. The Jewish scholars who wrote the Talmud did not take divine commands as the reason for action; if God commanded them to steal and murder, they would not be obligated to do so. By their nature, humans know what is right and wrong, and revelation is needed only to avoid all uncertainty over the application of moral precepts. Similarly, Moses Maimonides and other medieval Jewish thinkers refused to identify the good with the will of God.[16] The Roman Catholic tradition generally takes a similar, though more qualified, stand. According to St. Thomas Aquinas, to say that morality is determined simply by God's will is to suggest that God's will may sometimes not follow order and wisdom, and that stance would be blasphemous.[17]

RATIONALITY VERSUS TRUTH

The debate between relativism and objectivism has considerable theoretical importance. Most of us are led at one time or another to ask ourselves whether there is moral truth that is independent of human belief. But this issue is not the center of our concerns when we are wrestling with a real-life moral decision. We are interested rather in this sort of question: What is the best decision? Or perhaps: What is the right decision for me in this situation? Put more abstractly, the question is, What is the most rational decision? The question I must answer is not what decision is true in some absolute sense, but what decision is rational. The real issue, then, is not truth but rationality.

To make the most rational decisions, two things are necessary. First, I must use the most rationally defensible moral principles available. Second, I must apply these principles in the most rational way. Because we are concerned at this point with finding the most rational principles

---

[16] See Louis Jacobs, "The Relationship between Religion and Ethics in Jewish Thought," in Gene Outka and John P. Reeder, Jr. (ed.), *Religion and Morality* (New York: Anchor Books, 1973), pp. 155–172.

[17] Thomas Aquinas, *De Veritate*, 23.6, quoted in Eric D'Arcy, "Worthy of Worship: A Catholic Contribution," in Outka and Reeder, *Religion and Morality*, p. 191.

rather than applying them in the most rational way, let us look more closely at this first requirement.

Remember, to begin with, that whatever decision we make can be seen to follow from some moral principles. The principles may be implicit rather than explicit, but they are present in some form. If we decide that we are going to cheat on a test, we may be able to justify this decision only on the basis of egoism. If we decide that we will not use contraceptives because it is immoral to do so, we may be able to justify this decision only on the basis of natural law. Sometimes, however, our decisions may be justifiable in terms of several different moral principles—egoism and utilitarianism, perhaps. In any case, the question is not whether we will have moral principles but what they are.

Given this first point, the pressing practical question is whether the principles that underlie our actions are the best or most rationally defensible ones. The only way to answer this question is to look at various moral theories and attempt to determine which one is the most rationally defensible, all things considered. The moral principles justifiable by this theory (or these theories) would be those a morally responsible person should use. Whether these principles are true in the absolute sense may be hard to answer. Whether they are the most rationally defensible principles is a more manageable question. From a practical standpoint, this is the more important question regarding the objectivity of ethics. The task before us in the next several chapters, then, is to begin examining the four moral theories proposed for our analysis.

CONCEPT SUMMARY

One of the most widespread versions of moral objectivism is the view that moral truth is based on divine commands. One version of this theory holds that God, being omniscient, always commands us to do what is right. But this version of the divine command theory does not explain the source of God's ethical knowledge. A second version holds that the fact that God commands us to do something makes it true, but this seems to open the way for moral arbitrariness on God's part. A third version holds that "X is good (or bad)" means the same thing as "X is commanded (or prohibited) by God," but this view has implications for the relationship of God to morality that even many religious believers find implausible.

One way of circumventing the problem of the impasse in the debate between relativists and objectivists is to emphasize that rationality, not truth, is the central issue in the question of the objectivity of ethics.

CHAPTER

MORAL THEORIES

3

Socrates has as much right as anyone to be called the patron saint of philosophy. Few people have represented the ideal of philosophy more forcefully or eloquently, in either their words or lives. His conception of the nature and function of philosophy is closely connected with his personal "mission" in life: to coax and cajole the people of Athens into examining their values and beliefs. Socrates would engage individuals in conversation and get them to state their beliefs on some topic. Then he would examine these beliefs, pointing out difficulties and often leading people to reformulate their beliefs or perhaps abandon them altogether. Describing how he would treat someone who claims to have the truth, Socrates says:

> "I shall question him and cross-examine him and test him. If I think that he has not attained excellence, though he says that he has, I shall reproach him for undervaluing the most valuable things, and overvaluing those that are less valuable. This I shall do to everyone whom I meet, young or old, citizen or stranger, but especially to citizens, since they are most closely related to me."[1]

A little later Socrates gives what might be considered the theme of his philosophical mission: "An unexamined life is not worth living."[2]

Socrates tried to teach people to engage in critical reflection on their beliefs and values. Critical reflection involves attempting to give reasons for one's beliefs and values, examining those reasons, and being willing to modify or even abandon convictions that do not withstand rational scrutiny. This task is often very difficult and painful, as Socrates knew all too well. Sometimes members of his audience would simply decide they had

---

[1] Plato, *The Apology*, pp. 29–30; cited in *Euthyphro, Apology and Crito*, trans. by F. J. Church, rev. ed., introduction by Robert D. Cumming (New York: Liberal Arts Press, 1956), p. 36.

[2] Ibid., p. 38.

something better to do than listen to him. At other times they would become angry at having their faulty beliefs exposed in public. Many people also felt that Socrates was undermining the state's morals by coaxing people to question their most fundamental beliefs, and he was finally put to death on a charge of "corrupting the youth."

The kind of critical reflection that Socrates sought to stimulate is at the very center of the philosophical enterprise, and it is an essential task for anyone who wants to claim that his or her beliefs are rationally justified. Critical reflection on moral principles is the only way to determine which moral principles you want to use in making moral decisions in your own life. Critical reflection is an essential component of being a morally responsible person.

In this chapter, we shall consider some conceptual tools you can use in critically reflecting on your moral principles. First, we shall consider the relationship of moral theories to the larger and more informal stock of moral beliefs which we all possess. Second, we shall outline a standard conception of the structure of a moral theory. A *moral theory*, which can also be called a *moral philosophy*, is a systematic ordering of moral principles. Third, we shall consider some criteria for judging the adequacy of a moral theory. Finally, we shall discuss some typical problems you may encounter when you apply a moral theory to a particular moral issue and some reasons why critical reflection will not always resolve ethical disagreement.

COMMON MORALITY AND MORAL THEORY

We can call the stock of common moral beliefs, *common morality*. The term is used by analogy with the term *common sense*. Just as most of us share a common body of beliefs about the world and about what we must do in order to survive—a body of beliefs that we call *common sense*—so we share a common stock of basic moral beliefs. Common morality is a vast, complex and subtle set of beliefs which all of us call upon to maneuver our way through problems of moral decision. While this common stock may differ to some extent from one person to another, there is a surprising degree of agreement about the content of common morality. We also agree in many particular moral judgments. We not only agree that murder is wrong, but often we agree that particular actions are murders, and therefore wrong. This is not to deny, however, that differences occur with respect to specific practices, such as abortion, euthanasia, sexual morality, and capital punishment.

To examine common morality more closely and thereby determine the grounds of agreement and disagreement, it would be useful to formulate common morality in some way, rather than rest content with a haphazard attempt to bring up elements of common morality when a particular occasion of moral controversy arises. W. D. Ross is one theorist who has attempted to do this. Ross has constructed a list of basic duties or obligations, which he calls "prima facie" or conditional duties.[3] In using these terms, Ross intended to convey the idea that, although these duties are generally obligatory, they can be overridden in special circumstances.

Ross discliams "completeness or finality" for his list as an exhaustive account of common morality, but he believes the list is reasonably complete. We can summarize his primary duties in the following list, using "R" to refer to "Ross."

R1. Duties resting on our previous acts: (a) duties of fidelity (e.g., not to tell lies and to keep promises); and (b) the duties of reparation for wrong done

R2. Duties of gratitude (e.g., to parents and benefactors)

R3. Duties of justice (e.g., the promotion of a state of affairs in which happiness is proportional to merit)

R4. Duties of beneficence (e.g., to improve the condition of others)

R5. Duties of self-improvement (e.g., improving ourselves, either morally or intellectually)

R6. Duties not to injure others

Another theorist, Bernard Gert, has formulated a list of 10 "moral rules" which have many similarities to Ross's list of prima facie duties. Although Gert does not offer these rules as a summary of common morality, we shall take them as serving that purpose. Using "G" to refer to "Gert," here are the rules:

G1. Don't kill

G2. Don't cause pain

G3. Don't disable

G4. Don't deprive of freedom

G5. Don't deprive of pleasure

G6. Don't deceive

G7. Keep your promise (or don't break your promise)

G8. Don't cheat

---

[3]W. D. Ross, *The Right and the Good* (Oxford, England: Oxford University Press, 1988), pp. 20–22.

G9. Obey the law (or don't disobey the law)
G10. Do your duty (or don't fail to do your duty)[4]

Gert's rules are more specific and perhaps closer to common sense than Ross's more abstract duties. Gert, however like Ross, believes that moral rules will on some occasions conflict with one another. In this case, we must decide which rule takes priority, and this can only be done in the context of particular situations.

Gert believes that the precepts of morality fall into two broad categories. The first consists of the ten moral rules. In addition to the ten moral rules, however, Gert believes that common morality consists of ten "moral ideals," which differ from moral rules in at least two ways. First, while the rules are primarily negative and can be summarized as "Don't cause evil," the moral ideals are more positive in character and are oriented toward reducing the amount of evil in the world. Second, moral ideals are generally only encouraged by morality, whereas moral rules are required. We should not be punished for failing to follow moral ideals, but we often should be punished for failing to follow the moral rules.

The moral ideals can be formulated from the 10 moral rules by introducing the word "prevent" and changing the wording of the rules slightly. Thus the moral ideal corresponding to "Don't kill" is "Prevent killing," and the moral ideal corresponding to "Don't cause pain" is "Prevent the causing of pain."

Note that, while the lists of Ross and Gert do not entirely agree, they have many features in common. G1–G5 and G8 appear to be special cases of R6. G6 and G7 are included in R1a. R2–R5 seem to be of a more positive nature, but they have close affinities with Gert's moral ideals. The duty of beneficence is the most obvious example of a prima facie duty that includes many of Gert's moral ideals, but many of the duties of gratitude and justice can be included here as well. Ross's inclusion of a duty to self-improvement may represent a more fundamental difference between himself and Gert, because Gert does not appear to recognize any "duty to ourselves" as a part of common morality.

For some, the formulations of common morality given by Ross and Gert are sufficient, but some theorists have for various resons considered these formulations to be insufficient. One reason is that we might want to ask the question, "Is there some more fundamental principle or idea that formulates the deeper point or purpose of morality itself?" To put this question another way, "Can we point to something and say that this is what morality is all about?" Neither Ross nor Gert offer what we might call a

---

[4]Bernard Gert, *Morality* (New York: Oxford University Press, 1988), ch. 6–7.

"summarizing principle" of morality that would answer this question. They do not find, in their investigaiton of common morality, any deeper idea from which the various duties or rules spring, or to which they are all related in some important way.

It is in order to address this concern, among others, that the various moral "theories" presented in this book have been constructed. The ethics of self-interest is a theory which holds, at least in one of its formulations, that morality consists of a set of rules agreed to by self-interested people to enable them to more effectively pursue their own interests. The ethics of natural law holds that morality is a set of principles which sets out the implications for human conduct of the most important facts about human nature. The ethics of utilitarianism holds that morality is, or should be, designed to promote human happiness or well-being. The ethics of respect for persons holds that morality is a set of rules which protects individuals from unjustified interference by others. Virtue ethics holds that morality is not most insightfully formulated in terms of rules at all, but rather in terms of a series of virtues which the ideal person should manifest in his or her behavior. So being virtuous is what morality is "all about."

While there is some consensus among moral theorists that some of these theories are better accounts of common morality than others—for example, that the ethics of self-interest and natural law are not as adequate as the others—there is no consensus as to which one is *the* most adequate moral theory. It is very likely, in fact, that no single theory will ever be found. This may be in part because there are certain splits or divisions in common morality itself which these theories expose. Whatever may be the case, there is no reason that a person should feel compelled to commit to a single moral theory which he or she uses exclusively. In some situations one theory may be more appropriate and in other situations another. In some cases, it may be useful to use more than one theory. We shall return to some of the issues involved in applying the theories in Appendix 1. For now, let us look at the general structure of a moral theory.

THE THREE LEVELS OF A MORAL THEORY

How does a person engage in critical reflection about moral principles? By its very nature, critical reflection about moral principles is systematic. In justifying one moral claim, you will find yourself appealing to other moral claims and then to still other moral claims, so that you might finally be forced to reveal your most basic moral commitments in justifying a single ethical claim.

Let us consider a simple illustration. Suppose you and I are sitting at breakfast together reading the newspaper. Having just read a story about the execution of a criminal, I make the statement:

1. "John McRay should not have been executed."

You then ask me for a reason for this judgment, and I say:

2. "John McRay's execution is an instance of capital punishment."

Then I add:

3. "And capital punishment is wrong."

Notice that I began with a moral claim (1), made a conceptual claim about the scope of the concept of capital punishment (2), and then made another moral claim (3).

If I were asked to justify this last moral claim, I might make the following factual claim:

4. "Capital punishment is discriminatory. That is, if you are condemned to death, you are more likely to be executed if you are poor or a member of a racial or ethnic minority group."

We have already seen that moral claims cannot be derived from facts alone; so, to justify the moral claim that capital punishment is wrong, I must add another moral claim:

5. "Discriminatory actions are wrong."

What is the basis of this moral claim? I might justify it by making a factual claim about myself, namely:

6. "I would not want to be discriminated against in this way if I were condemned to death. I would at least want fair treatment."

Even this claim does not justify my judgment that discrimination is wrong without still another moral claim:

7. "In order for a principle of action to be right, I must be willing to have the same principle applied to me in similar circumstances."

If you asked me why I believed this claim, I might say that it is a fundamental belief of mine about how one determines what is right and wrong. So an attempt to defend my beliefs about capital punishment has led me back through increasingly general principles to one of my ultimate moral commitments.

This order of reasoning from more specific moral claims to very general ones gives the outline of any moral theory. A moral theory has three levels. The first level is represented by the first statement in our progression:

"John McRay should not have been executed." We shall refer to this kind of statement as a *moral judgment*. Moral judgments give moral evaluations of specific actions or individuals.

The second or intermediate level is represented by statements 3 and 5. We shall refer to these as *moral principles* or sometimes *moral rules*. They make moral evaluations of types or classes of action, such as capital punishment or acts of discrimination. They refer to many actions or individuals, not just one.

The third or highest level is represented by statement 7. This is the level that you eventually arrive at when you trace your moral convictions back to your most basic moral assumptions. We shall refer to this kind of statement as a *moral standard*. A moral standard gives the characteristic that, according to the moral theory, any action or person must have to be morally right. Rather than give evaluations of specific actions or individuals (as moral judgments do) or evaluations of types or classes of action (as moral principles do), moral standards give the *criterion* that *makes* any action or person right.

We shall discuss each of these levels, beginning with the moral judgment.

First Level: Moral Judgments

A moral judgment (MJ), as we have seen, gives a moral evaluation of individual people or actions. It represents the ultimate goal of moral reasoning: the point at which moral deliberation issues in a directive for action. By making the moral judgment "John McRay should not have been executed," I commit myself to a belief that the action was wrong. I would also have committed myself to making some attempt if the appropriate circumstances arise to reverse the execution if it had not already taken place. Because the execution has already occurred, I still commit myself to actions and attitudes that oppose similar executions in the future.

Three types of moral judgment can be made about an action, and a fourth type is sometimes relevant. Some judgments evaluate actions as *morally obligatory*—that is, they say it is right to do the actions and wrong not to do them. If the alternative to the action violates the moral standard, the action itself would be described as morally obligatory: we cannot be morally justified in refraining from performing the action. In most moral theories, the judgment that parents ought to care for their children would designate an obligatory action because the alternative to the action (that parents need not care for their children) violates the moral standard. If you are an egoist, it is morally obligatory for you to protect your property from theft because the alternative to the action (failing to protect your property from theft) violates your self-interest.

Other judgments designate *forbidden* or *morally impermissible* actions—those that are wrong to do and right not to do. Actions that violate the moral standard fall into this category. A valid example for most moral philosophies is the judgment that murder is morally impermissible because it violates most moral standards. For advocates of traditional natural-law moral philosophy, using "artificial" forms of contraception is morally impermissible because it is contrary to the value of procreation.

A third category is judgments that designate *morally permissible* actions. We might also refer to morally permissible actions as morally neutral actions because they do not themselves violate the moral standard, nor do the alternatives to them violate the moral standard. Because morally obligatory actions are also permissible, we might refer to this class of actions as merely permissible actions, to distinguish actions that are obligatory (and therefore obviously permissible) from those that are merely permissible. However, for convenience we shall call them morally permissible actions.

Permissible actions can be trivial or nontrivial. *Nontrivial permissible* actions are those that have important consequences, whereas *trivial permissible* actions are those that have relatively unimportant consequences. The decision to undergo a risky operation that might prolong your life a few more months and the decision to refuse the operation and die a few months sooner may in some cases be equally permissible by your moral philosophy. For example, as an egoist, you might conclude that the advantage of living a little longer would be balanced by the pain you would suffer even after the operation. If you had no other relevant considerations, both the decision to have the operation and the decision not to have it would be nontrivially morally permissible. On the other hand, the decision to give to one charity rather than another, when both are equally worthy, would be trivially morally permissible.

The final type of judgment is not usually as important as the other three, but it is essential in understanding the moral status of some actions. Sometimes moral philosophers designate an action as *supererogatory*—that is, "above and beyond the call of duty." Supererogatory acts can be acts of either omission or commission. Supererogatory acts of omission are actions that are good not to do but morally permissible to do. When you refrain from demanding immediate and total payment of a personal debt of a friend in financial trouble, you are doing something morally praiseworthy. However, it is still morally permissible to demand payment of a rightful debt. The decision not to demand immediate payment would be a supererogatory act of omission.

Supererogatory acts of commission are actions that are good to do but morally permissible not to do. It can be argued, for example, that a corporation is not morally obligated to perform such meritorious actions as contributing to the arts or helping solve the problems of inner-city unemployment and urban blight. For a corporation to perform these kinds of actions would be supererogatory. Others believe corporations have a moral obligation to do these kinds of things. Therefore, the question of whether these kinds of actions on the part of corporations are obligatory or supererogatory is often morally significant.

Acts of supererogation are commonly thought to be the actions of saints and heroes. However, some acts of kindness and generosity, although they are more than what duty requires and hence supererogatory in the strict sense, are certainly not the actions we associate with saints and heroes. Contributing small change to the Home for Little Wanderers may not be a duty, but neither is it saintly or heroic.

Given these considerations, we must distinguish between trivial and nontrivial supererogatory actions. *Nontrivial supererogatory* actions go beyond what is morally required and also involve the elements of risk and self-sacrifice. Trivial supererogatory actions do not involve the elements of risk and self-sacrifice. When an engineer risks his career to expose corruption or bad engineering in a public project in which he is not directly involved, he may not be doing something he has a positive duty to do, especially if the problems do not pose a serious threat to life. But he is certainly engaging in a nontrivial supererogatory act. Similarly, a lawyer who risks his professional career and perhaps his life by exposing and prosecuting gangsters engages in action that is risky, highly meritorious, yet not morally required. It is, then, a nontrivial supererogatory action.

Virtue ethics focuses moral evaluation on individuals rather than on actions. We can consider a person morally worthy if she manifests many or most of the virtues, morally unworthy if she manifests many of the vices. Of course these designations are matters of degree, since nobody is wholly good or wholly bad. Nevertheless, we would want to say that St. Francis was a morally worthy person and Adolf Hitler a morally unworthy person. If we are judging the morality of an action, some virtue ethicists hold that the commendable action in a given situation (one that is morally permissible, obligatory, or supererogatory) is the one that a good or virtuous person would do in that situation. Others would hold that the morally commendable action is one that manifests the appropriate virtues.

Second Level: Moral Principles

The next level of a moral theory consists of general moral principles. A moral principle (MP) is derived from the moral standard, and it serves as the basis for moral judgments. Moral principles apply to a wider area of conduct than moral judgments do but not as wide an area as the moral standard does.

Let us consider the function of moral principles in the moral philosophy known as egoism. Using her moral standard, the egoist may derive moral principles that denote kinds of goals she should pursue to achieve her self-interest. One such principle might be as follows:

MP: I should preserve my physical health.

Physical health is a necessary prerequisite to achieving one's self-interest, however one's self-interest is defined.

This moral principle might justify specific moral judgments:

MJ: I should start jogging at least three times a week.

A moral theory has many moral principles, whereas it ordinarily has only one moral standard. A useful first step in thinking about the moral principles appropriate to your own moral philosophy is to divide them into principles for personal ethics and principles for social ethics. *Personal ethics* has to do with the relationship of individuals to other individuals. Personal ethics can be further subdivided into *duties to self* and *duties to others. Social ethics* has to do with the relationship of individuals to groups and of groups to other groups. Let us consider personal and social ethics in more detail.

Regarding duties to oneself, the question to be asked is, What character traits and personal goals contribute most to the realization of the ideal set forth in the moral standard? The moral principle regarding preserving one's physical health is one answer to this question. An egoist may also find that she needs to develop her capacity to look at things rationally and calmly to determine what will lead to her own self-interest. So the obligation to develop the character trait of rationality follows from the egoistic moral standard.

An advocate of natural law may find that he has an obligation to get as much education as possible to better realize the natural tendency of all humans to know and understand. This obligation may be formulated in terms of a moral principle:

MP: People should develop their rational powers through education.

Duties may be negative as well as positive. As an egoist, I have a duty not to destroy my own health or to sacrifice myself to the welfare of others. Traditional natural-law theorists believe we have a duty not to violate our own natural tendency to preserve our own lives by committing suicide and not to practice forms of contraception that violate our own procreative function.

Some of the most important duties to others are negative. Most moral theories, for example, imply that in general we have duties not to lie to another person and not to perpetrate theft, fraud, or physical violence on others. Besides the duty not to harm others, however, some moral theories may imply the positive duties of preventing harm to others and even of doing good to others. Finally, family and sexual ethics are an important subcategory of duties to others.

Many important moral issues that all of us face as citizens fall into the category of social ethics rather than personal ethics. It is important, therefore, for any morally sophisticated person to work out ideas—consistent, of course, with his or her general moral philosophy—concerning the proper relationship of societies to one another and to individuals. The most general question to be answered is, What kind of social order is best suited to realize the goals set out in my moral philosophy? We can take two differing approaches to answering this question.

One approach, represented in its extreme form by libertarianism, advocates what one libertarian calls the *minimal state;* that is, the state should limit its functions to protecting citizens from violence, theft, and fraud and providing some mechanism for arbitrating disputes among citizens. Otherwise, individuals should be left alone to pursue their own goals with a minimum of governmental interference. Many egoists are sympathetic to the libertarian way of answering questions about social policy.

The other approach advocates a more active role for the state, one in which the state has a positive responsibility to promote the welfare of individuals or to promote some larger societal goals. Utilitarians for the most part have held that the state should take an active role in implementing policies that lead to the public's general welfare.

Third Level: Moral Standard

A moral standard (MS) is the most fundamental moral principle—the principle that provides the criterion for determining right and wrong for a theory. In the example, because we were reasoning from the moral judgment back to basic principles, the moral standard was the last moral principle stated: "In order for a principle of action to be right, I must be willing to have the same principle applied to me in similar circumstances."

Notice that a moral standard is different from both a moral judgment and a moral rule. A moral standard furnishes a *criterion* for determining what makes an action right or wrong. Rather than referring to an individual action, or even a class of actions, it designates a characteristic that all right actions must have. Consider a highly simplified version of the moral standard of egoism:

MS: Actions are right if and only if they promote the egoist's self-interest.

The criterion for the rightness of an action from the egoistic standpoint is that it must promote the self-interest of the egoist. Similar right-making characteristics can be found in the moral standard of every moral philosophy we shall discuss.

For uniformity in stating the moral standard, our phrasing of each moral standard will begin with the wording "Those actions are right that..." or "Actions are right if and only if..." or some closely analogous formula. The rest of the statement will supply the criterion that right actions must satisfy.

Each moral standard has certain terms that must be defined before the standard can be applied. In the egoistic moral standard, the crucial term is *self-interest*. Without clarification of this concept, the moral standard is useless. I cannot know which actions to pursue and which to avoid if I do not define my self-interest.

Often additional distinctions and definitions must be given before a moral standard can be used. The egoist, for example, must decide whether to pursue long-term or short-term self-interest. The utilitarian must decide whether to evaluate the utility of every action directly (a position called *act utilitarianism*) or to evaluate only the utility of general moral principles or rules (a position called *rule utilitarianism*). The natural-law theorist must decide how to determine what is "natural" before the ethics of natural law can be applied.

An outline of the three elements of a moral theory will be helpful. The order of the outline, however, will be different from our previous discussion. So far we have taken a "bottom-up" approach, beginning with moral judgments and proceeding through moral rules to a moral standard. This is the order two people would probably follow in an argument over a moral issue. In giving a general outline of a moral theory, however, it is more logical to take a "top-down" approach, starting with the moral standard and descending through moral rules to moral judgments. From the top-down standpoint, a moral theory has the following form:

I. Moral Standards
    A. Definitions of crucial terms
    B. Other relevant distinctions and principles

II. Moral Rules
    A. Personal ethics
        1. Duties to self
        2. Duties to others
    B. Social ethics

III. Moral Judgments
    A. Is the action morally obligatory?
    B. Is the action morally permissible?

    C. Is the action morally impermissible?

    D. Is the action supererogatory?

I will follow this outline in presenting the five moral theories treated in this book—namely, the ethics of self-interest, the ethics of natural law, the ethics of utilitarianism, the ethics of respect for persons, and virtue ethics.

I will furnish a "checklist" that will help you apply the moral theory to specific cases, and I will follow this checklist in discussing the cases presented. This organization should enable you to apply the theory to other moral problems as they arise in class or in your own experience.

Four Criteria for Evaluating a Moral Theory

Having looked at the structure of a moral theory, we are now ready to consider a set of concepts necessary to evaluate your moral beliefs—namely, criteria for evaluating a moral theory. Moral philosophers do not have an agreed-on set of standards for judging a moral theory. However, consistency and coherence are generally accepted standards for evaluating any theory, so it seems appropriate to apply them to a moral theory as well. The other three criteria we shall employ seem especially appropriate for a moral theory. They are the adequacy of the justification of the moral standard, agreement with your prior moral beliefs, and usefulness in resolving moral disagreements.

These four criteria fall into different categories. The joint criterion of consistency and coherence might be called a "formal" criterion because it has to do with the logical consistency of the moral theory. The second criterion might be described as a "rational" criterion because it concerns the rational justification of the moral standard. The third criterion might be referred to as a "common-sense" criterion because it compares the moral judgments generated by the moral theory with our "common-sense" moral judgments (that is, those we would make independently of the theory). The fourth criterion might be called a "pragmatic" criterion because it asks about the practical usefulness of the theory in resolving moral disagreements.

Criterion 1: Consistency and Coherence—Does the Theory Yield Consistent Judgments and Show Internal Coherence?

Consistency, by which we mean the making of logically compatible predictions or judgments, is a recognized criterion for evaluating the rationality of a belief or a theory. Suppose a scientific theory makes both the prediction that a liquid will freeze at a certain time and the prediction that the same liquid will not freeze at that same time. The theory would be inconsistent because it makes two logically incompatible predictions. Suppose Moral Theory X makes both the moral judgment that assisting Mrs. Wilkins, who is dying of cancer, to end her life is morally permissible and the judgment that assisting the same Mrs. Wilkins to end her life in the same circumstances is not morally permissible. Moral Theory X is inconsistent because it yields logically incompatible moral judgments.

If we assume different facts, then of course we can come out with different moral judgments, even though we subscribe to the same moral principles. For example, suppose two utilitarians are examining the moral permissibility of sex outside of marriage. One utilitarian thinks he has reason to believe that sex outside of marriage produces widespread pregnancies, greater disease, and greater psychological maladjustment in marriage. Another utilitarian thinks he has reason to believe that these adverse consequences do not occur and that in fact people are happier if they engage in premarital sex. Starting with the same moral standard that we should maximize human well-being, these two utilitarians would probably come out to different conclusions regarding the moral permissibility of premarital sex. This difference should not be considered a fault of the theory, however. It is the result of different factual assumptions.

A theory is *coherent* if it does not contain logically incompatible parts, such as standards, principles, rules, or concepts. Consistency is an *external criterion*, because it refers to the predictions or judgments generated by the theory, but coherence is an *internal criterion*, because it refers to the logical relationship of the parts of the theory itself. Suppose a theory of childhood delinquency contains two different and logically incompatible definitions of delinquency. The theory is internally incoherent. Suppose, to take an extreme case, we had an ethical theory with two moral standards of the following types:

MS1: An action is right if it leads to one's own self-interest.

MS2: An action is not right if it leads to one's own self-interest.

The ethical theory would be incoherent. Although this radical kind of inconsistency is unlikely, other kinds of incoherence are much more likely. An ethical theory might contain two different and incompatible definitions of self-interest, for example.

Here is a type of inconsistency that many moral philosophers believe appears in certain forms of ethical egoism. To be ethically acceptable, ethical egoists must be impartial. That is, they must admit that each person has an equal right to pursue her self-interest. As an egoist, then, I must advocate that others follow their self-interest, just as I follow mine. But in pursuing their interests, others can harm me. Thus, in advocating that others pursue their interests, I may be acting contrary to my own interests.

An inconsistency or incoherence does not necessarily mean that the moral theory should be abandoned. Perhaps no moral position is fully consistent and coherent. But the absence of logical incompatibility is an integral part of the concept of rationality itself, and we must regard inconsistency and incoherence as a significant weakness in a moral theory.

Criterion 2: Justification—How Well Can the Moral Standard Be Justified?

Every moral theorist attempts to give a rational justification for accepting his or her moral standard. We have already discussed two of the most popular ways of defending a moral standard: by an appeal to religion or by an appeal to social norms. However, many other ways to justify accepting a moral standard are possible.

The method of defending a moral standard must be fundamentally different from the method of defending moral rules or moral judgments within a theory. Moral rules and moral judgments can be defended by reference to the moral standard, but the moral standard cannot be defended by referring to a higher moral standard. Thus, a strict deductive proof of a moral standard is impossible. At best, a moral philosopher can show reasons why accepting one moral standard rather than another is plausible. We shall consider some of these arguments when we analyze each of the four theories.

Criterion 3: Plausibility—Does the Moral Theory Produce Moral Judgments That Agree with Our Prior Moral Beliefs?

One way to justify a moral theory is to work out its implications for particular moral issues and then compare these implications with our most strongly held moral beliefs. This is different from the type of justification described in Criterion 2. In Criterion 2, we look for a reason for accepting the moral standard. In Criterion 3, we inquire as to the plausibility of the moral judgments generated by the theory. Criterion 2 looks at justification from the "top" side of the theory (the moral standard), while Criterion 3 looks at justification from the "bottom" side of the theory (the moral judgments).

Consider a moral theory such as natural law, which holds that it is always wrong to take innocent human life directly. This principle implies the moral judgment that administering an injection to end the life of a dying cancer patient who requested to be put out of his misery is immoral. But you may believe that such an action is not immoral and is in fact an act of mercy. If so, a conflict exists between the moral judgments generated by natural-law moral theory and your own prior moral beliefs.

In the face of the conflict between natural law and your prior moral beliefs about mercy killing, you have four options: (1) give up your belief that mercy killing is sometimes morally permissible; (2) give up natural law moral theory altogether; (3) try to show that natural-law moral theory does not really condemn mercy killing; or (4) admit that in this instance your moral theory and your beliefs about mercy killing conflict. If you are strongly committed to natural-law moral theory (perhaps because you are a conservative Roman Catholic), you may be most attracted to the first and third options. If you have other reasons for questioning natural-law moral theory anyhow, you may choose the second option. The fourth option implies an admission that in this instance the implications of natural-law moral theory are implausible.

The most natural reaction to the criterion of plausibility is to say that it is a highly questionable test. If we evaluate a theory in terms of its agreement with our prior moral judgments and, at a later time, evaluate our moral judgments in terms of their agreement with the theory, aren't we involved in circular and therefore invalid reasoning?

The answer to this question is that the criterion of plausibility is only one test of the validity of a moral theory. Although a moral theory can be measured by its ability to generate those moral judgments about which we feel most confident, those moral judgments are not beyond question. It is possible that a moral theory that generates a moral judgment different from the one we were inclined to accept is more strongly justified by the other three criteria, so that we should modify the moral judgment that we originally held in such high confidence.

This view of the relationship of moral theory to moral judgments was classically described by John Rawls in his concept of reflective equilibrium, according to which there should be, ideally, an agreement between our moral theory and what he calls our "considered moral judgments." *Considered moral judgments* are those that are made with the greatest confidence. They are contrasted with "those judgments made with hesitation, or in which we have little confidence" or "those given when we are upset or frightened, or when we stand to gain one way or another. . . ."[5]

If the moral principles do not justify our considered moral judgments, then we should either change our moral judgments or modify our moral theory to bring the two back into equilibrium. Thus, the state of reflective

---

[5]John Rawls, *A Theory of Justice* (Cambridge, MA: Harvard University Press, 1971), p. 47.

equilibrium is a state in which there is an absence of tension between our moral theory and our moral judgments.

Criterion 4: Usefulness—Is the Theory Useful in Resolving Moral Disagreements?

Moral theories are of little practical use if they cannot help us resolve moral problems, either within our own thinking or between ourselves and others. A moral theory can fail to help us achieve this goal in several ways. We shall consider two general problems here. We shall consider other problems in the chapters devoted to particular moral theories.

One way in which moral theories can be deficient in their ability to resolve moral problems is that applying the principles derived from the theory may sometimes be difficult or controversial. A moral theory may show that bribery is wrong, but it may not provide a way for deciding whether paying a foreign official the customary $100 with an application to do business in his country is really a bribe.

Another way in which moral theories can fail to be useful is by providing conflicting directives, without showing how to resolve the conflict. For example, a moral theory may require us to keep promises and help those in distress. But it may not be easy to determine from the theory whether we should keep our promise to take a family member to a long-awaited social event or help a friend in emotional distress. We shall condider these in the next section.

CONCEPT SUMMARY

A moral theory has three levels. First, a moral standard is the basic criterion for determining right and wrong. Second, a moral principle marks a class of actions that is right or wrong. Moral principles give direction for the relationship of individuals to other individuals (personal ethics) and the relationship of individuals to groups or groups to other groups (social ethics). Finally, a moral judgment is a moral evaluation of particular actions or persons. Moral judgments can evaluate actions as obligatory, permissible, impermissible, or supererogatory. Virtue ethics evaluates people as morally worthy or unworthy.

The four criteria for evaluating a moral theory are (1) coherence and consistency; (2) the adequacy of the justification of the moral standard; (3) agreement of the moral judgments generated by the theory with prior moral beliefs; and (4) usefulness in resolving moral conflict. These criteria will be applied to each of the four moral philosophies that we shall consider.

PROBLEMS IN APPLYING MORAL PRINCIPLES

Moral thinking would be easier if moral theories provided simple and straightforward ways of arriving at moral judgments. "Just derive moral principles from the moral standard and then apply the principles to particular situations," we might be tempted to say. Unfortunately, deriving moral principles from moral standards is not always easy. Applying moral principles to specific circumstances to yield moral judgments can be even more problematic. Most of the problems in using moral principles to arrive at moral judgements fall into two groups. I shall refer to the first group of problems as relevance problems and the second group as conflict problems.[6]

Relevance Problems

A *relevance problem* occurs when we do not know whether a moral principle is relevant to a particular situation. Usually a relevance problem can be traced to a conceptual issue. You will recall that a conceptual issue has to do with (1) the meaning of a concept; or (2) its application to a particular situation. Sometimes we may not be sure how a concept such as "bribery" or "confidentiality" should be defined. At other times, we do not know what the appropriate application of a concept should be in a borderline situation.

In applying moral principles, therefore, you will find some circumstances in which they clearly apply and borderline circumstances in which their application is controversial. The clear cases in which the principle does apply we may call *paradigm cases*. The borderline cases in which application of the principle is controversial or ambiguous we may call *problematic cases*. Problematic cases give rise to relevance problems.

Consider the following example.[7] Most of us would agree to a moral principle or rule that says, "People should return or replace borrowed items."

---

[6]For a clear description of these two kinds of problems, see James D. Wallace, *Moral Relevance and Moral Conflict* (Ithaca, NY: Cornell University Press, 1988). See especially the introduction and the first chapter.

[7]For the suggestion of this example, which has been considerably modified and expanded, see Albert R. Jonsen and Stephen Toulmin, *The Abuse of Casuistry* (Berkeley: University of California Press, 1988), p. 324. Jonsen and Toulmin make a distinction similar to Wallace's distinction between relevance and conflict problems.

If we borrow a friend's car for the evening, we expect to return it the next day or as soon as possible. But what about "borrowing" a match? Does the principle that we should return or replace borrowed items apply here? Using quotation marks around the word "borrow" indicates that we may have come to an example where applying the concept of "borrowing" becomes problematic.

We could arrange examples of returning borrowed items to show the transition from paradigm cases in which the principle applies, through borderline or problematic cases, to cases in which the principle does not apply:

MP: "People should return or replace borrowed items."

1. Returning a borrowed car
2. Returning a borrowed book
3. Returning $10 that was borrowed
4. Returning borrowed money for a Coke
5. Returning a borrowed pencil
6. Returning three sheets of borrowed paper
7. Returning a borrowed match

You may find that the principle clearly applies to the first three examples, and you may also have little trouble deciding that the principle clearly does not apply to examples 6 and 7. But examples 4 and 5 may be troublesome. Should we consider these examples of borrowing, or should they be considered examples of gifts?

The most obvious thing to say is that the question whether the principle about returning a borrowed item applies is answered by determining the item's worth. This may well be the most important consideration, for it points to an obvious similarity between examples 1 through 3 and examples 6 and 7. The first three examples concern objects whose worth most of us would consider substantial, whereas the last two examples concern items that most of us would probably consider to be of trivial value. The amount of monetary value, however, does not by itself settle the issue of where we should draw the line, any more than the moral principle itself does. Exactly how much must an item be worth before it is subject to the rule that borrowed items should be returned or replaced?

To make matters more complicated, monetary worth is not necessarily the only consideration at issue in this example. How well I know the person may be a relevant consideration. Or whether we regularly borrow from each other may be important. Or my friend may know that I have a lot more money than he does, so we may have an implicit understanding that he can regularly borrow small amounts of cash without any need to return it. Or allowing a friend to borrow money without returning it may be a subtle way of repaying her for the help she gives me on homework.

Now let us consider a more morally significant example. In 1977, the U.S. Congress passed the Foreign Corrupt Practices Act (FCPA). The new law made it illegal for U.S. businesspeople and other citizens to "corruptly" pay, or authorize the payment, of money or anything of value to foreign government officials and foreign political parties. It was passed during the Carter administration as a result of the discovery that nearly 400 American companies had paid approximately $300 million to foreign officials for business favors. For example, Lockheed had paid $22 million to foreign politicians over five years to secure aircraft contracts, and Gulf Oil Corporation had made secret payments of $4 million to foreign politicians over the same period.

The FCPA was enacted, among other reasons, because of the widespread conviction that bribery is immoral. But it also raises the conceptual problem of the proper scope of the concept of bribery. Consider the following moral principle, with the accompanying set of examples:

MP: "It is wrong to pay or accept bribes."

1. Paying money to foreign government officials to obtain a contract from a foreign government
2. Paying money to foreign government officials so that the government will at least consider a product for possible purchase
3. Paying money to expedite the processing of an application to do business in a foreign country
4. Paying money to foreign government officials to ensure that your property will not be mysteriously destroyed by "vandals"

The first example is clearly a bribe, if we think of a bribe as paying money to a person or group for special considerations that are contrary to their role. The role of the purchasing officer is to select the best product for his government. The bribe leads the official to violate this requirement.

The second example is more problematic. Unlike paradigm cases of bribery, the payment in this case does not induce the foreign official to act contrary to his role. In fact, the foreign official should make his selection from all available products, so that he should consider your product anyhow. A second difference from paradigm cases of bribery is that the person who makes the payment does so to avoid an injustice that would otherwise accrue to himself and his company. Perhaps this payment should be called extortion rather than a bribe. Nevertheless, it has this feature in common with bribery: it gives the person who can afford to pay the fee an advantage over the person who cannot afford to pay it.

The third example usually involves small amounts of "grease money" and probably should not be considered bribery. In processing an application to do business efficiently, the government official is only doing what she should do anyhow. Furthermore, the amount of money involved would be so small that ordinarily one's competitors could afford to pay it too.

The fourth example would usually be considered an example of extortion or paying "protection money" rather than paying a bribe because it is paying a foreign official for what he should do anyhow. Furthermore, the payment is to avoid a harm rather than to obtain a benefit. If we apply the moral principle to these examples, and if we assume that extortion payments are not wrong, we can conclude that the first action is wrong, but the other three are not. These moral judgments are possible only after we have settled the conceptual problem about the meaning and scope of the concept of bribery.

Many other examples of relevance problems are encountered in applying a moral theory. Our moral theory may generate a moral principle such as "Deception is wrong." We may still wonder whether an advertisement for a children's cereal that portrays a muscular man eating the cereal is deceptive to children because children may be persuaded that eating the cereal will ensure that they will grow up to be strong and healthy. Or we may agree that our theory justifies the moral principle "Murder is wrong" but disagree whether euthanasia should be counted as murder. Or we may have a moral principle that condemns suicide but wonder whether the action of Captain Oates described in the first chapter should be considered suicide.

Now we can summarize several important points about relevance problems. First, relevance problems might not be resolvable by appeal to moral principles or even the moral standard. Although the moral standard and the derivative moral principles might give clear direction in the central or paradigm cases, they might not give direction in controversial cases. The relevance problem might also not be resolvable by making reference to a definition of the terms that is constructed independently of the particular context in which the conceptual problem appears. The "vertical" reasoning from moral standards, through moral principles, to moral judgments that apply in clear or paradigm cases, must be supplemented by "horizontal" reasoning that relies on analysis of similarities and differences between paradigmatic and problematic cases. We must determine when the similarities and differences justify placing an example under a particular concept and when they do not. Reasoning by analogy is thus an important tool in applying moral principles to ambiguous cases.

Second, the more ambiguous the case, the more we must know about the particular circumstances of the case to determine whether the case falls under a given concept. Whether money for a Coke should be returned may be decidable only with reference to a particular person and his or her relationship to the person who borrowed the money. Whether a payment of money is a bribe may depend on the extent to which the person accepting the money grants special favors to the person who pays the money.

Third, sometimes even the similarities and differences between particular cases are insufficient to make a convincing case for one decision rather than another. In such cases, it is often necessary to come to a general agreement on the proper scope of a concept. For example, in deciding when acceptance by a purchasing agent of gifts and amenities from vendors constitutes accepting a bribe, a company may have to stipulate that accepting a pen with the company's name on it is permissible but accepting a leather attaché case is not.

Conflict Problems

Sometimes we may find that more than one moral principle is relevant to a particular situation and that we can come up with different moral judgments, depending on which principle we think has priority. Then we have a *conflict problem*—that is, a situation in which two or more apparently conflicting moral principles are relevant.

Sometimes it is clear which of two relevant and conflicting moral principles should have priority. Suppose I promise to meet you for dinner at 6:00 P.M. Driving to your house, I pass two cars that have been in an accident. One of the victims signals for help. The police and ambulance have not yet arrived, and one of the other victims appears to have some injuries. I have some emergency medical training and might be able to help; I might even be able to save someone's life. If I do respond, however, I will be late for dinner with you. I have two conflicting moral obligations and cannot fulfill both. What should I do? Assisting someone in distress and possibly saving a life takes priority over being on time for a dinner appointment, so the resolution of this conflict is simple.

Some situations, however, are not as easily resolved. In a well-known incident from World War II, the French existentialist philosopher Jean-Paul Sartre tells of a young man who came to him for advice, asking whether he should stay with his aging mother or join the French Resistance.

If he left his mother, she would probably die; on the other hand, he believed he had an obligation to participate in the struggle to free France. What should he do?[8]

Philosophers have called this kind of conflict situation a *moral dilemma*. Literature furnishes many examples of moral dilemmas. In Euripides' play, *Iphigenia in Aulis*, Agamemnon is faced with the dilemma of having to sacrifice his daughter, Iphigenia, to the goddess Artemis—to persuade her to grant the Greek ships a favoring wind on their way to conquer Troy—or losing the war. His obligations to his daughter and his soldiers are on a collision course. In William Styron's *Sophie's Choice*, Sophie is ordered by a Nazi guard to shoot one of her children, or else he will kill both of them. Finally, in E. M. Forster's *Two Cheers for Democracy*, a disagreement arises over whether it is worse to betray a friend or one's country.

We have at least two ways of deciding issues when we are faced with a situation in which both of two equally important and incompatible principles appear to conflict.

First, we may be able to find a creative "middle way" between the two conflicting principles. In his struggle for civil rights for blacks, Martin Luther King, Jr., found such a creative middle way in his doctrine of nonviolent resistance. King faced a choice between his obligation to obey the law and his obligation to promote racial justice. On the one hand, he respected the laws of the United States and did not wish to destroy its legal system. On the other hand, he wanted to promote the cause of racial justice, and he believed he could not do so without breaking the law. His escape from this dilemma involved taking the path of nonviolent civil disobedience. Although he did break the law in some of his activities, he did so in a nonviolent way that involved a willingness to take the legal consequences of his actions.

In another example, which we mentioned earlier, Jeffrey Fadiman suggests a creative middle way may be available to American businesspeople facing the dilemma of whether to make payments to foreign nationals. If the payments are not made, valuable business opportunities may be lost. But if the payments are made, U.S. businesspeople may be doing something that is illegal or that violates their own consciences. Instead of yielding to either of these unattractive alternatives, Fadiman proposes the adoption of a "donation strategy." Rather than giving money or gifts to individuals, Fadiman suggests making donations to the community. A corporation might construct a hospital, for example, or it might

---

[8]J. P. Sartre, "Existentialism Is a Humanism," in Walter Kaufmann (ed.), *Existentialism from Dostoyevsky to Sartre* (Cleveland, OH: World, 1956), pp. 295–296.

offer jobs. In the 1970s, Fadiman points out, Coca-Cola hired hundreds of Egyptians to plant orange trees on thousands of acres of desert, thereby creating more goodwill than would have been generated by bribes made to individuals. In 1983, the British gained goodwill by assembling thousands of dollars worth of tools and vehicle parts and training Tanzanians to service the vehicles. This action enabled the Tanzanians to continue patrolling their wild-game preserves, an activity that had almost stopped because of the weakened Tanzanian economy. The British took this step instead of making a cash donation, which might well have been interpreted as a bribe.[9]

Second, resolving moral dilemmas can sometimes be accomplished by appealing to values that might not otherwise be relevant. Philosopher Isaac Levi provides an example of this kind of conflict resolution involving professional rather than strictly moral considerations.[10] According to a slightly modified version of Levi's example, an office manager must choose between two candidates for a secretarial position. She wants to select the person who is the best typist and the best stenographer, but, unfortunately, no single person has the highest rating on both the stenographer test and the typing test. John has 94 on the stenographer test and 90 on the typing test, whereas James has 90 on the stenographer test and 94 on the typing test. How does she decide what to do?

One option is to appeal to values that she might otherwise consider inadmissible. For example, although she generally is a staunch opponent of reverse discrimination, in this case she considers it admissible to hire John (who is black) rather than James (who is white). Or, if both candidates are members of minority groups, she might consider another value that she would ordinarily consider inadmissible—namely, the fact that James is much more handsome than John. Similarly, the debate described by E. M. Forster over loyalty to one's friends versus loyalty to one's country may be decided on the basis of personal ideals rather than moral principles. Does one want to be the kind of person who is loyal to friends at all cost or who takes loyalty to one's country as supreme?

Room for Disagreement

The first three chapters have shown that people who attempt to follow the Socratic ideal of critical reflection sometimes disagree over moral

---

[9]Jeffrey A. Fadiman, "A Traveler's Guide to Gifts and Bribes," *Harvard Business Review* (July–August 1986); excerpts reprinted in William H. Shaw and Vincent Barry, *Moral Issues in Business*, 4th ed. (Belmont, CA: Wadsworth, 1989) pp. 328–337.

[10]Isaac Levi, *Hard Choices* (Cambridge: Cambridge University Press, 1986), pp. 28–29.

issues for a number of reasons. People may disagree over the facts, moral standards, moral principles, and conceptual issues. We have just seen that relevance and conflict problems can also lead to different moral judgments.

Given these possible sources of moral disagreement, people who use their most careful critical reflection sometimes come to different moral judgments, especially in borderline cases. You may sometimes come to different conclusions than I do, even when you assume the same moral principles. In reading my discussions of cases in the following chapters, you should keep this in mind. When you do disagree, you should be able, however, to isolate the precise nature of your disagreement, using the concepts we have developed so far.

CONCEPT SUMMARY

Two types of problems in applying moral principles are relevance problems and conflict problems. Relevance problems arise when it is unclear whether a moral principle applies in a borderline case. In resolving relevance problems, we may often find it helpful to reason from clear or paradigm cases to problematic or borderline cases by observing similarities and differences. Also, the more ambiguous the case, the more we need to know about the particular circumstances. Finally, sometimes settling where the line is drawn is impossible except by stipulation and general agreement.

Conflict problems arise in situations where there are two or more relevant moral demands, both of which cannot be complied with in a particular situation. Sometimes we can find a creative "middle way" that does some justice to both demands. Failing this, we might be justified in appealing to considerations, such as personal interests and ideals, that would not otherwise be relevant.

People who are equally committed to critical reflection on moral issues sometimes disagree in their moral judgments. Using the concepts developed in the first three chapters, they should be able to isolate the nature of their disagreements.

THE ETHICS
OF SELF-INTEREST

Bryan Springer has a high-paying summer job as a forklift operator, which enables him to attend college without having to take out any student loans. He is now staring at a 50-gallon drum filled with used machine coolant.

Just moments ago, Bryan's supervisor, Max Morrison, told him to dump half of the used coolant down the drain. Bryan knows the coolant is toxic, and he has already mentioned this to Max. But Max was not swayed. He insisted, "The toxins settle at the bottom of the drum. If you pour out half and dilute with tap water while you're pouring it, there's no problem."

Bryan was not convinced, adding that Max's solution to the problem was against the law. But Max responded even more angrily:

> You aren't one of those "environmentalists," are you? You college guys spend too much of your time in the ivory tower. It's time to get real—and get on with the job. You know, you're very lucky to have a good-paying job like this, kid. In three months you'll be back in your cozy college. Meanwhile, how many other college kids do you think there are out there wondering if they'll be able to afford to go back—kids who'd give their eye teeth to be where you are right now?

Max then left, fully expecting Bryan to dump the used coolant. Bryan knows he is in danger of losing his job and jeopardizing his chances of returning to college in the fall. He wonders what he should do.[1]

We could say that this case illustrates a conflict between Bryan's desire to promote his own interests and his desire to act in a morally responsible way. But things may not be that simple. Could it be that Bryan's moral obligation *is* just to look out after his own self-interest and that this self-interest requires him to dump the coolant? Or perhaps Bryan's self-interest

---

[1] This case is adapted from Michael S. Pritchard, (ed.), *Teaching Engineering Ethics: A Case Study Approach,* June 1992, National Science Foundation Grant No. DIR 8820837. The case and accompanying commentaries are on pp. 162–171.

must be considered in some larger sense, so that his "enlightened" self-interest requires him not to dump the coolant?

There is a widespread belief that there is something important in the philosophy of egoism. Ayn Rand's *The Virtue of Selfishness* and her other books have sold millions of copies. Robert Ringer's *Looking Out for Number One* and David Seabury's *The Art of Selfishness* have evidently convinced many people of the validity of the egoistic point of view. Nevertheless, many philosophers seem so insistent on refuting egoism that they fail to take it seriously. In this chapter we shall attempt to resist this tendency by first untangling some of the conceptual knots encountered in attempting to think about the ethics of egoism, and then formulating a version of egoism that is as plausible as we can make it. We cannot assess the validity of ethical egoism until we have a plausible version of it.

In pursuing a plausible version of egoism, we must formulate it as a genuine *moral* philosophy. That is, we must formulate a version of egoism that satisfies the characteristics of a moral position set out in Chapter 1. In particular, we want to formulate a version of egoism that satisfies the criterion of impartiality. Recall that moral statements are supposed to take a universal point of view, in which each person's interests count the same. We shall be looking, therefore, at a formulation of *ethical egoism*, that is, a moral philosophy that affirms that *each person* ought to pursue what is in his self-interest.

This position should be distinguished from *individual ethical egoism*, which holds that everyone ought to pursue *my* best interests. This version does not meet the standard of impartiality. We are not willing for others to be egoists too. Rather, we want others to be *altruists*, in that they should promote the interests of others. However, the individual egoist is not even promoting a broad version of altruism, because he is advocating that others promote the interests of only *one other person, namely his own interests.*

The only morally acceptable version of egoism is what we shall call universal ethical egoism, namely the view that everyone ought to do what is in his or her own self-interest. This appears to be the version of egoism that many popular advocates of egoism promote. Ayn Rand says that "the objectivist ethics holds that the actor must always be the beneficiary of his action and that man must act for his own rational self-interest."[2] The term "man" refers to everyone, not just a single individual. The impartial standpoint characteristic of genuine moral positions forces the egoist to recognize that everyone has an equal right to pursue his or her own self-interest.

---

[2] Ayn Rand, *The Virtue of Selfishness* (New York: Signet Books, 1961), p. X.

THE PARADOX OF EGOISM

The State of Nature

Advocating that each person pursue his or her self-interest, however, produces a problem for the egoist. When everyone pursues his or her self-interest without restraint, the result is an intolerable state of conflict. Whenever it suits my interests and I believe I can get away with it, I will break moral rules. I will steal or cheat or lie or break my promises or even kill in order to achieve my goals. You, on the other hand, will behave the same way toward me. Many of the products of civilized society will be absent, and we will all live in a "dog eat dog" society.

Thomas Hobbes (1588–1679), one of the most important philosophical egoists, showed how human nature leads people to live in such a state, which he called the "state of nature." According to Hobbes scholar Gregory Kavka, Hobbes's account of the human condition contains six elements: (1) people are primarily concerned with their own well-being and act accordingly; (2) people want to avoid death and act accordingly; (3) people are concerned with what others think of them (reputation) and act accordingly; (4) people care about their future, as well as their present well-being, and act accordingly; (5) satisfaction of one person's desires often conflicts with another person's desire satisfaction, owing to such factors as material scarcity and competing claims to the same objects; and (6) people are roughly equal in their intellectual and physical abilities.[3] This combination of elements leads to the state of nature, which Hobbes classically defines in the following way:

> In such condition, there is no place for industry; because the fruit thereof is uncertain: and consequently no culture of the earth; no navigation . . . no knowledge of the face of the earth; no account of time; no arts; no letters; no society; and which is worst of all, continual fear, and danger of violent death; and the life of man, solitary, poor, nasty, brutish, and short.[4]

Hobbes's description of the state of nature shows that the universal adoption of egoism gives rise to what we might call the *paradox of egoism:* unrestricted pursuit of self-interest by everyone produces a state of affairs contrary to the egoist's self-interest. Put another way, the egoist faces

---

[3] Gregory S. Kavka, *Hobbesian Moral and Political Theory* (Princeton, NJ: Princeton University Press, 1986) pp. 33–34.

[4] Thomas Hobbes, *Leviathan,* ch. 13.

a dilemma. In order to have a position that is morally acceptable, he must be willing for others to be egoists too. But in doing so, he allows that others may act in ways that conflict with his own self-interest.

An Illustration

We can illustrate the way universal pursuit of self-interest generates a state that is less desirable from the standpoint of self-interest for everyone concerned. Let us take the example of the moral rule requiring us to refrain from stealing. Suppose Bob and Jane are neighbors and each has the opportunity to break into the other's home and steal some valuable antiques without being caught. We can consider various courses of action they might take and their outcomes, assigning numbers to the desirability of the outcomes. Let us assign 1 to the most desirable outcome, 2 to the next most desirable, 3 to the next most desirable, and 4 to the least desirable. If we let the first number in each quadrant represent the desirability of the option from Jane's standpoint and the second number represent the desirability from Bob's standpoint, a matrix of their options would look like this:

	Bob	
	Not steal	Steal
Jane		
Not steal	2,2	4,1
Steal	1,4	3,3

From the standpoint of Jane's self-interest, the most desirable option would be for her to steal and Bob not to steal (lower left quadrant), but she knows there is little chance of attaining this state of affairs. The best she can hope for is for both not to steal (upper left quadrant). The next most desirable option would be for both to steal (lower right quadrant), and the least desirable option would be for Jane not to steal and Bob to steal (upper right quadrant). From Bob's standpoint, the desirability of the options would be just the reverse.

Given that both are egoists and would not agree to the other's stealing while they refrain from stealing, the most rational thing for Bob and Jane to do would be to promise not to steal from each other, giving them the situation in the upper left quadrant. However, since both are egoists and know that the other would probably break their promises, they will both probably decide to steal from the other, giving them the situation in the lower right quadrant. Thus, egoists, following their own egoistic tendencies, will achieve a less-than-optimal situation, even from their own selfish standpoints.

Perhaps things are not quite this bad, however. This illustration shows only one choice situation—one "round" in the game between Jane and Bill. Suppose Jane and Bill continue to live as neighbors and have many opportunities for theft. Each has stolen from the other, and the other knows it. So, out of self-interest, both Jane and Bob decide they have had enough. They decide they will take a chance and stop stealing from the other, as long as the other does the same. Bob decides, for example, to adopt the rule:

> Refrain from stealing as long as Jane also refrains and steal only if Jane steals first.

Jane adopts a similar rule with regard to Bob.

There are still two significant problems. First, this state of affairs is inherently unstable and so not satisfactory from an egoistic standpoint. Even though he has adopted this rule, if Bob can find a way to steal without Jane's knowing he is stealing, he will steal, and Jane will try to do the same thing. If either finds out, the vicious cycle will start all over again, and they will both fall again into the less desirable situation described in the lower right quadrant. The state of nature reappears.

ESCAPING FROM THE PARADOX OF EGOISM

This second problem points a way to a solution to the paradox of egoism. Suppose, however, that Bob and Jane believed that it was simply wrong to violate promises—or, for that matter, to violate the other basic moral prohibitions of morality—in order to achieve their own self-interest. They believe it is wrong to kill, lie, steal, break promises, or cheat, even to achieve their own goals. They believe this, not because they have made any agreement with other egoists, but because they think it is simply wrong to do these things. Let us say that they have *moral side constraints* on their pursuit of their self-interested goals. They are egoists, to be sure, but only within certain limits.

You may be inclined to say, "Well, this is no longer egoism, or at best only a watered-down form of egoism." But remember that the impartiality requirement itself prohibits us from adopting positions in which each person's interests do not count the same. If we break the rule against stealing to further our interests, others may do so as well. Even some well-known advocates of egoism seem to recognize the legitimacy of moral side constraints. Consider a statement from one of the best-known contemporary egoists, Ayn Rand. In a continuation of the quotation given earlier, she says that an egoist's right to do as he pleases is constrained by ethical principles:

> . . . his right to do so [pursue his own self-interest] is derived from his nature as man and from the function of moral values in human life—and, therefore, is applicable only in the context of a rational, objectively demonstrated and validated code of moral principles, which define and determine his actual self-interest. It is not a license to "do as he pleases". . .[5]

In other places she points out that this code of moral principles includes a set of rights possessed by all individuals (such as the right to life) that guide the relationship of individuals to each other.[6] Pursuit of self-interest operates within a context of moral side constraints.

It is tempting to reassert that this is not genuine egoism, but note that the side-constrained version of egoism is still different from the views of most non-egoists. The moral side constraints are "negative" in orientation. In general, the side-constrained egoist will not feel obliged to comply with the "positive" demands of morality. She will not feel any obligation to help others in distress unless it is in her interest to do so. She will not be inclined to enter sympathetically into the suffering of others. She certainly will not feel obligated to promote the public good or the general welfare unless it can be shown to be a means (and, in fact, the best way) of furthering her own interests. She will not ordinarily perform saintly or heroic acts. Engaging in a high-risk military mission to defend her homeland might be justifiable for the egoist, however, if the defense of her homeland is important to her own well-being.

Let us put the distinction between negative and positive obligations in a different way. Philosopher Bernard Gert distinguishes between moral rules and moral ideals. Moral rules include prohibitions of such actions as killing, causing pain, disabling, depriving of freedom, depraving of pleasure, deceiving, breaking promises, cheating, disobeying the law and failing to perform one's duties.

Moral ideals, on the other hand, include positive obligations, such as preventing killing, preventing the causing of pain, preventing disabling, and so forth. In other words, moral ideals comprise the positive obligations associated with the moral rules.[7] The side-constrained egoist accepts the

---

[5] Ayn Rand, *The Virtue of Selfishness*, op. cit., p. X.

[6] Ayn Rand, *The Virtue of Selfishness*, op. cit., p. 92.

[7] Bernard Gert, *Morality: A New Justification of the Moral Rules* (New York: Oxford University Press, 1988), p. 157 and ch. 8.

prohibitions embodied in the moral rules and advocates that others accept them as well. On the other hand, she does not accept the moral ideals as imposing obligations, and does not advocate that others accept them. She believes that, within the side-constraints of the moral rules, everyone should pursue his or her own self-interest.

THE MORAL STANDARD

Before we formulate the moral standard of this side-constrained form of ethical egoism, several additional clarifications must be made.

First, the moral standard must provide a method for deciding which action is right when several alternative actions would each contribute to a person's good (or well-being). Suppose action A provides ten units of good and action B provides 50 units of good; both acts would promote a person's self-interest. In this case, action B should be obligatory. To consider another possibility, suppose actions A, B, and C each contribute ten units of good and no action contributes more than ten units of good. In this case, actions A, B, and C should be equally desirable. Thus, an act cannot be right simply because it promotes my well-being. The course of action to be followed should be the one that produces the most good, or at least as much good as any   alternative action.

Second, the moral standard must take account of situations in which no available action contributes to a person's good. If I am faced with several alternatives, all of which detract from my well-being, the proper course of action is the one that will diminish my well-being the least. The moral standard should reflect this requirement.

Third, the moral standard should reflect what we have called "universal ethical egoism" and should incorporate the side constraint on egoism that requires people not to pursue their self-interest at the expense of violating fundamental moral rules.

Fourth, the moral standard should give direction not only for the actions of individuals, but also for general policies or rules. Here we should make a distinction between two kinds of egoism. *Act egoism* focuses on the actions of individual egoists and specifies that I should evaluate every act in accordance with whether it promotes my well-being within the moral side constraints. *Rule egoism* focuses on questions of social policy and general social import. It looks for rules that would meet egoistic criteria if generally followed. This means that the rules must be those (such as the prohibition of killing) that would (1) in general benefit the individual proposing them; (2) secure agreement from other egoists; and (3) conform to the moral side constraints.

Rather than evaluating his actions directly by asking whether they promote his self-interest, the rule egoist evaluates his actions by asking whether they conform to certain rules, the rules themselves being justified by these three criteria.

Fifth, we shall use the term "audience" to refer to those whose self-interest will be (or could be) affected by the act or rule being evaluated.

Given these considerations, the moral standard can be formulated as follows:

> MS: Those actions (or rules) are right if and only if, within the moral side constraints, they promote the person's self-interest at least as much as any alternative action or if they harm their self-interest the least or as little as any alternative action. Moral rules must also be agreeable to the audience of egoists, within the limits of the moral side constraints.

Now we are ready to provide checklists for applying act and rule egoism.

CHECKLIST FOR APPLYING ACT EGOISM

I.   Determine the alternative actions that are possible in the situation and their consequences.
II. Within the limits of the moral side constraints, choose the action that promotes the egoist's self-interest at least as much as any alternative action or harms the egoist's self-interest the least, or as little as any alternative action.
   A.   An action that promotes the egoist's self-interest more than any alternative action or harms it the least is morally obligatory.
   B.   An action that promotes the egoist's self-interest less than an alternative action or harms it more than an alternative action is morally impermissible.
   C.   If several actions equally promote the egoist's self-interest or equally harm the egoist's self-interest (and they are the only options available), they are all morally permissible.

CHECKLIST FOR APPLYING RULE EGOISM

I.   Determine the alternative rules that are possible in the situation.
II. Within the limits of the moral side constraints, determine which rule is most likely to promote the egoist's self-interest and to be agreeable to the audience of egoists.

III. If the rule is to be applied to a particular action, evaluate the action in the following way:
   A. An action that is more consistent with the relevant rule than any alternative possible action is morally obligatory.
   B. An action that is less consistent with the relevant rule than any alternative possible action is morally impermissible.
   C. Actions that are equally consistent with the relevant rule are all morally permissible.

CONCEPT SUMMARY

Egoists believe that a person should pursue his or her self-interest. To have a morally acceptable version of egoism, however, egoists must be willing to allow others to be egoists too. This produces the paradox of egoism: unrestricted pursuit of self-interest by everyone produces a state of affairs contrary to the egoist's self-interest. The paradox of egoism can be overcome if the egoist accepts moral side constraints on his or her pursuit of self-interest. Egoists agree, that is, to refrain from violating basic moral rules, such as the prohibitions of killing, stealing and lying, even when these restrictions impede their ability to pursue their self-interest.

The egoistic moral standard should, within the moral side constraints, direct egoists to maximize self-interest, or at least act to diminish self-interest the least. This standard should also apply to everyone. Act egoism focuses on individual actions, whereas rule egoism focuses on those policies that, while benefitting their proposer and conforming to the moral side constraints, can be agreed to by the audience of egoists.

THE PERSONAL AND SOCIAL ETHICS OF EGOISM

Duties to Self

As an egoist, my primary concern is to promote *my* self-interest, within the limitations imposed by the moral side constraints. I will not kill, lie, steal or cheat, for example, even to achieve my own goals.

As an egoist, I must first define my self-interest. I may define it primarily in terms of such conventional goals as a good job, a respectable social position, and a good family life. I may define it in terms of great wealth or political prominence. Or I may define it in terms of prestige in the professions, a happy life as a hermit, a life of creativity as a writer, or a life devoted to sensual pleasure. I must also decide whether I am more interested in long- or short-term realization of my goals.

I must then come up with a strategy for achieving my goals. What kind of lifestyle will I want to adopt? How much education do I need? What kinds of friendships should I cultivate? What kind of career do I want to pursue? Even more basic than these concerns, however, is the question of what kind of person I need to be to realize my goals. The kind of person I am is determined by the virtues or character traits I have.

Ayn Rand argues that certain virtues will promote a person's well-being, no matter how it is defined.[8] One of these character traits is *rationality*. To achieve my long-range goals, I must never let any belief or emotion get in the way of my ability to see the world clearly and to think about it logically. Another virtue is *productiveness*. I must select a career that is commensurate with my abilities and pursue it with as much energy as possible. Finally, *pride* is the ability to "hold oneself as one's own highest value by achieving one's own moral perfection...."[9] Having pride also means that I will never accept unearned guilt and will rectify flaws in my own character. I will not consider myself as a "sacrificial animal" and will never allow any wish or fear or mood of the moment to override my self-esteem.

Duties to Others

As an egoist, I can justify many apparently other-regarding actions that might initially seem incompatible with my self-interest. Suppose I am a wealthy man whose wife is dying of a disease that can be cured only at great expense. I might spend my entire fortune to save her if her life is crucial for my happiness. Similarly, my children's happiness is important to me, so I may be willing to make considerable sacrifices to ensure their education for a good career. I might also become the chairperson of a fund-raising drive for the local charity hospital because I know the publicity will help my career. I will cultivate friendships and go out of my way to help my friends because I know that this is the only way to have friends, and friends are important for my happiness. I will also refrain from theft, fraud, and violence against others, because of the moral side constraints I have embraced.

As an egoist, however, I must reject all positive obligations to others, unless I have reason to believe that these obligations promote my own

[8] See especially Ayn Rand, *The Virtue of Selfishness*, pp. 25–27.

[9] Rand, *The Virtue of Selfishness*, p. 27.

interests. Do I have a duty to rescue a drowning person, if that person's survival is not important to my own welfare? It would seem that I do not.[10] Do I have a duty to help my neighbor who is in trouble financially, or to warn him that he is about to make a disastrous financial decision? Again, the answer is that I do not have any such obligations, unless these actions promote my own interests.

Social Ethics

As an egoist, I am willing to agree to rules that other egoists will accept, within the limits of the moral side constraints. What kinds of rules for social organization could be expected to result from negotiation with other egoists?

One proposal is that the state should be limited, and its function should be primarily negative. Following philosopher Robert Nozick, we can call this state the *minimal state*, which is a political order limited to protecting individuals against physical violence, theft, and fraud.[11] The minimal state allows me the maximum opportunity to pursue my interests freely in competition with others. It also embodies a set of rules to which other egoists might agree. This political philosophy, known as *libertarianism*, might appear to be the most obvious outcome of negotiations in Hobbes's state of nature. It provides the most basic protection from the most violent and destructive tendencies of human beings. Here are three characteristics of the minimal state, according to Nozick.

First, the minimal state will have two explicit limitations. There will be no enforced benevolence. Even though voluntary benevolence is perfectly permissible (and we have seen that the egoist may sometimes want to help others for her own benefit), the state has no right to tax one person to support another. Thus, few if any welfare programs will be available to aid the disadvantaged. The only possible exceptions might be programs that counteract a clear and present danger of civil disturbance or that aid victims of natural and war-related disasters. Even an egoist might prefer to spend tax dollars on relief for the poor rather than have riots in the streets.

The other limitation is that the state will not engage in paternalism—that is, forcing persons to do or not to do something for their own good

---

[10] Rand says that "...it is morally proper to save him [a drowning stranger] only when the danger to one's own life is minimal." (*The Virtue of Selfishness*, op. cit., p. 45) She does not explain whether "morally proper" means "morally permissible" or "morally obligatory." It may be morally permissible to save such a person, if one gets a certain satisfaction out of doing it. There is no basis in Rand's egoism, or in the egoism we have developed, for saying saving the drowning person is morally obligatory, even if we can do it without endangering our own life.

[11] Robert Nozick, *Anarchy, State and Utopia* (New York: Basic Books, 1974).

or protection. Paternalism requires a limitation of individual freedom of action that many egoists believe is contrary to their desire to run their own lives. Because of this undesirable feature of paternalism, the libertarian state will not require people to use seat belts or wear crash helmets, even though these behaviors would be for their own protection. It will not require people to put away part of their income for retirement. However, a voluntary social security program, in which persons receive after retirement the contribution they made to the program, plus interest, would be acceptable, as long as one person's earnings were not distributed to others.

In opposing all strictly paternalistic laws, the libertarian will examine carefully the laws against the use of drugs such as marijuana and even heroin. The minimal state may prohibit the use of drugs only to the extent that they cause crime that limits the rights of others. Any law must be rejected that can only be justified paternalistically.

Second, because the only justification for state coercion is the protection of individuals from one another or from other states, the minimal state will not prohibit conduct simply because someone thinks it is immoral. Thus, no laws will be enacted against pornography unless legislators can show that pornography substantially increases sex crimes or in some other way threatens the basic rights of others. Similar considerations apply to laws against homosexuality or other kinds of sexual behavior that some people consider immoral. Laws forbidding certain kinds of commercial activity on Sunday must be eliminated. Laws prohibiting people from having more than one spouse would have no justification in the minimal state. You can probably think of other laws that must be eliminated for the same reason.

Third, egoists generally believe that their moral position is most compatible with laissez-faire capitalism. Capitalism is an economic system characterized by private accumulation of capital, private ownership of the means of production, and a free-market system. An economic system compatible with egoism will grant maximum freedom for an individual to pursue her own self-interest in terms of profit, as long as she does not violate the basic rights of others.

Does the minimal state offer enough protection for individuals who are intent on pursuing their interests? Some egoists might conclude that it does not. Suppose I have a heart problem requiring extensive medical care or worry that my elderly parents might not have saved enough to provide for themselves in old age. These considerations might lead me as an egoist to come up with a very different set of principles to govern the social order.

Philosopher John Rawls has come up with several principles that some would say an enlightened egoist might endorse.[12] Two principles are especially important. The first one is the *principle of liberty:*

> Each person is to have an equal right to the most extensive total system of equal basic liberties compatible with a similar system of liberty for all.[13]

The libertarian might not have any objection to this principle. It simply assures that each egoist has the maximum liberty to pursue his own interests, that is, as much liberty as is compatible with other egoist's having the same liberty.

The second one is the *difference principle:*

> Social and economic inequalities are to be arranged so that they are both (1) to the greatest benefit of the least advantaged; and (2) attached to offices and positions open to all under conditions of fair equality of opportunity.[14]

The libertarian would not accept this principle because it can justify massive infringements of the liberties of individuals, to maximize the benefits to the least advantaged members of society or to ensure that the more desirable social positions are equally accessible to everyone.

As an illustration of the way the difference principle works, consider the fact that physicians have higher incomes than most citizens. According to the difference principle, this discrepancy can be justified only (1) if paying physicians above-average salaries benefits the least advantaged members of society by attracting talented people into medicine *whose services are then available to all citizens;* and (2) if everyone has an equal opportunity to become a physician. This last condition could only be met if everyone of sufficient talent had an opportunity to go to medical school, regardless of their financial means. More than likely, this condition in turn could only be met if the government, through the

---

[12] See John Rawls, *A Theory of Justice* (Cambridge, MA: Harvard University Press, 1971). Rawls would not consider himself an ethical egoist, but his principles of justice are arrived at by agreement among hypothetical "negotiators" who are concerned only with their own interests. Rawls specifies, however, that the negotiators operate under a "veil of ignorance," so that they do not know the circumstances of their own lives (for example, interests, abilities, intelligence, health status, social position). Thus, they can only negotiate to guarantee an acceptable life, no matter what their particular circumstances might be. I am assuming that a group of egoists who *know* their own condition but who must negotiate with other egoists living in very *different* conditions might agree to principles similar to the ones Rawls develops. Thus, Rawls's principles of justice are rules that at least some egoists might endorse.

[13] Rawls, *A Theory of Justice,* p. 250.

[14] Rawls, *A Theory of Justice,* p. 83.

use of tax dollars, paid the medical school tuition of poor but talented students.

The contrast between libertarian and Rawlsian principles shows that egoism can lead to very different social principles, depending on how egoists define their own well-being, how they assess their own situations, and what principles they can negotiate with other egoists. There is no such thing as one egoistic social ethics. We can only point out some of the courses that egoists can take in developing their positions

CONCEPT SUMMARY

As an egoist, I must first define *my* own self-interest, and then develop those character traits necessary to realize my interests. Some egoists maintain that rationality, productiveness, and pride are character traits important in realizing almost any interests. I can also justify many apparent altruistic activities, such as caring for my family and being a loyal friend, because they ultimately promote my own well-being. I will reject all positive obligations to others, however, unless the actions contribute to my own self-interest.

The society in which egoists live will be determined by the rules to which I and other egoists can agree. As an egoist, I might well agree to a minimal state that protects citizens from violence and fraud by others and allows everyone the maximum freedom to pursue his or her own interests. I might, however, want to be protected from the worst conditions that could befall me or be assured that I will have the necessary conditions for my own self-actualization. In this case, I might agree to rules constituting an expanded state, structured according to Rawls's principle of liberty and his difference principle.

APPLYING THE ETHICS OF EGOISM

Now we shall examine, from the egoist's standpoint, several cases requiring a moral decision. These examples will help you to understand how an egoist would analyze a situation requiring moral choice and decide what he should do. We shall follow the methodology outlined in the checklist. When it is useful, we shall also refer to the distinctions among factual, conceptual, and moral questions and to the notions of relevance and conflict problems.

Case 1: Bryan's Dilemma

Let us consider the case presented at the beginning of this chapter. We shall first analyze it from the perspective of a version of act egoism, in which Bryan defines his self-interest in terms of career success.

1. The two most obvious alternatives open to Bryan are obeying Max and not obeying him. Another alternative is to try to find some middle way between these two choices. Bryan should consider carefully the con sequences of each of these three alternatives.

    If he obeys Max, Bryan will be able to continue his summer job. Because Max has dumped the coolant for some time without reprisals from his superiors or the law, Bryan may assume that he could continue to do so without fear of punishment, at least long enough to allow him to finish his summer employment. On the other hand, if Max runs into trouble for his practice of dumping the coolant, Bryan might share in the blame. The outcome could cost Bryan his job or possibly result in legal expenses that he cannot afford. Perhaps Bryan could defend himself by arguing that he is a junior employee who was just following orders, but this defense might not be successful in court.

    There is another consideration with regard to this alternative, however. As a moral egoist, Bryan may not violate any of the moral side constraints. If his action involves breaking the law (thereby perhaps breaking an implicit commitment as a citizen to abide by the law) and probably engaging in deception regarding his practice, he must not obey Max.

    If Bryan disobeys Max, he might lose his job. This course of action would protect him from legal repercussions. On the other hand, Max's supervisors might not know about his practice of dumping the coolant and might not approve if they knew. Then, if they did learn about Max's practice, Bryan's refusal to go along with it would probably increase his standing in the firm and might even help him get a permanent job there.

    If he could find a middle-way solution, Bryan might be able to meet the moral obligations in the relevant side constraints without jeopardizing his job. He might find a way to avoid dumping the liquid this time and then try to find a cost-effective way of treating or recycling the liquid. He might decide that he must obey Max this one time and then try to find an acceptable alternative. Or he might try to convince Max that the legal consequences of continued dumping could be unpleasant for both Max and the firm. Another option is to inform Max's superiors of Max's action, in the hope that managers would protect Bryan and perhaps place him under someone else's supervision.

2. If our analysis of the facts is correct, Bryan should try to find a middle-way solution, because both of the other two solutions are undesirable. If no middle-way solution is possible, Bryan should honor the moral side constraints by refusing to follow Max's orders.

Let us now look at the same case from the standpoint of rule egoism.

1. The alternative courses of action are the same three described earlier: obey Max, disobey Max, or find a middle-way solution.
2. Most egoists would probably agree on the rule that everyone should obey the law. The alternative, in which everyone disobeys (or at least attempts to disobey) the law when it is in their interest to do so, would not only violate the moral side constraints, but also produce a chaotic situation close to Hobbes's state of nature. This would be contrary to the interests of most egoists.
3. Applying this rule to Bryan's situation, obeying Max is impermissible, because it requires Bryan to break the law. Finding a middle-way solution, however, would allow Bryan to promote his own interests, while still obeying the law. Therefore, either finding a middle way (if it is possible) or disobeying Max is morally required.

Case 2: The Legalization of Homosexual Acts Between Consenting Adults

In 1957, the Wolfenden Committee in Great Britain recommended that Britain's laws on homosexuality be liberalized, so that homosexuality between consenting adults would no longer be a crime. Sir Patrick Devlin, who served on the Queen's Bench, objected to this recommendation, arguing that legalizing such activities could cause the disintegration of the social order. Devlin believed that agreed-on moral values are a part of the binding force that holds society together and that the view that homosexual acts are wrong is a widely shared value in British society. Tampering with the moral consensus on such issues is tampering with the social fabric. Therefore, homosexual acts between consenting adults should not be legalized. What position would an egoist take on this issue?

This is not an individual decision, but a matter of social policy. Therefore, the rule-egoist approach is more appropriate. In this case, the same answer would probably be given by the libertarian or by Rawls's principle of liberty. Let us assume that the egoists in the audience have agreed to Rawls's principle of liberty and apply it to this case.

1. The two options we shall consider are either advocating the legalization of homosexual acts between consenting adults or advocating their continued criminalization.

2. The relevant rule is Rawls's principle of liberty: Each person is to have an equal right to the most extensive total system of equal basic liberties compatible with a similar system of liberty for all. We shall assume that this rule has been agreed to by the egoists in the audience.

  This rule seems to clearly yield the conclusion that the egoist should favor decriminalizing homosexual acts between consenting adults. But the egoist would be concerned with Devlin's claim that legalizing homosexuality can threaten the social fabric. If legalization produces or tends to produce social chaos, the government's ability to protect citizens against conditions prevailing in the state of nature will have been impaired. Therefore, the egoist will look carefully at the evidence for the view that legalizing homosexual acts would contribute substantially to social disintegration.

  Unfortunately, evidence on either side of this issue is difficult to obtain. One reason is that we cannot easily establish causal relationships between two historical events that enable us to say that one event (for example, a change to a more tolerant attitude toward homosexuality) might cause or even contribute to another event (for instance, disintegration of the social order). Another reason is that we often have difficulty distinguishing between social disintegration and mere social change. The social changes that may follow changes in moral values are not necessarily signs of disintegration.

  Given these problems, the egoist would probably conclude that the evidence to justify the claim that legalizing homosexual acts between consenting adults would materially contribute to social disintegration is inadequate.

3. We must conclude that the rule egoist who embraces Rawls's principle of liberty (and, almost certainly, any libertarian as well) would find laws that suppress homosexual conduct between consenting adults morally impermissible.

This conclusion does not imply that egoists favor giving adults freedom to molest children, either homosexually or heterosexually. Protecting children from harm by others is an essential function of the state, for egoists. Even genuinely paternalistic action can be justified, when the paternalism is exercised toward children. If we assume that children are incapable of making a free, informed decision about participation in sexual activity because of their lack of experience, cognitive development, and emotional maturity, we can easily justify paternalistic intervention on behalf of children.

Case 3: Should a Lawyer Reveal the Truth?

David Spaulding was badly injured in an automobile wreck and sued the driver responsible for the injury.[15] David's examining physicians reported to his lawyer that David might have a permanent brain injury caused by the accident and recommended refusing to settle the case for one year. The driver's defense lawyer, John Zimmerman, also had his physician examine David. This physician discovered an even more serious problem, an aortic aneurism, apparently caused by the accident, that the boy's doctor had not found. The physician's report contained the following statement: "This aneurism could dilate further and it might rupture with further dilation and this would cause his death." Apparently because David was a minor and the physician was employed by the defense lawyer, the physician reported this information only to Zimmerman, not to David or his attorneys. Zimmerman realized that David's attorney would ask a higher settlement if they learned of the aneurism. He also knew that, according to the code of ethics for lawyers, he was not required to reveal the information. His responsibility was to keep secret the information gained in the professional relationship whose disclosure would likely be detrimental to his client. If Zimmerman is an egoist, should he reveal the information?

Because the decision to withhold or disclose the information to David's lawyer has important implications for Zimmerman's career and personal well-being, the perspective of act egoism is relevant. Because a practice of legal ethics is involved, we must also consider the question from the standpoint of rule egoism. Let us begin with an act-egoistic analysis.

1. If Zimmerman reveals the information to the youth's lawyer, his ability to defend his client will be substantially weakened. This result may lead to his having to settle for a higher payment from his client, which will harm his standing as a competent defense lawyer and perhaps lead to fewer cases in the future. He also knows that, if he decides not to reveal the information, he has a basis for defending himself in the legal code of ethics, thus preserving his standing as an ethical as well as a successful lawyer. A consideration of these consequences suggests that he should not reveal the information.

   If he does reveal the information and the boy dies, however, his reputation as an ethical lawyer will be damaged, regardless of the provisions of the legal code. Furthermore, he may believe that preserving confidentiality in this situation violates the moral side constraints against dishonesty and is therefore impermissible.

2. Zimmerman must carefully investigate the consequences of breaking confidentiality with his client in this case. He must also think

---

[15] This case is based on *Spaulding v. Zimmerman*, 116 NW.2d 704 (1962).

carefully about the relationship of the two roles he occupies: as a lawyer subject to professional guidelines and as an individual who must honor the moral side constraint of honesty. He must also acknowledge that he might be violating the moral side constraint of loyalty if he failed to abide by the rule of preserving confidences and secrets of his clients.

Zimmerman will not find it easy to decide which decision would most effectively promote his interests or what the moral side constraints require in this case. Whether the moral side constraint against dishonesty overrides the moral side constraint of loyalty may be difficult to decide. Much will depend, therefore, on how he assesses the likelihood that his concealing the information from David's lawyer will be discovered and how much the discovery will damage his economic well-being and professional reputation. If we can assume that Zimmerman would suspect that the information would eventually be made public in some way, he should reveal it now.

Now let us look at this issue from the standpoint of rule egoism.

1. We shall assume that the only two actions available to the lawyer are revealing or not revealing the existence of the aneurism.

2. A strict prohibition of lawyers' revealing information gained in the professional relationship whose disclosure would likely be detrimental to clients might appear to be in the interests of lawyers, so that they would mutually agree to its enforcement. The prohibition would enable the lawyers to protect their clients' interests more effectively and thereby be more professionally successful themselves. Lawyers could, however, experience disadvantages from adherence to a strict rule. In situations such as the present one, where the rule produces unfortunate or even tragic consequences, the reputations of individual lawyers and even the legal profession could be severely damaged. In addition, there are questions whether adherence to an unbending rule is compatible with the moral side constraints.

    A rule enforcing confidentiality without exceptions invariably produces a negative reaction by the public when it leads to tragic consequences for individuals. The public standing of the legal profession should be a primary consideration in deciding which rules the egoistically oriented lawyer should support. Therefore, we shall conclude that the strict prohibition as it has been stated is not justified from the standpoint of rule egoism.

3. If these conclusions are valid and an exceptionless rule favoring confidentiality is not justified by rule egoism, the present circumstances should surely constitute such an exception. Applying the rule to this situation would lead to the conclusion that concealing the

information about the aneurism from David Spaulding's lawyers is impermissible.

EVALUATING EGOISM AS A MORAL THEORY

We are now ready to evaluate egoism, using the four criteria established in Chapter 3. Keep in mind that some criticisms can be made of every moral theory; no theory is perfect. You should also note that a subjective element necessarily arises in evaluating a moral theory. The evaluations in this and the following chapters are my own, although they usually reflect widely held positions among moral philosophers. These evaluations are for your consideration rather than uncritical acceptance.

Criterion 1: Coherence and Consistency

A theory is coherent if it does not contain principles that are logically incompatible. Is egoism incompatible in this sense? Certainly an egoistic theory could be internally incoherent, if, for example, it incorporated both Rawls's difference principle and libertarian severe restrictions on the power of the state. But a given egoistic theory need not be incoherent in this way. It can adopt either of these approaches to social ethics.

A theory is consistent if it does not give rise to logically incompatible moral judgments. Insofar as two egoists have differing personal goals, they may also come to differing moral judgments. Suppose Egoist A and Egoist B are in competing businesses. As long as they do not violate any moral constraints, Egoist A may attempt to put Egoist B out of business ("I should put B out of business") and Egoist B may attempt to put Egoist A out of business ("I should put A out of business"). But this is not an inconsistency, in terms of the egoistic position we have developed. Within the moral side constraints, egoists are permitted to pursue their own goals, even if they conflict in this way.

Criterion 2: Justification of the Moral Standard

The most common justification of the egoistic moral standard is an appeal to psychological egoism. *Psychological egoism* is the view that human behavior is always and necessarily motivated by self-interest. The usual argument for ethical egoism on the basis of psychological egoism proceeds as follows. First, the ethical egoist claims that a person never has an obligation to do something he cannot do. We could never, for example, have a moral obligation to pick up 10,000 pounds of steel because it is physically impossible for us to do it. Second, the ethical egoist appeals to psychological egoism in claiming that people are always motivated by considerations of self-interest and cannot have any other motivations. Then the ethical egoist concludes that the only legitimate obligation human beings have is to act out of considerations of self-interest.

This argument might be attacked by questioning the first premise. Perhaps we do have an obligation to do something we cannot do, namely act for reasons other than self-interest. The fact that we cannot act from non-self-interested motivations may only show that human beings are not capable of moral behavior. At any rate, there is nothing inconsistent about saying that we always act out of self-interest but that doing so is still wrong.

The second premise of the psychological egoist's argument can also be questioned. Do we always act out of motives of self-interest? Most of us would probably say that the psychological egoist has a great deal of truth on her side. Many apparently altruistic acts really are done because of self-interest. But some human actions do appear to be motivated by considerations other than self-interest. Parents often make sacrifices for their children that are difficult to explain in terms of selfishness. Heroic actions on the battlefield and in civilian life also seem to involve more than considerations of one's own well-being.

Morally praiseworthy actions are not the only actions that have motivations other than self-interest. Malice and hatred may be no more selfish than are actions we admire. People often attempt to harm their enemies at great cost to themselves. They may try to kill or injure the enemy even when doing so will cost them large sums of money, reputation and social status, or even their own lives.

The convinced psychological egoist might reply that whatever a person does he does because he gets satisfaction from it. If a mother sacrifices for her children, she does so because she gets more satisfaction from seeing them have a happy childhood or a good education than from anything else. If a person spends his life's savings to get revenge on his enemy, he does so because he finds more satisfaction in getting the revenge than in having his money.

Perhaps an example will show the limitations of this argument. A story (perhaps apocryphal) is told that Abraham Lincoln was once trying to convince a friend that all men were prompted by selfishness in doing good. As the coach in which they were riding crossed a bridge, they saw an old razor-backed sow on the bank making a terrible noise because her pigs had fallen into the water and were in danger of drowning. Lincoln asked the driver to stop, lifted the pigs out of the water, and placed them on the bank.

When he returned, his companion remarked, "Now, Abe, where does selfishness come in on this little episode?" "Why, bless your soul, Ed, that was the very essence of selfishness. I should have had no peace of mind all day had I gone on and left that suffering old sow worrying over those pigs. I did it to get peace of mind, don't you see?[16]

Lincoln's argument is based on a misconception. If he had not cared for the pigs' welfare, he could not have derived pleasure from helping them. Had he not had a prior desire for something other than his own happiness, he would not have experienced satisfaction from helping them. His own satisfaction was not the *object* of his action but rather the *consequence* of his preexisting desire for the animals' welfare. This example illustrates the fact that all actions cannot be egoistically motivated. If my welfare consists of the satisfaction of desires, some desires must exist before the desire for my own welfare. In Lincoln's case, this preexisting desire was for the relief of the pigs' suffering.

Although most philosophers have found the thesis that all human behavior is motivated by self-interest implausible, they may still concede that a great deal of human behavior is so motivated. Hobbes scholar Gregory Kavka calls this position *predominant egoism*, which he defines as the view that "self-interested motives tend to take precedence over non-self-interested motives in determining human actions."[17]

Criterion 3: Plausibility of the Moral Judgments

One way to justify a moral philosophy is to provide a foundation for its moral standard, as the previous argument from psychological egoism attempts to do. Another way to provide confirmation for a moral theory is by showing that it produces moral judgments that we find plausible. According to the theory of reflective equilibrium, as we have seen, this is not the end of the story. Our most plausible moral judgments may be in error, and we can critique them by evaluating the moral theory that produces them. Nevertheless, the plausibility of the moral judgments generated by a theory is one measure of the theory's adequacy. What can we say about ethical egoism from the standpoint of the criterion of plausibility?

---

[16] Quoted from the *Springfield* (Illinois) *Monitor*, in Joel Feinberg, "Psychological Egoism," in his (6th ed.), *Reason and Responsibility* (Belmont, CA: Wadsworth, 1985). Feinberg's chapter is a valuable discussion of psychological egoism, and the argument based on this example is derived from it.

[17] The claim that non-self-interested motives usually give way to self-interested motives is much more plausible and may still provide a reasonably strong foundation for ethical egoism. The egoist could still claim that, because most actions are egoistically motivated, egoism is more compatible with the facts of human nature than is any other moral philosophy. This point would still be a strong argument in its favor.

The principal difficulty with ethical egoism in this regard is that it provides no justification for positive concern for the well-being of others, where their well-being does not contribute to our own. We have no obligation to help a drowning person, unless helping him promotes our own self-interest. Although, by definition, supererogatory acts (acts above and beyond the call of duty) are not obligatory, we can say that people often feel a moral motivation to perform them. This motivation would be difficult to explain on egoistic grounds, even on the grounds of the version of egoism we have developed in this chapter. Therefore, we can conclude that egoism cannot generate all of the moral judgments we ordinarily consider correct.

Criterion 4: Usefulness

One of the functions of any moral philosophy is to assist in the resolution of conflicts between human beings. The kind of egoism we have advocated can resolve some of those conflicts. It can do so by showing that some degree of cooperation is in the self-interest of egoists themselves and that there are moral side constraints against violating such negative moral rules as the prohibitions against killing, lying, stealing, and cheating.

This leaves many areas of conflict in which egoism provides no guidelines, however. Within the moral side constraints, each person is simply advised to pursue his or her own interests. No moral basis is provided for cooperation in the production of some higher goal.

Consider this example. When the Second World War was over, the British press published a story regarding two female counterspies. During the war, the Allies had finally broken the Nazi code, and the British War Office discovered that the Nazis knew the true loyalties of the two counterspies. The War Office also knew that, if the women returned to Nazi Europe, they would almost certainly be caught, tortured, and killed. Yet, if they did not return, the Nazis would probably infer that their code had been broken and would change it. The British and their Allies then would lose their major source of intelligence about Nazi war plans for at least two more years. As a result, the two counterspies were sent back to Europe without the knowledge that their identity was known by the Nazis. They were never heard from again.

What was the right thing to do? How does one resolve the conflict of interests? The egoist can only advise each person to pursue his own interests, but the interests are different. The interests of the War Office personnel were to keep the code intact. The interests of the counterspies were to preserve their own lives. Which interests should prevail?

Egoism does not provide guidance because it cannot embrace any higher interpersonal good.

The restriction that people should pursue their interests only within the guidelines of the moral side constraints does not help to resolve this conflict. What moral side constraint should prevail? On the one hand, the side constraint of honesty would prevent the War Office personnel from misrepresenting the situation to the counterspies. On the other hand, the side constraint requiring loyalty to superiors and country would require the personnel to conceal the information from the counterspies. Egoism, then, seems to provide little guidance as to which side constraint should take priority.

Utilitarianism, by contrast, would require that the welfare of the majority of citizens take priority, suggesting that the War Office personnel should send the counterspies back to the Continent without knowledge of their fate. The problem again is that *egoism does not specify any overall interpersonal good to be pursued,* so it does not always provide an effective means of reconciling conflicting private interests.

This example also exposes another problem in applying the version of egoism proposed in this chapter. It is not always easy to specify just what the moral side constraints are. We have specified that the side constraints must be only negative obligations, but it is not always easy to distinguish between "positive" and "negative" obligations. For example, it is not easy to know whether the obligation of loyalty by the War Office personnel should be considered a positive obligation (an obligation to promote the welfare of the country) or a negative obligation (an obligation not to break presumed commitments to the War Office or to the country).

Finally, as we have seen in this case, arbitrating conflicting side constraints is often difficult. How do we arbitrate the conflict between loyalty and honesty in Case No. 3, for example? Some egoists would argue, however, that these kinds of conflict are difficult to arbitrate from the standpoint of any moral theory.

Concept Summary

A moral theory is incoherent if it has principles that conflict with one another. Although individual egoists may adopt different principles (for example, some might adopt Rawls's Difference Principle and others would not), this should not be seen as an incoherence in the egoistic position itself. It reflects only a difference in how an individual egoist or group of egoists would construct an egoistic theory. A moral theory is inconsistent if it yields different and contradictory moral judgments. Even though one individual egoist may certainly promote his or her own interests at the expense of other egoists, this again reflects how an individual egoist applies the basic guidelines of egoism.

The most important justification of the moral standard of egoism is psychological egoism, namely the claim that all human behavior is necessarily motivated by self-interest. The major objection to psychological egoism is that the most plausible interpretation of human behavior is that it is not always motivated by self-interest. Nevertheless, predominant egoism (the view that self-interested motives tend to take precedence over non-self-interested ones) is plausible, and this is enough to give some support to the claim that ethical egoism is at least a plausible moral position, although not the only possible one.

The plausibility criterion asks whether the moral judgments generated by egoism are in agreement with our most considered moral judgments. The most obvious problem with this criterion is that egoism does not justify any positive obligations to others. For example, according to the version of egoism we have developed, an egoist has no moral obligation to save a drowning person, even if we can do so easily, if it is not in the egoist's self-interest to do so.

With regard to the criterion of usefulness, one of the problems with applying egoism is that it does not provide any conception of an overall interpersonal good, so some disputes between individuals are difficult to settle. Another problem is that specifying the scope of the moral side constraints is problematic. One of the reasons for the difficulty is that the distinction between "negative" and "positive" moral obligations is not always clear. Conflicts between competing side constraints are also difficult to arbitrate.

THE ETHICS
OF NATURAL LAW

Cardinal Joseph Ratzinger, the then head of the Congregation of the Doctrine of the Faith of the Roman Catholic Church, criticized a statement of American Roman Catholic bishops that gave implicit permission to church hospitals and agencies to provide information on condoms as a potential safeguard against AIDS. This permission was later rescinded after criticism from Rome.

A document on this subject released in Rome under Cardinal Ratzinger's approval said, "The safe-sex approach to preventing HIV/AIDS, though frequently advocated, compromises human sexuality and can lead to promiscuous sexual behavior." The document continued by warning, "Not only is the use of prophylactics an attempt to halt the spread of HIV technically unreliable; promoting this approach means, in effect, promoting behavior which is morally unacceptable."

The Rev. Albert Ogle, an Episcopal priest who directs the All Saints AIDS Service Center in Pasadena, California, criticized the bishops' reversal on the question of condoms and AIDS for "not addressing what is really happening in their communities." "The reality," Ogle said, "is that young people in our parishes are being infected by the virus and will get sick and die and infect others because the church has painted itself into a corner over birth control."[1]

This controversy reflects the continuing influence of the tradition of natural-law moral philosophy, which condemns both sexual promiscuity and the use of "artificial" forms of birth control such as condoms. This tradition is especially associated with the Roman Catholic Church, but its influence is not confined to that institution. Many people have a deep-seated feeling, especially with regard to sexual conduct, that if something is "unnatural," it is also immoral. Even the law sometimes makes

---

[1] Russell Chandler and John Dart, "Bishops' Panel Rejects Condoms in AIDS Battle," *Los Angeles Times*, October 13, 1989, p. A3.

reference to "unnatural acts" with the obvious intent of condemning them as wrong. The words *unnatural* and *immoral* are closely connected in popular thought. On the other hand, the connotation of the word *natural* is strongly positive. We tend to think that if something is "natural," it must also be right.

We shall see that much of this talk of what is and is not "natural" has little to do with the more sophisticated versions of natural law. Nevertheless, natural-law moralists do teach that human nature and the ethical life are connected. Our primary life goal should be to realize as fully as we can our potential as human beings. This statement resembles egoism but has an important difference. Whereas the egoist strives to realize his own individual preferences, whatever they may be, the natural-law theorist advocates realizing those goods specified by a nature that he has in common with his fellow human beings. Thus, the moral standard in natural law has an objective quality that egoism lacks.

We can easily see why the natural-law tradition provides an attractive approach to the problem of determining a moral standard. If ethics is supposed to regulate human conduct, the purpose of this regulation must surely be for the good of human beings themselves, and it is reasonable to believe that this good is determined by the requirements of human nature. What more reasonable foundation could any ethical system have than human nature itself?

Nevertheless, the appeal to human nature as a basis for making moral judgments encounters difficulties. Does this appeal imply that "doing whatever comes naturally" is right? Can a person who has a natural tendency to lie justify her lying behavior by an appeal to natural law? How do we determine the standards of conduct that our human nature presumably entails? In this chapter, we shall look at the tradition in moral philosophy that raises such difficult questions and yet continues to influence our moral thinking.

THE NATURAL-LAW MORAL STANDARD

What Is Natural Law?

The term *natural law* can be misleading. It implies that ethical laws are like "laws of nature" or scientific laws. An example of a scientific law is Boyle's law in physics, which states that the product of the pressure and the specific volume of a gas at constant temperature is constant. But scientific laws are *descriptive;* they state how phenomena in nature do in fact always behave. Ethical laws, on the other hand, are *prescriptive;* they stipulate how people *should* behave, whether or not they do so.

Natural-law theorists assume that human beings have free will and that they can decide whether to act as they ought to act. This discussion implies that the word *law* has more in common with civil laws than with natural laws because both civil and ethical laws can be disobeyed. Natural phenomena presumably always act according to the laws of nature, whereas people do not always behave either legally or morally.

But the analogy with civil laws can also be misleading, for the point of the term *natural* is to contrast ethical laws with the laws of governments. When the Roman jurists were looking for legal concepts that could apply throughout the Roman empire, they turned to the philosophy of natural law precisely because it proposed that certain ethical laws are "natural" rather than "conventional"; that is, they apply equally to all human beings, regardless of the conventions, customs, or beliefs of their particular society. These natural laws for all human behavior could thus serve as a basis for judging people's actions throughout the Roman empire. Therefore, we can say that *natural law* refers to ethical guidelines or rules that stipulate what people ought to do rather than what they in fact do and that the guidelines apply equally to all humanity because they are rooted in human nature itself.

The term *natural law* can be misleading because it inevitably brings to mind some kind of ethical legalism—the belief that hard-and-fast guidelines cover every possible detail of conduct. This characterization, however, is unfair to the natural-law tradition. The greatest exponent of natural law, Thomas Aquinas (1224–1274), believed that the basic outlines of proper human behavior are relatively clear. But he also taught that the closer we come to particular moral judgments, the more prone we are to error and the more room we must make for differences of opinion. Some contemporary natural-law theorists even believe that natural law has a historical dimension, so that what is right in one epoch may not be right in another. Whether or not the view is accepted, the lively discussions of ethical issues in the Roman Catholic Church, where natural-law thinking is especially prominent, show that natural-law theorists by no means believe that all ethical problems have already been solved. The word *law* merely refers to the prescriptive character of the rules that should govern human behavior.

The natural-law theorist does, however, believe in an objective standard for morality. Moral truth exists just as scientific truth exists. The natural-law theorist cannot be an ethical relativist or an ethical skeptic; rather, he is committed to some form of moral realism. He generally believes we know the basic outlines of this standard, but this belief does not mean we have interpreted the implications of this standard correctly in every case. In ethics, as in science, human beings continually search for truth. The belief in objective truth should be no more stifling of human freedom and creativity in ethics than it is in science.

Human Nature and Natural Inclinations

What is the standard of truth in natural-law ethics? As an approximation, we can say that the standard is human nature. People should do whatever promotes the fulfillment of human nature. How, then, do we determine what human nature is?

Let us consider some analogous situations that illustrate the difficulty in describing human nature. We often find it useful to describe something's nature in terms of its function, the purpose it serves. For example, we can describe the nature of a pencil in terms of its function of enabling humans to make marks on paper. A "good" pencil is one that performs this function well, without smudging, scratching, or breaking, for example. Similarly, if an automobile's function is to provide transportation, a good automobile is one that provides comfortable, reliable transportation. The function of a tomato plant is to produce tomatoes, and a good tomato plant is one that produces many high-quality tomatoes.

We can also determine the function of human beings if we confine a person to one particular social role. The function of a farmer is to grow food, and a good farmer produces food efficiently and with proper care for the animals and land for which he has responsibility. By similar reasoning, we can say that a good father is one who attends diligently to his children's welfare. But now let us take human beings out of their social roles and ask simply, "What is the function of a human being?" Here we see the problem faced by those who attempt to base ethics on human nature. Generally speaking, the more complex the animal, the more varied its behavior and presumably the less clearly defined its function. The freedom of action possessed by human beings makes it plausible to argue, as some philosophers have, that human beings are characterized precisely by the fact that they have no set nature or function. How can we make sense out of natural law in the face of these problems?

Fortunately, we can take another, more promising approach to discovering what human nature is like. One way to determine a thing's characteristics is to observe its behavior. In chemistry, we learn about the nature of iron by observing how it reacts with other elements. Perhaps we can find out what human nature is like by ascertaining those "natural inclinations," as Aquinas puts it, that human beings have in common. To phrase it another way, perhaps we can discover what human nature is by identifying those goals that human beings generally tend to seek. These values would presumably reflect the structure of our human nature, which natural law directs us to follow. Therefore, we shall propose the following statement as the moral standard of natural law:

> MS: Those actions are right that promote the values specified by the natural inclinations of human beings.

How do we find out what these natural inclinations are? We might first consult psychologists, sociologists, or anthropologists. Some contemporary natural-law theorists use studies from the social sciences to defend their conclusions. However, the natural-law tradition developed before the rise of the social sciences, and a more informal method of observation was used to discover the basic human inclinations. Most natural-law theorists would maintain that these observations are still valid. We can divide the values specified by natural human inclinations into two basic groups: (1) biological values, which are strongly linked with our bodies and which we share with other animals; and (2) characteristically human values, which are closely connected with our more specifically human aspects. (We will not call this second group uniquely human values because some of the inclinations that point to these values, such as the tendency to live in societies, are not unique to human beings.) We can summarize the values and the natural inclinations that point to them as follows:

I.   Biological Values
    A.   *Life*—From the natural inclinations that we and all other animals have to preserve our own existence, we can infer that life is good, that we have an obligation to promote our own health, and that we have the right of self-defense. Negatively, this inclination implies that murder and suicide are wrong.
    B.   *Procreation*—From the natural inclination that we and all animals have to engage in sexual intercourse and rear offspring, we can infer that procreation is a value and that we have an obligation to produce and rear children. Negatively, this inclination implies that such practices as sterilization, homosexuality, and artificial contraception are wrong.
II. Characteristically Human Values
    A.   *Knowledge*—From the natural tendency we have to know, including the tendency to seek knowledge of God, we can infer that knowledge is a value and that we have an obligation to pursue knowledge of the world and God. Negatively, this inclination implies that the stifling of intellectual curiosity and the pursuit of knowledge, including the pursuit of the knowledge of God, is wrong. It also implies that a lack of religion is wrong.

B. *Sociability*—From the natural tendency we have to form bonds of affection and love with other human beings and to form groups or societies, we can infer that friendship and love are good and that the state is a natural institution and therefore good. We thus have an obligation to pursue close relationships with other human beings and to submit to the legitimate authority of the state. We can also infer that war can be justified under certain conditions if it is necessary to defend the state. Negatively, this inclination implies that activities that interfere with proper human relationships, such as spreading slander and lies, are wrong. Actions that destroy the state's power are also wrong, so natural law finds a basis for an argument against revolution and treason, except when the state is radically unjust.

These natural inclinations are reflections of human nature, and the pursuit of the goods they specify is the way to individual fulfillment. Aquinas himself makes it clear that his enumeration of basic values, which closely parallels our account, is incomplete; other natural-law theorists have expanded the list to include such things as play and aesthetic experience. However, the list given here has had the greatest historical influence, and we shall assume it is basically adequate.

The more important issue raised by this list is the potential for conflict between the various values. What should we do when our need to defend ourselves requires that we kill someone else? What should we do when sterilization is necessary to prevent a life-threatening pregnancy? What should be done when contraception seems necessary to limit family size so that families can properly educate the children they already have? In each of these examples, one aspect of natural law seems to conflict with another, and the question arises whether these values have a hierarchy on which a decision can be based. The answer to this question brings into focus one of the most important and controversial aspects of natural-law morality—namely, its moral absolutism.

MORAL ABSOLUTISM AND THE QUALIFYING PRINCIPLES

Moral Absolutism

Suppose you are on a military convoy from the United States to England during World War II. Your ship is attacked and sunk. Your life raft is carrying twenty-four persons, although it was designed to carry only twenty. You have good reason to believe that the raft will sink unless four people are eliminated, and four people on board have been so seriously injured in the catastrophe that they are probably going to die anyhow. Because no one volunteers to jump overboard, you, as the ranking officer on the boat, decide to have them pushed overboard. Are you morally justified in doing so? Many of us would say that under the circumstances you were, but natural-law theorists would say that you were not justified, even if everyone on the raft would have died otherwise.

Consider another wartime example. Suppose you know that some prisoners have information that will save a large number of lives. The only way to obtain the information is to threaten to kill the prisoners, but you know that they will not reveal what they know unless your threat is absolutely serious. To show them how serious you are, you have another prisoner, who has done nothing to deserve death, shot before their eyes. As a result of your action, the information is revealed and many lives are saved. Is this action justified? Many people would say that under these extreme circumstances it is justified, but natural-law theorists would say that it is not.

These examples illustrate natural law's absolutism. *Moral absolutism* is the view that "certain kinds of actions are always wrong or always obligatory, whatever the consequences."[2] This is because natural-law theorists believe that *none of the values specified by natural inclinations may be directly violated.* Innocent people, for example, may not be killed for any reason, even if more innocent people can thereby be saved. The procreative function that is a part of our biological nature may not be violated by such practices as contraception and sterilization, even if these practices are necessary to preserve other values, such as providing for a child's education or even protecting the mother's life. Similarly, homosexuality violates the value of procreation and is prohibited, even if it is the only kind of sex a person can enjoy.

Natural-law theorists believe that basic values specified by natural inclinations cannot be violated because *basic values cannot be measured or compared;* that is, basic values cannot be quantified or measured by some common unit, so they cannot be traded off against one another. For example, we cannot divide the good of knowledge into units of value and the good of procreation into units of value so that the two can be compared on a common scale. Nor can the good of a single life be compared with the good of several lives; thus, we cannot say that a single life may be sacrificed to preserve many other lives. This idea is sometimes called the "absolute value" or "infinite value" of a human life, suggesting that a human

---

[2] *The Oxford Companion to Philosophy* (Oxford: Oxford University Press, 1995), p. 2.

life cannot be weighed against anything else, including another human life. Natural-law theorists also make this point by saying that basic values are *incommensurable*. Because we cannot measure values, we cannot calculate which consequences of an action are more important. Therefore, consequences cannot be used to determine the moral status of actions.

Another characteristic of natural law is that it is nonconsequentialist in character, even though it may not rule out consideration of consequences. Natural-law theorists insist that *moral judgments must include an evaluation of the intentions of the person performing the action*. The intention of an action is what a person wants to accomplish or "has in mind," as we say, in performing the action. For example, a person can give money to charity because he wants a good reputation in the community. The consequences of the action are good, but the person's intention is not morally praiseworthy. Some moral philosophers distinguish between a moral evaluation of the action and a moral evaluation of the intention of the person performing the action. Using this distinction, we can say that the action of giving money to charity is praiseworthy, but the person giving the money is not to be commended because his intention was not praiseworthy.

Qualifying Principles

Because values are incommensurable and may not ever be directly violated, we may find ourselves in a moral dilemma in which any action we could perform violates some value and hence is immoral. For example, self-defense may sometimes require that we override the natural inclination of another human being to self-preservation. If we do nothing, we allow ourselves to be killed; if we defend ourselves, we kill someone else. To avoid the paralysis of action that would result from such moral dilemmas, natural-law theorists have developed two principles that are crucial in making moral judgments: the principle of forfeiture and the principle of double effect.

The Principle of Forfeiture   According to the *principle of forfeiture*, a person who threatens the life of an innocent person forfeits his or her own right to life. (An innocent person is one who has not threatened anyone's life.) Suppose you are a pioneer tilling his land one morning when two men approach you and say they are going to kill you and your family in order to take your land. Is it morally permissible for you to defend yourself, even to the point of killing them? Natural-law theorists answer the question in the affirmative. Even though you might have to kill your would-be assailants, they have forfeited their innocence by unjustifiably threatening your life. Therefore, they have forfeited their claim to have their natural inclination to self-preservation respected. We can make this point by distinguishing between killing and murder. *Killing* is taking the life of a noninnocent person, whereas *murder* is taking the life of an innocent person. When you take the life of a person who is attempting to kill you, you are killing him but not committing murder.

The principle of forfeiture can be used to justify not only acts of individual self-defense but also war and capital punishment. A defensive war may be justified under certain conditions, even though it involves killing other people, because the aggressors have forfeited their rights to life. Similarly, murderers may justly be put to death because they have forfeited their rights to life by killing others.

The Principle of Double Effect   According to the *principle of double effect*, it is morally permissible to perform an action that has two effects, one good and the other bad, if the following criteria are met:

1. The act, considered in itself and apart from its consequences, is good, or at least morally permissible. An act of murder violates this criterion because murder is bad in itself and apart from its consequences.
2. The bad effect cannot be avoided if the good effect is to be achieved. The moral significance of this criterion lies in the belief that if an alternative method that does not produce the bad effect is available and not used, we must assume that the bad effect was intended. This criterion illustrates the important place that consideration of intent has in natural law. An action with improper intent is morally unacceptable even if it does not otherwise violate natural law. Another test must be passed, however, before we can say that an action is unintended. It is embodied in the next criterion.
3. The bad effect is not the means of producing the good effect but only a side effect. If the bad effect is a necessary means of achieving the good effect, the bad effect must be intended along with the good effect for which it is a necessary means, so the action is morally impermissible. This criterion also illustrates the importance of intention in natural law.
4. The criterion of proportionality is satisfied, in that the good effect and the bad effect are more or less equally balanced in importance. If the bad effect of an action is far more significant than any good effect, the action should not be done, even if the other criteria are met.

If these four criteria are met, the violation of a fundamental value may be considered as indirect rather than direct. Although we may still be said to *bring about an evil*, we cannot be said to *do* an evil, according to natural law. The best way to explain the principle of double effect is by example, so let us consider several applications.

In the first example, a pregnant woman who has tuberculosis wants to take a drug that will cure her disease, but the drug also has the effect of aborting the fetus. Is taking the drug morally permissible? The principle of double effect justifies taking the drug in this case, because all four of its conditions are met.

First, the act of taking the drug to cure a disease is itself morally permissible. In fact, considered in itself and apart from its consequences, it is morally obligatory for the mother to take the drug, for she is obligated to do what she can to preserve her own life.

Second, if we assume that the drug is the only one that will cure the disease and that the mother cannot put off taking the drug until after the baby is born, then the bad effect is unavoidable. By this criterion, then, the death of the child is not intended. We must clarify here what natural-law theorists mean. The bad effect is certainly foreseen; the woman knows the drug will produce an abortion. But an effect may be foreseen without also being intended, that is, without being the goal of the action. If another drug were available that would cure her tuberculosis without causing the abortion, presumably the woman would take it. Otherwise, it would be difficult to argue that she did not intend to have an abortion.

Third, the bad effect is not the means of achieving the good effect. An abortion is not a necessary step in curing a person of tuberculosis; rather, it just happens that the only drug that will cure the woman also causes an abortion. The abortion is an unfortunate and unintended side effect, due to the particular nature of the drug.

Fourth, a proportionally serious reason exists for performing the abortion. The death of the fetus is at least balanced by the saving of the mother's life. If the bad effect were serious (as in this case), but the good effect were relatively insignificant, the action would not be justifiable by the principle of double effect, even if the other conditions were met.

The criterion of proportionality is an exception to the earlier statement that values are incommensurable and that human lives cannot be weighed against one another. We have seen that it may also be considered an exception to the claim that consequences are not considered in moral evaluation. Here, consequences do play a part in natural-law reasoning. But note that consequences can be considered only when the other three conditions have been met. A more accurate statement, therefore, is that in natural-law theory, the consideration of consequences occupies some place in moral evaluation, but it is of secondary importance.

Two other examples will further illustrate how the principle of double effect functions. Suppose I want to turn on a light so that I can read a book on ethics, but I know that throwing the switch on the wall that turns on the light will result in the electrocution of a workman on the floor below. Is it morally permissible to throw the switch?

First, turning on a light to read a book on ethics is in itself a permissible—even praiseworthy—action.

Second, the bad effect is unavoidable if the good effect is to be achieved. If another light could be turned on and I deliberately failed to use it, knowing the consequence is the death of the workman, then I could not argue that I did not intend to kill the workman.

Third, the bad effect (killing the workman) is not a means to reading philosophy but rather only an unfortunate and unintended side effect. Killing someone is not ordinarily a consequence of turning on a light.

But the fourth condition of the principle of double effect is not satisfied. The killing of a human being is not outweighed by the value of reading a book on ethics. Therefore, turning on the light is not justified by the principle of double effect.

Consider another example.[3] In the process of attempting to deliver a fetus, a physician discovers that the fetus is hydrocephalic. The fetus's large cranium makes normal vaginal delivery impossible; both the woman and the fetus would die in the attempt. Neither the mother nor the fetus would survive a cesarean section, so the only way to save the mother's life is to crush the skull of the fetus (craniotomy), thus rendering a vaginal delivery of the stillborn fetus possible. Would the craniotomy be justifiable by the principle of double effect?

First, the act of attempting to save the mother's life is morally permissible, even commendable.

Second, there is no way to save the mother's life except by killing the fetus. The bad effect cannot be avoided if the good effect is to be achieved.

Third, the bad effect can only be seen as the means of producing the good effect. It makes no sense to talk about crushing the head of the fetus without also killing it. Because the death of the fetus must be considered the means of achieving the good effect, the third criterion is not satisfied. Each of the four criteria must be met for the action to be permissible, so we already know that the craniotomy is impermissible. However, for the sake of completeness, we shall consider the fourth criterion.

Fourth, both the fetus and the mother will die if the abortion is not performed; thus, the criterion of proportionality is satisfied. But because

---

[3] For a discussion of this case, see L. W. Sumner, *Abortion and Moral Theory* (Princeton, NJ: Princeton University Press, 1981), p. 116.

the third criterion is not met, the craniotomy may not be performed, and the fetus and mother must both die.

Natural-law theorists admit that this is a tragic case, and various attempts have been made to justify the craniotomy on other grounds. For example, some natural-law theorists argue that the principle of forfeiture can be invoked, because the fetus should be considered an aggressor on the life of the mother. Even though the fetus is innocent of any conscious motive to harm its mother, the actual effect of its growth is to threaten the mother's life. Natural-law theorists sometimes say that the fetus, having no malicious intent, is *subjectively innocent* but not *objectively innocent*, because it does threaten the mother's life. Whether this argument justifies an abortion will be left for you to decide.

CHECKLIST FOR APPLYING NATURAL-LAW ETHICS

I.   Determine whether an action is in accord with the four fundamental values specified by human inclinations or whether there is some apparent violation of one or more of these values.
II. If there is an apparent violation, determine whether the qualifying principle of forfeiture applies to the action.
III. If there is an apparent violation, determine whether the qualifying principle of double effect applies to the action. For the principle of double effect to apply, all four of the following criteria must be met:
  A. The act itself must be good, or at least morally permissible.
  B. The bad effect of the action must be unavoidable if the good effect is to be achieved.
  C. The bad effect must not be the means of producing the good effect but only a side effect.
  D. The criterion of proportionality must be satisfied, in that the good effect must be at least as morally desirable as the bad effect is morally undesirable.
IV. Make a final decision on the morality of the action.
  A. If the action is in accord with the fundamental values, or if it is not in accord but is excused by one of the qualifying principles, the action is morally obligatory.
  B. If the alternative to the action is a violation of a fundamental value, the action is morally permissible.
  C. If the action is a violation of a fundamental value and the qualifying principles do not apply, the action is morally impermissible.

CONCEPT SUMMARY

The basic idea of natural law is that a person should promote those values that are the object of our fundamental human inclinations or tendencies. The realization of these values in a person's life will lead to a fulfillment of his human nature. As analyzed by natural-law theorists, these values include the biological values of life and procreation and the characteristically human values of knowledge and sociability.

Because natural law stipulates that no fundamental values may be directly violated, the question arises as to what action should be taken when situations seem to force a person to violate one of the values regardless of what is done. The qualifying principles of forfeiture and double effect are designed to remedy this problem. According to the principle of forfeiture, a person who threatens the life of an innocent person forfeits his own right to life. The principle of double effect provides four criteria that must be met for an action to be considered only an indirect violation of a fundamental value.

THE PERSONAL AND SOCIAL ETHICS OF NATURAL LAW

Duties to Self

In natural-law ethics, a person's primary duty to herself is to promote the realization in her life of the four fundamental values of life, procreation, knowledge, and sociability. The duties to oneself have positive and negative dimensions. I have a positive obligation to promote the values specified by natural law and a negative obligation not to act directly against those values.

Keep in mind that the negative obligations are more binding than the positive ones. Because of the absolutist orientation of natural law, we are never justified in directly violating a fundamental value, but we need not always actively promote these values. A certain amount of discretion is called for in determining when and how the fundamental values of natural law are to be promoted. For example, a person who decides not to marry and have a family so that she can devote herself to the service of God does not violate the requirements of natural-law morality. She may be failing to use her procreative powers, but she is not directly violating them. It is generally easier to determine when a person has violated a negative obligation than when she has violated a positive obligation. Not surprisingly, therefore, some of the best-known moral judgments of natural law are negative.

The moral duties to oneself arising from the biological values of life and procreation have received more attention than the moral duties derivable from the characteristically human values of knowledge and sociability. As we have already seen, self-defense is a positive duty, justified by the value of life. The value of life also requires us not to commit suicide, because suicide directly violates that value. Therefore, suicide has been condemned in the natural-law tradition.

However, some actions that appear to be suicide may not be, because the principle of double effect applies. When a soldier throws himself on a grenade to protect his comrades, he is acting directly to save the lives of his fellow soldiers, which itself is morally permissible. His own death is a tragic but unintended consequence of his actions. He may foresee his own death, but he does not directly intend it, for his death is neither a means to the good effect of saving other lives nor avoidable if his comrades are to be saved. Furthermore, the criterion of proportionality applies, because his death saves other people's lives.

The value of procreation leads to what is probably the most widely discussed conclusion of natural-law theory: the prohibition of "artificial" contraception. Because the use of contraceptive devices could be considered a violation of a duty to oneself, we can appropriately discuss it here. To show that contraception is intrinsically immoral, we need only point out that it violates the value of procreation, and this violation is not excused by either the principle of forfeiture or the principle of double effect.

We have seen that merely failing to use one's procreative powers to pursue another value, such as knowledge of God, is permissible. But, when a person chooses to have intercourse with his or her spouse and does something to prevent conception, he or she is directly acting against the value of procreation. Therefore, the action cannot be acceptable from the standpoint of natural law.

Attempts to avoid this conclusion by appealing to the principle of forfeiture and double effect are unsuccessful. The principle of forfeiture is inapplicable, because neither the parents nor the fetus may be considered noninnocent. In applying the principle of double effect, we might possibly argue that, when parents use contraceptive devices, their intention is to promote the value of knowledge by limiting their family size so that they can provide more effectively for their children's education. However, the prevention of conception is a direct means chosen by the parents to attain this end. Therefore, contraception must be considered a violation of natural law and hence immoral.

That sterilization is morally wrong is even more obvious from the natural-law standpoint. Although one might argue that the parents' intention is to provide more effectively for their children's education or to promote some other laudable end, the means to this end is the prevention of conception.

The situation is quite different if an action that produces sterility is taken for a reason that is legitimate in itself. Suppose a woman with uterine cancer has her uterus removed to save her life. The woman will no longer be able to bear children, but her action is still morally justifiable because sterility is not a necessary means to the end of saving the woman's life but merely an unintended side effect. Moreover, because life is a fundamental value, the woman must do what she can to save her life, as long as her action is not directly contrary to another basic value.

Natural-law theorists have not devoted as much attention to the negative and positive duties to self that might be derived from the values of knowledge and sociability, but these duties should be just as binding. An interesting exercise would be to consider the duties arising from these values. Obviously, a person has an obligation to develop her ability to pursue knowledge through education and to develop her capacities for relationships with other people. But what kinds of actions should be counted as a direct violation of these values? Do we directly violate the value of knowledge if we discontinue a promising education or if we stifle our scientific or philosophical curiosity?

Finally, it is not surprising that many people think that the pursuit of pleasure might be a duty to self. Many people seem to have a natural inclination to pursue pleasure, so why should it not be listed as a fundamental value? Natural-law theorists believe that, if we examine our motivations closely, we find that we do not pursue pleasure for its own sake. To understand this claim, consider the following possibility. Suppose you could be connected to an "experience machine" that would produce any sensations you desired.[4] You could have the pleasures of sex, the joy of eating, the euphoria experienced after jogging ten miles, or any number of other delightful experiences—all just by pressing various buttons on the machine. Suppose you could spend your entire lifetime connected to such a machine. Would you do it?

Most of us would probably choose to spend very little if any time connected to such a machine. The reason is that we want more than experiences. We want to do things, to be a certain kind of person, and to interact genuinely with other human beings in specific ways. Pleasure for its own sake is not a fundamental pursuit. You may be interested in considering whether you agree with this claim and whether you accept the

---

[4] For a modified version of this idea (used for different purposes), see Robert Nozick, *Anarchy, State and Utopia* (New York: Basic Books, 1974), pp. 42–45.

natural-law theorist's claim that fame, power, and wealth are also not fundamental human pursuits.

Duties to Others

The biological and characteristically human values provide the basis for many negative duties to others. Besides the duty not to kill another person directly, including a human fetus, we also have a duty not to act directly against the values of knowledge and sociability. Deliberately discouraging a child's curiosity, for example, violates the value of knowledge. Lying is also an offense against another person's inclination to know the truth. Actions that destroy people's ability to relate to one another, such as slander and malicious gossip, violate the value of sociability. You can probably think of many other negative duties that follow from the biological and characteristically human values.

The extent of one's obligation to help others is controversial. Our obligation to help others is clearly limited by the requirement not to violate another basic value directly. I cannot donate my heart to save your life while I am still in good health, but some cases provide interesting problems for natural law. Consider the following case as an example.[5] In 1956, Leon and Leonard Madsen, nineteen-year-old brothers, presented themselves to Peter Brent Brigham Hospital in Boston. Leon's only hope for life was a kidney transplant from Leonard. The hospital had performed the first successful kidney transplant in two adult identical twins in 1954. Is Leonard's donation of one of his kidneys morally permissible by natural law?

The question hinges on whether, in giving one of his kidneys to his brother, Leonard is acting directly against the value of his own life. The loss of a kidney is not a serious danger to life, but many natural-law theorists believe the donation nevertheless violates the integrity of the human body because it is potentially life-shortening. The principle of double effect cannot justify the action because it is a means to the good effect. Natural-law theorists have generally taught that our obligation to help others falls short of this action. Could you set up any general guidelines for the limits of benevolence according to natural-law theory?

Social Ethics

Three principles characterize the natural-law approach to social ethics. First, the state has a right to defend itself against international and external

---

[5] See Paul Ramsey, *The Patient as Person* (New Haven, CT: Yale University Press, 1970), pp. 165–197.

enemies, as long as it is fundamentally just. Sociability is a natural human inclination, and humans cannot find fulfillment apart from association with other human beings. Consequently, the state is a natural institution for human beings, not an arbitrary, oppressive invention of tyrants. War is thus justifiable in certain circumstances if it is necessary to preserve the social order. But a war must be just, and natural-law theorists have developed a theory of the "just war" to define the legitimate conditions of war.

The first of these conditions is that a war must be declared by a lawful authority in the state and not by private individuals. Second, the war must have a just cause; that is, there must be a violation, attempted or accomplished, of the state's legitimate rights. Examples of just causes would include carrying off part of the population, seizing territory or resources or property, or casting a serious blow to the nation's honor that would weaken its authority. Third, the cause must not only be just but also known to be just by the rulers who declare the war. The rulers must have the right intention in starting the war. Fourth, the conduct of the war must include the right use of means. To seek a good through the direct violation of a basic value is morally wrong. The direct killing of innocents, for example, must be avoided.

A second principle of natural-law social ethics is that natural law is always more binding than the human laws of a particular state. As long as the laws of the state do not seriously violate the principles of natural law, citizens have an obligation to obey them. Nevertheless, when the moral wrongs perpetrated by the state are great, and when it can be reasonably predicted that a rebellion would succeed, revolution may be justified.

Outright rebellion is not, of course, the only way a citizen may act contrary to the laws of his country. In considering such actions as conscientious objection, for example, natural-law theorists often distinguish between the question of whether a citizen's action is *objectively correct* (in accordance with natural law) or *subjectively correct* (performed because of the right intentions). A conscientious objector's action in refusing military service may be objectively correct, because the war is actually unjust, but subjectively incorrect, because the objection is based not on moral grounds but perhaps on the fear of losing one's life. Or the objector's action can be objectively incorrect and subjectively correct, as when the war is just but the objector genuinely thinks it is not and so refuses to serve in the military. Of course, a citizen might believe a war is just when it is not, in which case military service would also be objectively incorrect but subjectively correct.

Natural-law theorists have always held that one's duty is to follow one's own conscience; that is, one's action should always be subjectively correct.

At the same time, we also have an obligation to keep our consciences from being corrupted by factors like self-interest.

The third principle of natural-law social ethics is that the state should be organized for the common good. The state exists for the good of individuals; individuals do not exist for the state's benefit. Therefore, promoting the common good is nothing more than providing the conditions necessary to realize the four values of life, procreation, knowledge, and sociability. Natural-law theorists have insisted, for example, that citizens should be accorded a "just wage" that is sufficient both to allow them to enjoy an appropriate level of dignity and productiveness and to realize the moral values of natural law in their lives. Exploitation by private business or the government is wrong. Many natural-law theorists have been sympathetic with socialism and welfare-state policies as the most appropriate means for realizing these goals. Whether natural law is compatible with an enlightened form of capitalism is a question worth considering.

If the state is obliged to give citizens the opportunity to realize the values prescribed by natural law, does it follow that the state should force the values of natural law on its citizens? This conclusion has often been drawn by moral theologians, as the following passage by Bernard Häring illustrates:

> The state has a duty to assume an unequivocal position in relation to natural and supernatural revelation. The Church was repeatedly forced to condemn the principle of the "liberal" state according to which every option, every doctrine, whether true or false, good or bad, has an equal right to be publicly expressed and defended through free speech and press. These so-called "liberal" principles, apart from dishonor to God, would ultimately lead the state to its own destruction. For its own survival, not to speak of progress, it must possess at least a minimum of certain and unassailable principles regarding truth and error, good and evil. Only through the unconditional possession of such principles can the state avoid the dilemma of anarchy which forbids nothing or legislation which is utterly arbitrary in its sheer legal positivism.
>
> To avoid very grave disunity in the public life of a nation, however, it is justifiable at times for the state to restrict its protection to the truths universally accepted by the major groups in its domain representing basic attitudes to life. And from a merely practical standpoint, it may go still further and grant the same freedom to any and every doctrine. However, such a situation is far from ideal.[6]

Häring's statement represents a completely different stand on the enforcement of morality from the egoist's libertarian position. What is

---

[6] Bernard Häring, *The Law of Christ*, trans. Edwin G. Kaiser (Paramus, NJ: Newman, 1966), Vol. 3, pp. 120–121. Used with permission.

the basis of this extreme position on the obligation of the state to enforce the principles of natural law? Häring argues that actions contrary to natural law dishonor God and eventually result in the destruction of the state. However, he also admits that the conclusions of natural-law morality might not be accepted by a given population. In this case, the generally accepted moral views should be allowed to prevail, even though the situation would be far from ideal—the ideal being the enforcement of moral precepts derived from natural law.

Häring believes that the conclusions of natural law are objectively right, that they are matters of reason rather than revelation. Its conclusions are available to all those willing and able to use their faculty of reason. Thus, in asking the state to enforce natural-law morality, Häring does not believe he is calling for the enforcement of a uniquely Catholic, or even Christian, moral perspective. Like any natural-law moralist, Häring believes that he is advocating only what is in accord with human nature. From the standpoint of natural law, therefore, by allowing the advocacy and practice of actions contrary to true human inclinations, the state is not promoting human self-realization but, rather, the distortion of human nature.

Nevertheless, Häring's statements shock most people who have been raised in a democratic tradition. An interesting question is whether natural-law theorists can work out a political philosophy more genuinely supportive of individual freedom. Many sophisticated attempts have already been made in this direction, and Häring himself provides one possible avenue. Recalling the distinction between the objective and subjective morality of an action, we can see what is behind Häring's observation that some people may genuinely not be persuaded by the arguments of natural law. Because individuals should not do what they think is wrong and should do what they think is right, regardless of the objective morality of the actions, the state must be careful in forcing natural-law morality on its citizens. Even if natural-law moralists were to allow more freedom in behavior than Häring does, however, they may still believe the state is obliged to prevent immoral teachings and immoral behavior from unduly influencing other people. In any case, the criterion of the common good provides an instructive basis for a philosophy of the obligations of government to its citizens.

Concept Summary

Duties to self are governed by the principle that a person has an obligation to promote the realization in his or her life of the basic values specified by our natural inclinations and not to do anything that directly obstructs the realization of those values. Most of the duties to self discussed in traditional natural law have concerned the biological values of life and procreation. An interesting question to ask yourself is what positive and negative duties follow from the characteristically human values of knowledge and sociability.

Duties to others include the duty not to kill another person directly or to violate the values of knowledge (for example, by lying) or sociability (for example, by slander). Many other duties follow from the four fundamental values. The extent of one's positive obligations to others is limited by the duty not to violate obligations to oneself. The question of donating vital organs poses an interesting test case of the limits of others' duties.

Three principles characterize the natural-law approach to social ethics. First, the state has a right to defend itself against internal and external enemies, as long as the state is fundamentally just. Second, natural law takes priority over human laws, and it may sometimes provide a justification for civil disobedience or even revolution. Third, the state should be structured in a way that promotes the realization of the four values of natural law in its citizens' lives.

APPLYING THE ETHICS OF NATURAL LAW

We can now apply natural law to some cases involving moral decisions, following the methodology outlined in the checklist.

Case 1: AIDS and Condoms

Let us consider the controversy over the use of condoms as a way to prevent AIDS, which was described at the beginning of this chapter.

Because of the different moral issues that arise in various instances of the use of condoms to prevent AIDS, it will be helpful first to treat the use of condoms to prevent AIDS in heterosexual vaginal intercourse between married couples and then consider all other uses of condoms to prevent AIDS. We shall refer to this first category of sexual relations as *procreative intercourse*, because married couples would have intercourse in a context in which procreation would be justified from the standpoint of natural law. Natural-law theorists hold that the natural mode for producing children for human beings is in the context of monogamous heterosexual marriage. Other sexual relationships would include nonvaginal intercourse between married partners, vaginal and nonvaginal intercourse between unmarried heterosexual partners, and oral and anal intercourse between homosexual partners. We shall refer to this second category of sexual relations as *nonprocreative intercourse,* because the mode of intercourse is incapable of producing children, or the partners would probably not wish to produce them. To sharpen the issue further, we shall focus on the morality of actually *using* condoms rather than the morality of *advocating* the use of condoms.

I.   The use of condoms is an "artificial" mode of contraception and a violation of the natural tendency to procreation. Therefore, it is morally illegitimate unless the principles of forfeiture or double effect can be invoked.

II. The principle of forfeiture is inapplicable to either procreative or nonprocreative intercourse. A person with AIDS has done nothing worthy of death, so he has not forfeited his own right to life.

III. If the use of condoms to prevent AIDS is morally permissible, it must be because the principle of double effect is satisfied.

Let us begin by considering procreative intercourse. To apply the principle of double effect, we must describe the action and its effects. In this case, the action is the use of condoms in marital vaginal intercourse. The good or morally desirable effect is the prevention of the transfer of the HIV virus. The bad effect is the prevention of conception.

A.   Married couples who have a long-standing monogamous relationship would not need to use condoms, but we can consider a newly married couple, where one or both of the partners had been sexually active before marriage. Here the use of condoms would be desirable to prevent the spread of the HIV virus, assuming the couple had not taken the test for its presence, or the test is not reliable, or some suspicion exists that the couple might still be sexually active outside the marriage. Although sexual activity outside the marriage cannot be justified by natural law, the use of condoms in marital intercourse is a different issue.

If it makes sense to consider the use of condoms apart from the consequence of preventing conception or the transmission of the HIV virus, then we should consider the action in itself morally permissible.

B.   If one partner has the HIV virus, or there is a suspicion that he or she has, then the bad effect of using condoms can be avoided while achieving the good effect only by refraining from intercourse altogether. Because natural-law theorists usually consider intercourse an obligation of married partners, this alternative is not acceptable. Therefore, if there is reason to believe a partner might have the HIV virus, the use of condoms might be considered unavoidable.

C. The application of the third criterion is controversial. The prevention of conception is not, strictly speaking, the means of controlling the spread of AIDS. Condoms are used to prevent the entrance of the HIV virus into the other partner's body, not to prevent conception. From this perspective, the use of condoms might appear morally permissible. However, in attempting to control the spread of the HIV virus, the transmission of all bodily fluids from one sexual partner to the other must be stopped—including sperm, which can carry the virus. Hence, the prevention of the transmission of sperm (and therefore the prevention of conception) must be a part of the means employed. So the use of condoms in heterosexual vaginal intercourse by a married couple would seem to violate the third criterion.

D. If we consider the risk of loss of life through HIV infection a greater evil than the violation of moral principles involved in the use of condoms, then the principle of proportionality is satisfied.

Because criterion c is violated, procreative intercourse, using condoms to prevent AIDS, is morally impermissible.

Now let us consider nonprocreative intercourse in its various forms. To apply the principle of double effect, we must again describe the action and its effects. In this case, the action is the use of condoms in nonprocreative intercourse. The good or morally desirable effect is the prevention of the transfer of the HIV virus. The bad effect is the provision of a degree of safety that allows nonprocreative intercourse to occur more easily. That is, the bad effect is the encouragement of promiscuity.

A. The use of condoms, considered in itself and apart from its consequences, will again be considered morally permissible.

B. The transmission of the HIV virus can be prevented by refraining from nonprocreative intercourse, so the bad effect is not unavoidable in promoting the good effect.

C. The provision of an environment in which intercourse that is impermissible from natural law's standpoint can more easily take place is a means of preventing the spread of the HIV virus. Therefore, the bad effect is a means to the good effect.

D. If we consider the risk of loss of life through HIV infection a greater evil than the violation of moral principles involved in the use of condoms, then the principle of proportionality is satisfied.

Because criteria b and c are violated, nonprocreative intercourse with condoms is also morally impermissible.

IV. We can conclude that the use of condoms to prevent AIDS is morally impermissible in both procreative and nonprocreative intercourse.

Case 2: The Morality of Obliteration Bombing

During World War II, both the Germans and the Allied Forces bombed civilian residential areas, a practice called "obliteration bombing." Probably the two most famous examples of this practice, in which conventional explosives were used, were the German bombing of London and the Allied bombing of Dresden, Germany. Let us confine ourselves to the bombing of Dresden and ask whether this action was permissible by the principles of natural law.

I.   The focus must be on the killing of civilians in Dresden. This feature of the action makes it an apparent violation of natural-law morality. Hence, we must ask whether the principles of forfeiture and double effect serve to make the bombing morally permissible.

II. The principle of forfeiture raises the conceptual problem of whether the civilians in Dresden should be considered innocent. If we assume that the criteria of just-war theory were met—that is, the Allied Forces were fighting a just war and the Germans were not fighting a just war—then the Germans in uniform were noninnocent, and attacking them was morally justified. But most civilians in large cities were connected with the war effort in a very indirect way. Unless civilians are employed in the production of military hardware, most natural-law theorists would probably count them as innocent. Many Germans may have had little knowledge of the reasons for the war; in a nondemocratic state, they certainly had no part in starting it. Therefore, the civilians in Dresden should be considered innocent, and the principle of forfeiture does not justify the bombing.

III. Some have argued that an appeal to the principle of double effect could justify the bombing. According to this argument, the direct and intended effect of the bombing was to destroy war industries, communications, and military installations, whereas the damage to civilian life was unintentional and indirect. But a careful analysis of the conditions of the bombing will not sustain this argument.

  A. We shall consider the action under analysis to be the bombing of Dresden, the good effect to be the shortening of the war, and the bad effect to be the deaths of innocent civilians. Bombing an enemy city cannot be said to be intrinsically immoral. We have shown that war can be justified by natural law, and we shall assume that the Allied cause could be defended by just-war criteria. Therefore, the Allies had a right to attack German cities.

B.   Let us assume that there was no other way to shorten the war except by bombing cities. If the desirable end is described as "shortening the war," bombing the cities would be unavoidable in achieving that end, so the second criterion of the principle of double effect is met.

C.   Destroying German morale through terror was, on the testimony of military documents themselves, an object of the bombing. And the means of inducing terror and consequent demoralization was the deaths of innocent civilians. Therefore, the third condition of double effect is not met.

D.   We can also question the allegation that the principle of pro-portionality was satisfied by the belief that obliteration bombing would shorten the war. That goal was speculative, futuristic, and problematic, whereas the evil effect was definite, immediate, and widespread. Thus, we shall conclude that this criterion is also not met and that the principle of double effect does not apply.

IV.   Because the Allied attack on Dresden involved the destruction of innocent human life, and because the principles of forfeiture and double effect do not excuse it, we must conclude that the action was morally impermissible by natural-law theory.

Case 3: The Suppression of Galileo

Galileo Galilei (1564–1642) has a strong claim to the title of founder of modern science. At first he accepted the Ptolemaic theory that the sun and planets revolved around the earth. But his invention of the telescope and the discovery of the satellites of Jupiter led him to confess his adherence to the Copernican system in 1610. In 1616, the Office of the Holy Inquisition took the important step of entering the works of Copernicus on the list of forbidden books and declaring his teaching heretical. In 1632, Galileo published his *Dialogue on the Two Principal Systems of the World*, in which he contrasted the Ptolemaic and Copernican systems of astronomy. He thought that, if he merely gave an "objective" account of the differences between the two systems, he would not offend the Inquisition and would thereby avoid persecution.

Galileo's sympathies with the Copernican system were all too evident, however, and the Inquisition banned his book and summoned him to Rome for a hearing. After being threatened with torture, Galileo was forced, on June 22, 1633, to go down on his knees and renounce the doctrine that the earth revolves around the sun and to swear that he would cease any further promotion of Copernican astronomy. He lived for several more years under conditions of virtual house arrest but was still able to produce his greatest scientific book. However, the spectacle of Galileo's persecution inhibited the advance of science. Can the silencing of Galileo be justified by the principles of natural law?

I.   This issue raises the problem of how to properly promote the natural inclination to know. Natural law requires that we promote the natural inclination of humans to know, but the question is how best to accomplish this. The leaders of the Inquisition would no doubt have described their action of silencing Galileo as promoting the inclination to know, arguing that they were defending truth against error by defending the astronomical system that seems to be in agreement with Holy Scripture. From our perspective, their action should probably be described as obstructing the inclination to know by silencing free inquiry, which we regard as essential to the discovery of truth.

What is implied by the natural-law requirement to promote knowledge: defending the truths of Holy Scripture or defending free inquiry? In Galileo's time, there were different conceptions of the authority of Scripture in science and the value of free inquiry, and it is not clear that contemporary views are an appropriate basis for evaluating actions that took place centuries ago. However, adopting the contemporary perspective is probably more instructive for us today, so I shall assume that the proper way to promote the natural inclination to know is to promote free inquiry. However, I shall also assume that from the natural-law viewpoint, protecting Holy Scripture has some value as well. Because suppressing free inquiry is, by this account, a violation of a natural inclination, the only way to avoid the conclusion that the Inquisition's action was morally impermissible is to find an excusing condition in one of the two qualifying principles.

II. Galileo had not threatened anyone's life; he had done nothing to forfeit his own right to life. This consideration is important, because Galileo was threatened with torture and possible death. Natural-law theorists might argue that a person can do other things to forfeit his status as an innocent person, such as teach heretical doctrines that endanger the souls of others. However, this point presupposes that Galileo was wrong, so I shall assume that the principle of forfeiture is not relevant.

III. To analyze the action of the leaders of the Inquisition from the standpoint of the principle of double effect, we must be able to distinguish an action, a good effect, and a bad effect. The action, as we have described it, was forcing Galileo to renounce his adherence to Copernican astronomy. The good effect was promoting Scripture's authority. The bad effect was denying individual freedom to state one's views and seek truth. Can the action of the Inquisitors be justified by the principle of double effect?

   A. Forcing Galileo to renounce his public adherence to a scientific view is an act that seems inherently contrary to the inclination to know, even if we consider the act apart from any future consequences regarding the inhibition of free inquiry. Therefore, I shall assume that the first criterion is not met. There is no need to continue the analysis, because the principle of double effect cannot be used here. But, in this case, it will be instructive to proceed with the rest of the analysis.

   B. The Inquisitors would probably have argued that denying freedom of expression was unavoidable if the authority of Scripture was to be preserved, so that the second criterion was met. Recent historical experience with religious pluralism, however, has probably convinced most of us that freedom of expression and belief in the authority of Scripture (at least on the part of those committed to religious faith) are compatible. So we shall assume that bad effect is avoidable and the second criterion was not met.

   C. The means used to achieve the end of protecting Scripture was the denial of freedom of inquiry. So this criterion is also not met.

   D. The leaders of the Inquisition would probably have said that their action passed the test of proportionality, because the negative consequences of Galileo's suppression were outweighed by the fact that Scripture was defended. But this claim is questionable, because the suppression of opinion (even if it is false) is probably not the best way to defend Scripture. Besides, the test of proportionality is relevant only if the other tests are met. We may conclude that this criterion is also not passed.

IV. Because the action of the leaders of the Inquisition violates the value of knowledge by suppressing the right to dissent, and because the two qualifying principles are inapplicable, we must conclude that the Inquisitors' action was morally impermissible.

This case illustrates the difference that factual assumptions and conceptual issues can make in the ethical analysis of a case. The Inquisitors had very different ideas from most of us about the place of free discussion and the authority of Scripture in the pursuit of truth. I shall leave it to you to determine whether, using the ideas prevalent in their time, the Inquisitors could have justified their action from the standpoint of natural law.

EVALUATING NATURAL LAW AS A MORAL THEORY

We are now ready to evaluate natural law, using the four criteria set up in Chapter 3. I will give you my own evaluations and try to defend them.

Criterion 1: Consistency and Coherence

Natural-law ethics is, for the most part, internally coherent, but some theorists have found a problem in the use of the principle of forfeiture to justify the direct taking of life. Traditional natural-law theorists take an absolutist position regarding the values of life, procreation, sociability, and knowledge, and they maintain that these values can never be directly violated for any reason. But the principle of forfeiture has seemed, even to some natural-law moralists, to be a violation of the absolute value of life, for it allows the direct taking of life. Killing in war and self-defense can be justified by the principle of double effect, because we can argue (although perhaps implausibly) that the direct intent of these actions is to protect the country or one's life. However, the principle of double effect cannot justify capital punishment, because it can only be counted as a direct taking of life. Here the principle of forfeiture is required if the taking of life by capital punishment is to be justified. Because capital punishment has been considered morally permissible by traditional natural-law moralists, the principle of forfeiture has been essential. It is interesting to consider whether the principle of forfeiture is a legitimate part of natural-law morality or whether its use in natural-law arguments is inconsistent with the theory.

We have also pointed out that the criterion of proportionality seems like an exception to the claim that values are incommensurable and cannot be weighed against one another. It also seems to be an exception to the view that consideration of consequences plays no part in natural-law ethical analysis. The response of the natural-law moralist to this possible incoherence is that weighing values and considering consequences is permissible only within the confines of the principle of double effect and even then only after the other criteria have been considered. Perhaps we would be correct in saying that weighing values and considering consequences is only a secondary method of ethical analysis and not a primary method as it is in consequentialist theories.

Criterion 2: Justification

Natural-law morality has been associated with religion since the advent of Christianity, so we might suppose that its advocates would attempt to justify the moral standard of natural law by an appeal to the will of God or divine revelation. But natural-law theorists have held that ethical truth is available to all human beings through the natural use of their reason, whether or not they accept a particular religious revelation. Certain religious injunctions, such as observing the Sabbath in Judaism or partaking of the Lord's Supper in Christianity, are derived exclusively from revelation. But, apart from such special commands, revelation is not necessary for us to know how we ought to live. What, then, is the basis of our knowledge of ethical truth that is equally available to all people? We have seen that it is human nature or, more specifically, the natural inclinations of human beings, but we still have not explained how these natural inclinations are known or how they establish ethical truth. Let us consider one account of the foundations of natural law.[7]

We can begin by considering some of the principles or norms that underlie our thinking in areas not necessarily related to ethics. For example, in science we assume that all occurrences in nature have an adequate reason, even if we do not know what this reason is. In ordinary experience, we assume that the things we see are real unless we have reason to believe we are experiencing an illusion. Such principles cannot be proven, for they would be presupposed in any possible proof. But, although they cannot be proven, they are obviously valid to anyone who has any experience with scientific inquiry or even practical living. To deny them is to disqualify oneself from the pursuit of knowledge. In this sense, these principles are self-evident.

Some natural-law theorists believe that certain ethical theses underlie our action in the same way. In particular, we assume in our action that value exists in life, procreation and child rearing, sociability, and knowledge. One way to see the self-evident nature of these values is to observe that anyone who denies them finds that he has refuted himself. We can illustrate this claim by showing self-refutation in the skeptical assertion that knowledge is not a good. One natural-law theorist states the contradiction in the skeptic's assertion in this manner:

---

[7] See John Finnis, *Natural Law and Natural Rights* (Oxford: Clarendon, 1980), pp. 59–75.

One who makes such an assertion, intending it as a serious contribution to rational discussion, is implicitly committed to the proposition that he believes his assertion is worth making, and worth making qua true; he thus is committed to the proposition that he believes that truth is a good worth pursuing or knowing. But the sense of his original assertion was precisely that truth is not a good worth pursuing or knowing. Thus he is implicitly committed to contradictory beliefs.[8]

Some natural-law theorists believe that similar demonstrations can be given for the other basic values, although the arguments have not been worked out in detail.

An important point is that, according to this version of natural-law theory, something is not good because we have a natural inclination to pursue it. Rather, we have a natural inclination to pursue it because it is good. Natural inclinations are indicators of those goods that we tend to pursue. Yet it is also true that, if our human nature or the general human condition were different, we might pursue different goods.

Even if we accept the argument that knowledge is a good, similar arguments for the other three values of natural-law morality are not readily available. Nor does this argument establish that these values can never be violated—that, for example, the good of procreation could not be violated to care better for the children we already have. In other words, the natural-law theorist finds it difficult to establish the absolutism that characterizes her position, in both of the senses in which this term is used. She encounters difficulties in identifying natural inclinations and establishing that the values specified by these inclinations are objectively valid. She also faces difficulties in establishing that the values of natural law can never be violated. Thus, the claim of the natural-law theorist that the values of natural law are clear and objectively valid for all people has not been demonstrated.

Criterion 3: Plausibility

As we have seen, a moral theory can be evaluated in part by comparing the moral judgments it produces with our own prior moral beliefs about these issues. Natural law produces a number of moral judgments that many of us find difficult to accept. Although our objection is inconclusive, because our moral judgments may be incorrect, the comparison is important. These seemingly implausible judgments produced by natural law fall into two primary categories.

---

[8] Ibid., pp. 74–75.

First, in situations of "life against life," in which human life will be lost regardless of what decision is made, natural law teaches that innocent people must never be directly killed, even if the result is greater loss of life in the long run. For example, natural-law moralists hold that, when a choice must be made between pushing a person off a life raft or letting everyone drown, we must choose the second option. When the choice is between bombing civilians and shortening a war, thereby saving many lives, or not bombing civilians, thereby producing greater overall loss of life, we must again choose the second option. Finally, even when both the mother and the fetus will die if an abortion is not performed, natural law teaches that an abortion is immoral, unless the principle of double effect is applicable. These conclusions seem implausible, even cruel, to many people, yet they follow from the absolutist character of natural-law ethics—the view that a fundamental value must never be directly violated.

Second, natural law often seems to place excessive emphasis on the physical or biological values, giving them importance equal to or greater than the characteristically human values. The most widely known example of this tendency is the emphasis on procreation in marriage. Traditional natural law holds that the primary function of marriage is procreation and that the secondary function is companionship; that is, primary emphasis is placed on the biological function of reproduction, a function that human beings have in common with other animals. Characteristically human qualities, such as the capacity for love and commitment, are given secondary status. This view seems inconsistent with the form of natural law we have advocated, according to which the biological and characteristically human values are of equal importance. However, our proposed concept of natural law prohibits the use of contraception because it is a direct violation of the value of procreation. Most people probably feel that the value of procreation should be violated to allow a couple more fully to enjoy a love relationship or more adequately to care for the children they already have. Why should procreation be a value that can never be violated?

Some contemporary natural-law theorists have agreed that the characteristically human values should be given priority over the biological values. These theorists criticize traditional natural-law theory for being too "physicalistic" or exhibiting the trait of *physicalism*, which is the understanding of human acts in terms of their physical or biological function.[9] Some natural-law theorists would regard as excessively physicalistic any version of natural-law theory that gives greater or even equal importance to the physical or biological values of life and procreation. For example,

---

[9] See Charles E. Curran, "Natural Law and Contemporary Moral Theology," in his *Contemporary Problems in Moral Theology* (Notre Dame, IN: Fides, 1970), pp. 97–158.

they might argue that, in marriage, love (sociability) and the proper education of children (knowledge) should have priority over any obligation to produce more children. Similarly, a concern for the quality of life as exhibited in the capacity for meaningful relationships (sociability) might justify euthanasia in situations in which a person is dying of cancer. By the same kind of reasoning, the traditional natural-law prohibitions of sterilization, homosexuality, masturbation, and many other practices could also be reversed. Do you believe this restructuring is compatible with natural-law morality?

Criterion 4: Usefulness

To help people think clearly about moral issues and reach conclusions in difficult cases, a moral theory must provide a clear, plausible method for resolving moral controversies. Natural law has been reasonably successful in this regard. Natural-law moralists generally agree on many important ethical issues. However, the determination of whether a fundamental value has been violated is sometimes difficult, which impairs the usefulness of natural-law moral theory. Recall that a basic value may never be directly violated, but it may be indirectly violated when the principles of double effect and forfeiture apply. The application of these principles is often difficult, impairing the usefulness of the theory.

CONCEPT SUMMARY

Some natural-law theorists believe that traditional natural-law theory is inconsistent in using the principle of forfeiture to justify the direct taking of life, as in capital punishment. The use of the criterion of proportionality also raises problems of consistency with regard to the natural law claim that basic values must never be weighed against one another and that consequences are not crucial in ethical analysis. Natural-law moralists also have difficulty justifying their fundamental values. They sometimes attempt to justify the basic values of natural-law morality by arguing that the values are necessarily assumed in all human activity; however, this demonstration has not been completely worked out. Furthermore, the arguments do not show that basic values may never be violated.

Natural-law theory also does not agree with our prior moral beliefs in several important respects. First, it does not agree with our previous moral beliefs in its claims that life can never be taken. Most of us would probably agree, for example, that a mother should have an abortion when both she and the fetus will otherwise die. Second, natural law also disagrees with most people's moral convictions in its insistence that the biological values have an importance equal to or greater than the characteristically human values. This tendency to understand human action in terms of its biological or physical function is called *physicalism*.

The usefulness of natural-law ethics is limited by the fact that we sometimes have difficulty determining when a fundamental value has been directly violated.

THE ETHICS
OF UTILITARIANISM

In 1958 and 1959, the *New England Journal of Medicine* reported a series of experiments performed on patients in the Willowbrook State School, a home for retarded children in Staten Island, New York.[1] The experiments were designed to confirm the usefulness of gamma globulin as an immunization against hepatitis, improve the serum, and learn more about hepatitis. The school was already experiencing a low-grade hepatitis epidemic. Researchers obtained the consent of the parents, because the children were both under-age and retarded. The children were divided into experimental groups and control groups that received hepatitis virus at various levels of infectiousness and gamma globulin inoculations at various strengths. Some of the gamma globulin was given below the strength known to be effective. Children who contracted the disease suffered the usual symptoms (enlargement of the liver, vomiting, anorexia), but all of them recovered.

When these experiments became public knowledge, they produced a storm of controversy. Many people objected that the children had been "used" in a morally unacceptable way. But the experimenters pointed out that the children would have been exposed to the virus anyhow, none of them had died, and valuable medical knowledge was gained from the experiments. Judged in terms of overall human well-being, the experiments do seem to be justified.

If the argument of the experimenters appeals to you, you may be a utilitarian. The basic question a utilitarian asks in determining the moral status of an action is "Will this action produce greater overall human well-being?" For the utilitarian, human well-being is the only good,

---

[1] Robert Ward, Saul Krugman, Joan P. Giles, A. Milton Jacobs, and Oscar Bodansky, "Infectious Hepatitis: Studies of Its Natural History and Prevention," *New England Journal of Medicine* 258, No. 9 (February 27, 1958), pp. 407–416; Saul Krugman, Robert Ward, Joan P. Giles, Oscar Bodansky, and A. Milton Jacobs, "Infectious Hepatitis: Detection of the Virus during the Incubation Period and Clinically Inapparent Infection," *New England Journal of Medicine* 261, No. 15 (October 8, 1959), pp. 729–734.

although some utilitarians also include the well-being of animals. Utilitarians also consider everyone's well-being to be of equal value. Utilitarianism is thus midway between egoism and altruism. The egoist is concerned only with her own happiness, and the altruist is concerned only with the happiness of others. For the utilitarian, her own well-being is neither more nor less important than the well-being of anyone else.

Utilitarianism has its roots in eighteenth-century England, but it flowered in nineteenth-century England, particularly in the writings of Jeremy Bentham and John Stuart Mill. Utilitarianism greatly influenced liberal legislation in England and the United States in the twentieth century and is probably the basic moral philosophy of most nonreligious humanists today.

Utilitarianism is one of the most powerful and persuasive traditions of moral thought in our culture. In fact, many moral controversies, such as the debate over euthanasia, can best be understood as a conflict between utilitarianism and traditional Hebrew-Christian morality. Jewish and Christian theorists generally condemn active euthanasia (for example, taking an injection of poison), even though passive euthanasia (for example, termination of lifesaving medication) may sometimes be allowed. Their reasoning is usually based on the belief that God created human life, and only He has the prerogative of directly ending it.

But what if one does not believe in God? What if one believes that human life is solely the product of nonconscious forces and that the only source of value in the universe is human existence? Then one might conclude that the only possible good is the well-being of humanity. If an individual who is dying of incurable cancer sees only suffering for himself and those he loves, with no discernible good to come out of that suffering, why should he not take his life? If this course of action will produce the most overall human good or well-being, what better way of determining the right thing to do?

Even someone who takes a religious perspective might well find utilitarianism attractive. Would a loving God not be concerned primarily with human welfare? Some religious utilitarians maintain that the utilitarian perspective is compatible with religious values. Thus, for both religious and nonreligious people, utilitarianism is an attractive moral position.

THE UTILITARIAN MORAL STANDARD

Before we formulate a utilitarian standard, we must mention the concept of "audience." In deciding what is morally right, I must take into account all those affected by my action. We shall refer to those affected by a course of action as the *audience* of the action. Thus, from the utilitarian standpoint, the audience of an action includes all of those whose well-being could be either increased or decreased by one's action.

The well-being of each member of the audience should count equally. Each person should count for one and none for more than one. But because the utility (welfare) of various members of the audience is sometimes incompatible, the best I can do is to seek the greatest total utility. Also, many (probably most) utilitarians now believe that the evaluation of particular actions should be based on the utility of the general moral rules underlying these actions, not on the actions themselves. Taking both of these considerations into account, we can formulate the utilitarian moral standard in the following way:

> MS: Those actions (or moral rules) are right that produce the most utility, or at least as much utility as any other actions (or rules).

Now we are in a position to discuss several aspects of this moral standard in more detail.

The Definition of Utility

How shall we define *utility*? Some utilitarians have maintained that utility is synonymous with *happiness* or even *pleasure*. But, unfortunately, these terms are defined differently by different people. And if we specify a particular definition of happiness or pleasure, we seem to be forcing our own values on others.

For example, John Stuart Mill, an important nineteenth-century utilitarian, argues that human beings have capacities that animals do not have and that, when we are aware of those capacities, we cannot regard anything as happiness unless it includes them. In particular, we must give "pleasures of the intellect, of the feeling and imagination, and of the moral sentiments a much higher value as pleasures than those of mere sensation."[2] Mill believes we can confirm the judgment that these pleasures have a higher value than the pleasures of food and sex, for example, simply by asking those who have experienced both kinds of pleasure which they prefer. Would you really want to exchange places with a person who has had all of his physical desires satisfied but who has no close personal relationships, no intellectual or artistic interests, and no goals other than pleasure? Most of us would conclude, Mill believes, that it is better to be a dissatisfied Socrates than a satisfied fool.

---

[2] John Stuart Mill, *Utilitarianism* (New York: Liberal Arts Press, 1957), p. 10.

However, not everyone who has experienced both the pleasures of the intellect and the pleasures of sex will always choose the former over the latter. The novelist D. H. Lawrence believes that we relate most meaningfully to other human beings and obtain our deepest communication with the nature of things through sexual acts. So, as Mill himself acknowledges, the most we can say is that a majority of people who have experienced the various kinds of pleasure usually prefer the pleasures of the intellect, feelings, and imagination. But even so, have we established that the majority is right? It seems that the utilitarian cannot really define utility in terms of the "higher" pleasures without being arbitrary.

Perhaps it would be better to define utility as the satisfaction of any preferences or desires a person might have. But this definition seems too broad and permissive. Jack the Ripper satisfied his preferences by killing people. Must the utilitarian advocate that Jack satisfy his preferences even though they conflict with the desire of his victims to live?

There may be a way out of this dilemma. For the utilitarian, the satisfaction of any preference must be considered a "good" in some sense, but it need not be a good toward which the utilitarian aims. The utilitarian's goal is the greatest total amount of satisfaction of preferences or desires. Some desires, such as the desire to become a cancer researcher, contribute at least potentially to the satisfaction of others' desires as well, such as those who have cancer. Most of our desires are relatively neutral with respect to the desire satisfaction of others. Thus, my desire to buy an ice cream cone after class neither contributes to nor detracts from your desire to go back to your apartment. Still other desires, like those of Jack the Ripper, decrease the ability of others to satisfy their desires. These categories of preferences or desires can be classified according to their claim to satisfaction, beginning with those that have the highest claim:

1. Preferences whose satisfaction contributes to the preference satisfaction of others
2. Preferences whose satisfaction is neutral with respect to the preference satisfaction of others
3. Preferences whose satisfaction decreases the preference satisfaction of others

When we arrange the categories of preference satisfaction into such a hierarchy, we can see that the utilitarian should aim at the satisfaction of preferences in the top two categories if he wishes to achieve the greatest total amount of preference satisfaction. Although this solution to the problem of defining utility is not without its difficulties, it does seem to avoid the problem of arbitrariness inherent in the first attempt. We can therefore be content with our definition of *utility* as preference or desire satisfaction.

Distribution versus Quantity of Utility

This solution assumes that the utilitarian wants to do what produces the *greatest total amount* of utility or preference satisfaction. This means that, when we have a choice between an action that produces the greatest total amount of utility and one that produces the greatest distribution of utility, we must choose the former. Consider a situation represented by the following table:

Action	Number of People Affected	Units of Utility per Person	Total
Act 1	2	100	200
Act 2	50	2	100

Note that act 1 affects only two people, but it gives each of them 100 units of utility and gives no one any disutility, so that the total quantity of utility is 200 units. The alternative act affects 50 people, but it produces only two units of utility each, for a total of 100 units. The act producing the greatest quantity of utility would not provide for its widest distribution, and the act producing the widest distribution would not produce the greatest quantity. Which action should be performed?

In accordance with the guideline set out in the previous section, a utilitarian must choose act 1. If a utilitarian chooses act 2, he can justify his choice only by adding another criterion, having to do with the distribution of utility, to the utilitarian moral standard. For example, the moral standard might say that those actions (or moral rules) are right that produce the most utility, or at least as much utility as any other actions (or rules), *provided the utility is equally distributed.* This addition not only severely restricts the ability of the utilitarian to maximize utility, but one has to ask, "What is its basis?" It seems to have a basis in a concern for justice (equal distribution) rather than anything connected with the utilitarian standard.

Most utilitarians have therefore concluded that this addition would introduce serious inconsistencies into the utilitarian position and so must be avoided. Nevertheless, eliminating any direct consideration of the distribution of utility raises questions about the compatibility of utilitarianism with ordinary standards of justice. We shall return to this issue later.

The Place of Animals

The third and final question concerns the types of beings whose preferences are to be considered. Should the audience over which utility is maximized be confined to human beings? If utilitarianism takes the satisfaction of preferences as the only thing that is good in and of itself, why should only the preferences of human beings be considered? Do not all animals have preferences or, at least, wants or needs? Mill seems to admit the force of this observation when he says that happiness should be secured not only to human beings but, "so far as the nature of things admits, to the whole of sentient creation."[3] Even though we use the concept of preference satisfaction rather than happiness, the point is the same.

One of the most eloquent and moving pleas for the consideration of animals is made by Jeremy Bentham, the founder of modern utilitarianism. In a passage written when black slaves in parts of the British Empire were treated the way we treat animals today, Bentham says:

> The day may come when the rest of the animal creation may acquire those rights which never could have been withholden from them but by the hand of tyranny. The French have already discovered that the blackness of the skin is no reason why a human being should be abandoned without redress to the caprice of a tormentor. It may one day come to be recognized that the number of legs, the villosity of the skin or termination of the *os sacrum,* are reasons equally insufficient for abandoning a sensitive being to the same fate. What else is it that should trace the insuperable line? Is it the faculty of reason, or perhaps the faculty of disclosure? But a full-grown horse or dog is beyond comparison more rational, as well as a more conversable animal, than an infant of a day, a week, or even a month old. But suppose it were otherwise, what would it avail? The question is not, Can they reason? nor Can they talk? but, Can they suffer?[4]

Here Bentham makes the capacity to suffer (and, of course, he would include the capacity to enjoy) the characteristic that entitles a being to consideration from a utilitarian standpoint. The capacity for suffering and enjoyment is not just another characteristic like the capacity for language or higher mathematics. It is a prerequisite for having any claim to ethical consideration at all. A stone does not have any such claim precisely because it cannot suffer or enjoy. Animals have such claims because they can suffer and enjoy. Therefore, we have little justification for considering only human beings in our utilitarian calculations.

---

[3] Ibid., p. 16.

[4] Jeremy Bentham, *Introduction to the Principles of Morals and Legislation,* ch. 17, Sect. 1, note; quoted in Peter Singer, *Practical Ethics* (Cambridge, MA: Cambridge University Press, 1979), pp. 49–50.

The human-centered ethical orientation of much Western ethics has been called "speciesism" by Peter Singer, a utilitarian advocate of the rights of animals.[5] Just as the white racist fails to regard the interests of blacks as having the same importance as the interests of whites, so the speciesist excludes animals from having a claim to our consideration. Humans may suffer more intensely than animals because of their greater self-consciousness and ability to anticipate the future. Therefore, human interests can often outweigh animals' interests. Nevertheless, equal suffering should count equally, according to the advocates of animal rights. So, in a utilitarian calculation, animal suffering or enjoyment should count equally to that of human beings in considering the morality of actions or rules, insofar as it is of the same degree or intensity. This position has some interesting implications for issues such as eating animal flesh, using animals in experimentation, wearing animal skins, hunting of all types, and keeping animals as pets and as circus and zoo exhibits.

Act Utilitarianism and Rule Utilitarianism

One of the most frequently discussed issues in utilitarian theory is the distinction between act utilitarianism and rule utilitarianism. Because the difference in applying these two versions of utilitarianism can be difficult to understand, let us begin our discussion with an example.

John finds himself with a final average in a philosophy course that is ten points below passing. Without a passing grade, he cannot graduate and take the coaching job he has been offered. He approaches his professor with the following argument:

> If you give me the ten points on my final average, I will not tell anyone. I know the information would hurt both of us. I'm married and have a small son. I will be out of school soon, and my job is in another state. If I do not graduate, I will lose the job offer, and my family and I will endure considerable hardship. In fact, I may have to drop out of school, because I am out of money. I studied as much as I could, but I find philosophy hard to understand and work forty hours a week. This has been a tough semester for me.

Suppose you are the professor and you know that John's story is true. Your concern is not simply to protect your own interests; rather, you want to do whatever produces the greatest total utility for those affected. What should you do?

---

[5] Singer, *Practical Ethics*, ch. 3.

The answer to this question depends in part on whether you are an act utilitarian or a rule utilitarian. Here is a summary of the difference between these two forms of utilitarianism:

> *Act utilitarianism* judges the morality of an action by whether the action itself produces the most utility, or at least as much utility as any other action.
>
> *Rule utilitarianism* judges the morality of an action by whether the moral rule presupposed by the action, if generally followed, would produce the most utility, or at least as much utility as any other rule.

What conclusions will these two versions of utilitarianism lead to in this particular case? Applying act utilitarianism, you would determine whether to give John the ten points on his final average by deciding which of the two alternative actions (giving or not giving the ten points) would produce more utility in this particular situation. To make this determination, you must consider how everyone in the audience would be affected by the two alternatives.

A good argument can be made that, according to act utilitarianism, you should give John the ten points on his final average. Assuming the arrangement is kept secret, you would suffer no negative consequences, except perhaps a general feeling of uneasiness or guilt. If you are a confirmed act utilitarian, you may not feel any remorse because by your own moral standard your action is justifiable.

The other people who are directly affected by the action are John, his family, and the other students in the class. If John gets the ten points, his own desires will be met; he will graduate and get the job he has been promised. His family will then enjoy the benefits of a father and husband with a stable income. He may suffer some loss of pride, knowing that he has not fully earned his degree, but very likely this loss will be offset by the fact that he has a good job and can care for his family. He can also justify his action by remembering that he probably did the best he could under the circumstances.

The welfare of the other students will not be adversely affected to any significant degree. Assuming that you do not allow the one higher grade to influence the grades you give to other students, their standing in the class will not be affected, so you will conclude that greater total utility will be produced by giving John the ten points than by refusing his request.

Rule utilitarianism probably leads to a different conclusion. To see the difference, you must compare the utilities of the two alternative rules involved in this case. If you give John the ten points, the rule underlying your action could be formulated as

> Professors should assign grades according to the needs of students, not their merit.

If you decide not to give the ten points, the rule underlying your action could be formulated as:

> Professors should assign grades according to merit, not the needs of students.

As a rule utilitarian, you will ask, "Which of the two general rules will produce the greater overall utility?" You will not be comparing the utility of two specific actions but that of two different policies. Would more utility be produced if professors generally graded according to need or if they graded according to merit?

Let us consider first the consequences of a general policy of grading according to need rather than merit. If this policy became widespread, grades would become relatively meaningless. Other teachers and prospective employers could not make any inference from grades to a student's true academic merit. They would have to spend a great deal of time talking to professors and asking questions such as, "I know John received an A in your course, but was he really an A student?" Grades would no longer have the prestige they once had, which might reduce many students' incentive to do well in school. Students could more easily deceive parents, teachers, fellow students, and prospective employers about their academic achievement.

Requiring that professors assign grades on the basis of merit seems not to have the same disadvantages. Although the present system of determining grades by merit is not without fault, it seems to produce more overall utility than the alternative system. Therefore, if the second rule is more justified by the utilitarian moral standard, it must be applied to John. He must be judged by merit rather than need, and his request must be denied.

As this example suggests, rule utilitarianism often leads to different, more plausible conclusions than act utilitarianism. Rule utilitarianism also does more justice to our belief that morality should be a matter of following rules; that is, it agrees with a widespread belief that a morally acceptable action is one we would willingly have others follow. Not surprisingly, then, many philosophers have favored rule utilitarianism over act utilitarianism. Following this tradition, we will use utilitarianism to mean rule utilitarianism. When we discuss act utilitarianism, we will specify so.

Act utilitarianism is an important adjunct to rule utilitarianism. It can be used, for example, when a rule and its most reasonable alternative produce approximately equal amounts of utility, in which case rule utilitarianism provides no basis for making a decision. If you cannot decide which of two alternatives is morally right by evaluating the utility of the rules underlying the two alternatives, look directly at the utility of the two actions themselves. If neither has appreciably greater utility, then either action is permissible by the utilitarian moral standard.

Keep in mind that for the utilitarian, nothing but utility is good in itself, and nothing but disutility is bad in itself. Particular actions and general rules must be evaluated by their consequences. Murder, rape, fraud, and theft are not somehow wrong in themselves; they are wrong only because they do not produce as much utility as alternative behaviors. If two or more actions or rules have the same utility, they are of equal moral worth.

FURTHER CONSIDERATIONS IN APPLYING RULE UTILITARIANISM

The basic idea of utilitarianism is simple: Rules or actions are right insofar as they promote utility and wrong insofar as they promote disutility. We have already seen some complications in applying this simple idea. Two additional issues, which we will encounter when we begin to apply utilitarianism, are (1) whether others will obey the rules that utilitarians find most desirable and (2) how we should go about formulating the rule presupposed by a particular action.

Will Others Obey the Rules?

In the example of the student who asked for a higher grade, we assumed that professors could realistically be expected to follow either of the two rules we formulated. Our assumption was most likely valid; college teachers would probably be able to adopt either rule. But, in some cases, the rule that produces the most overall utility is unlikely to be generally adopted under any circumstances we can reasonably imagine. Is a rule utilitarian still morally obligated to follow the ideal rule?

Let us first consider a trivial example to illustrate the point and then proceed to a more serious example to show how important this issue can be. Suppose you are walking to your class, and the most direct route is across the grass along a path that is well worn by frequent use. A sign posted nearby reads, "Please do not walk on the grass," but most people disregard it. Should you disregard the sign too? From a rule-utilitarian perspective, the rule that "Everyone should walk on the sidewalks rather than on the grass" will probably produce more utility than the rule "One may walk wherever one wishes." If everyone follows the first rule, we experience only minor inconvenience, the campus will have a neater appearance, and the maintenance crews will avoid the unnecessary expenses of filling the ruts and planting new grass, which will then be destroyed again.

But suppose you have good reason to believe that few people will follow this first rule. Moreover, from an act utilitarian standpoint, you should probably take the path across the grass like everyone else. You will avoid a minor inconvenience, and the grass will not be any worse because one more student takes the easier way. Many utilitarians would say that you are not obligated to obey the sign "Please do not walk on the grass" until you have reason to believe that it will be generally followed, even though a rule requiring obedience to the sign would actually produce greater utility if generally followed.

Now let us consider a more serious example. Suppose you are a manager for a foreign operation of a multinational corporation. Your plant is in a country where racial discrimination is still widely practiced. Ideally, you would like to provide housing for your employees without regard to race or ethnic origin, but you know that such a policy would cause serious problems for your business. The plant might even be forced to close, and your employees would lose their jobs. You feel confident that, if everyone were to adopt it, the rule that "Business should provide housing for employees without regard to race or ethnic origin" would produce greater utility in the long run than the alternative rule of following discriminatory policies. You are just as confident, however, that few companies would freely adopt the ideal rule.

So the rule that could actually produce more utility, because it has a greater chance of being adopted, is "Business should adopt a policy of racially discriminatory housing in areas where this policy is the only practical one that can be followed." By following this rule, your business will at least be allowed to remain open and provide needed jobs. However, you do have to consider the example you are setting in following the traditional racist policies. If you have reason to think your example will cause others to rethink their practices, you should probably break precedent.

A general guideline for such circumstances might be as follows: When you have reason to believe that the ideal utilitarian rule will not be generally followed and that a less desirable rule, because it more likely would be generally adopted, would produce more utility, you should follow the less desirable rule.

How Should the Rule Be Formulated?

So far we have discussed rule utilitarianism as if only one rule and one clear alternative can be presupposed by a course of action. However, many actions can be described by more than one rule. It is important to use a rule that (1) describes all of the features of the action that are relevant from a utilitarian standpoint, (2) does not describe features that are morally irrelevant, and (3) is as general as possible. Let us consider each of these three guidelines.

First, the rule should describe all relevant features of the action from a utilitarian standpoint. Suppose you are driving along a highway and see an orchard full of ripe apples. You are hungry and wonder whether it would be morally acceptable to stop and pick several apples. The rule presupposed by the action might be stated as follows:

> A person should pick and eat fruit when he is hungry.

However, this rule does not adequately describe the situation and is therefore not an appropriate rule on which to base a moral decision. Its most obvious deficiency is its failure to mention at least one morally relevant fact: the apples belong to someone else, and they would be taken without the owner's permission. Because this fact is relevant to the utility that would be produced by the general adoption of the rule, you should restate the rule to include it:

> A person should pick and eat apples that do not belong to him when he is hungry.

This rule is a better description of the circumstances of the case and superior to the first rule for this reason. This is not to say that the utilitarian would find this rule justifiable from the utilitarian standpoint, but it is a more appropriate rule to test for its utility because it is a more adequate account of the morally relevant factors.

This rule still might not fully describe the situation under which you took the apples, however. Suppose you are experiencing severe dehydration and the apples are the only available source of water. You might formulate the rule to take this need into account:

> A person should pick and eat apples that do not belong to him if the apples are the only means of avoiding serious dehydration.

This rule would apply only to a small number of people, and its general adoption would probably produce more utility than the alternative rule requiring that the apples not be picked even under these extreme circumstances.

Second, the rules should not describe features that are morally irrelevant. If your name is Susan Brown and you are driving home after your first year in college, you might formulate the moral rule underlying your action as follows:

> Everyone whose name is Susan Brown and who is returning from her first
> year in college should pick and eat apples that do not belong to her if
> the apples are the only means of avoiding serious dehydration.

This rule incorporates morally irrelevant features. It violates a criterion discussed in Chapter 1—namely, that moral statements have an impersonal character. Thus, names, dates, and places should not be included in moral rules.

Third, the rules should be as broad as possible, without being too broad. The rule must strike a balance between being too broad and too narrow. The first two guidelines indicate some of the factors that can make a rule too broad or too narrow. When relevant moral factors (such as the apples' belonging to someone else) are ignored, the rule is too broad. When irrelevant factors (such as Susan Brown's name) are included, the rule is too narrow. But rules can be too broad or too narrow in other ways. For example, as a utilitarian, you might well conclude that a rule covering many other types of actions would be acceptable. Rather than limit the rule to the circumstance having to do with picking apples and the possible harm of dehydration, it would be better to say:

> Everyone should engage in petty theft if it is necessary to avoid serious harm.

Remember that the rules you are evaluating are supposed to be ones that could be adopted in a society. This rule is more likely to be a part of a moral code of a society than is a rule limited to the particular case of eating apples. For this reason, it is probably a more adequate rule to test than any of the others are.

Because moral rules are part of a larger system of moral rules, some utilitarians argue that the standard of utility should not be applied to particular rules, one at a time, but to a whole set of rules, even an entire moral code. We must ask of a moral code whether its general acceptance by most people in a given society would produce more or less utility than would the general acceptance of an alternative moral code. We have not used this version of rule utilitarianism because it is difficult to apply. Evaluating the utility of an entire moral code is no easy task, and it would take us far afield from our consideration of particular moral issues. Furthermore, it is still possible to modify a particular rule within a moral code by testing the rules much as we have been doing. So our method of testing particular rules would seem to be a part of any more elaborate version of rule utilitarianism.

The following two checklists cover rule and act utilitarianism. The first checklist covers rule utilitarianism, the form favored by many utilitarians. However, we must appeal to act utilitarianism in situations in which two rules produce equal utility or in which rule utilitarianism just does not seem to be appropriate. Also, it is often important to see the different conclusions reached by act and rule utilitarianism on the same issue.

CHECKLIST FOR APPLYING RULE UTILITARIANISM

I. State the rule that is presupposed by the action you are evaluating. The rule should be specific enough to describe those features of the situation that would produce positive or negative utility but not so specific or impractical that it could not realistically be adopted by a society.

II. State the most reasonable alternative rule or rules, keeping in mind the precautions stated in step 1.

III. Determine the proper audience for the rule—that is, the people or animals that would be affected by the rules.

IV. Identify the rule that would produce the greatest total utility, assuming that it could realistically be followed.
   A. The rule that produces the greatest utility or whose alternative produces the least utility is morally obligatory.
   B. Rules that produce less utility overall are morally impermissible.
   C. If two rules produce equal utility, or if for any reason a rule cannot be formulated, it is permissible to resort to act utilitarianism to decide the issue.

V. Apply the obligatory or permissible rule to the particular action. If no rule is justified, move to act utilitarianism.

CHECKLIST FOR APPLYING ACT UTILITARIANISM

I. Describe the action and the most reasonable alternatives to the action.

II. Determine the proper audience for the act—that is, the people or animals that would be affected by the action.

III. Identify the action that would produce the greatest total amount of utility, assuming it could realistically be followed.
   A. The action that produces the greatest total amount of utility is morally obligatory.
   B. Actions that produce less overall utility are morally impermissible.
   C. If two or more actions produce equal utility, they are equally morally permissible.

CONCEPT SUMMARY

Utilitarianism is a highly influential moral philosophy in contemporary society. One of the most widely accepted forms of utilitarianism defines utility as preference or desire satisfaction. The most consistent form of utilitarianism is one that disregards the distribution of utility (that is, whose preferences are satisfied) and aims simply for the greatest total utility or preference satisfaction. A consistent utilitarianism must take account of the preferences of animals as well as humans, especially the natural tendency of all animals to avoid suffering. However, because humans have a higher degree of self-consciousness and the ability to anticipate the future, they have greater capacity to suffer and enjoy. This capacity justifies giving human preferences special consideration.

Act utilitarianism focuses on the utility produced by a particular action, whereas rule utilitarianism focuses on the utility produced by the general acceptance of the rule presupposed by an action. These two forms of utilitarianism can sometimes lead to different moral conclusions, and many utilitarians favor rule utilitarianism as the more adequate version of utilitarian theory. However, act utilitarianism is still useful in determining what to do when two rules seem equally acceptable from a utilitarian standpoint.

In applying rule utilitarianism, it is important to ask yourself whether the rule that would produce the greatest utility is one that others would be likely to follow. If others are not likely to follow it, the best procedure is to adopt a rule that does have a chance of being generally accepted. Several guidelines for selecting the rule to test in rule utilitarianism are available: (1) the rule should describe all the features of the action that are relevant from a utilitarian standpoint; (2) the rule should not include features that are morally irrelevant; (3) the rule should be as broad and inclusive as possible, without leaving out morally relevant features.

UTILITARIAN PERSONAL AND SOCIAL ETHICS

In applying utilitarianism thus far, we have resolved moral problems by referring to the utilitarian moral standard; that is, we have analyzed the rule presupposed by an action and then tested the action by the standard of utility. But analysis is aided by knowing generally what the implications of utilitarianism are—that is, what kind of personal and social ethics the utilitarian moral standard supports. This section is devoted to clarifying these issues.

We must first, though, enter a cautionary note. Utilitarianism, like egoism, judges the morality of actions by their consequences. In both moral theories, knowledge of the consequences of actions (or rules, in the case of rule utilitarianism) is of central importance. The egoist cannot know which form of economic organization is justified by egoism unless he knows which one produces consequences that are most compatible with his own self-interest. Similarly, the utilitarian cannot know what character traits or types of behavior or forms of social organization are justified by the utilitarian moral standard unless she knows what consequences they produce and which consequences are most conducive to utility.

This point means that any discussion of the general implications of utilitarian theory must presuppose the truth of certain factual assumptions. If these assumptions are questioned, the implications drawn from them must also be questioned. It is important, therefore, for you to identify the factual assumptions made in the following discussion and decide whether you agree with them.

Duties to Self

In the personal ethics of utilitarianism, a person's actions must be governed by those rules that in general lead to the greatest total utility. But this statement does not mean that I will make my maximum contribution to the well-being of others if I am doing something that I am unsuited for or that I detest. If I find my greatest satisfaction in being an engineer or a gardener, a physician or a plumber, I should follow that occupation. I will probably make my greatest contribution to the general well-being by doing what gives me the greatest satisfaction.

This observation shows that self-realization has a legitimate place in utilitarian ethics, although it must always be the means to the promotion of utility. Of course, if my greatest talent is robbing banks, I should not realize this talent because it will not contribute to the general welfare. Nevertheless, utilitarianism clearly takes account of the psychological egoist's observation that all of us are powerfully motivated by considerations of self-interest. The utilitarian can argue that, in large measure, utilizing these motivations for utilitarian ends is possible.

In some important areas of duties to self, utilitarianism leads to different conclusions than traditional Hebrew-Christian morality does. We have seen that natural-law ethics condemns suicide and euthanasia as violations of the sanctity of human life. A moment's consideration of this issue shows that the utilitarian will take a very different stance than a natural-law theorist will. Just as we must count a desire to go on living as a reason against killing, so we must count a desire to die as a reason for killing. One can have a preference for dying as well as a preference for living.

Utilitarianism can even justify "active" as well as "passive" euthanasia. The Hebrew-Christian tradition has placed great emphasis on the distinction between acts and omissions. But utilitarians judge the morality of an action by its consequences—in particular, those consequences that affect the satisfaction of preferences. If two actions, one a commission and the other an omission, both have the same consequences in terms of preference satisfaction (or, as some might say, the same "bottom line" in terms of utility), they should not have different moral evaluations from the utilitarian standpoint.

Suppose a terminal cancer patient is receiving life-sustaining medication. The patient asks the physician to help him end his life. In one version of the story, the physician administers a lethal injection; in the other, she omits administering the life-sustaining medication. If the death is equally swift and painless in both cases, the utilitarian would have to evaluate the two acts as morally equivalent. In this situation, the physician would probably omit the life-sustaining medication, but if the lethal injection produced a faster and less painful death, the utilitarian would find this "active" method to be the more morally desirable. In any event, the active-passive distinction would not be the deciding factor.

One qualification should be made in the claim that it is only the "bottom line" with which the utilitarian must be concerned. Although this claim is true, all the consequences of a general practice (in the case of rule utilitarianism) or all the consequences of a particular act (in the case of act utilitarianism) must be considered. For example, suppose it could be shown that the widespread practice of active euthanasia resulted in a diminished regard for human life that is contrary to utility. This consideration must be considered as one effect of euthanasia, and it might be sufficient to overbalance any positive effects of the practice.

You can probably think of other issues within the category of duties to oneself for which the utilitarian would reach conclusions different from traditional Hebrew-Christian beliefs, especially the beliefs of natural-law theorists. What would utilitarians say about the morality of sterilization, masturbation, or the self-giving of vital organs, for example? A measure of the influence of utilitarianism is that the moral beliefs of many people already appear to be undergoing a change in the direction of the utilitarian approach to these issues.

Duties to Others

Utilitarianism can easily justify many of the common rules of morality relating to other people. Prohibitions against murder, theft, and fraud follow from the observations that such activities, if generally practiced, would not promote the general welfare. A more interesting case to consider from the utilitarian standpoint is the controversial case of abortion.[6] The utilitarian believes that human beings do not deserve special consideration simply because they supposedly have a soul. Rather, consideration must be based on possession of traits that allow a being to have interests or preferences, such as rationality and self-consciousness, and the ability to experience pain or enjoyment. Killing is wrong when it conflicts with the interest of living beings in staying alive, and the degree of interest a being can have depends on the extent to which it possesses these traits. The fertilized egg immediately after conception cannot possibly feel pain or be aware of anything. It cannot, therefore, have interests that deserve to be considered in a utilitarian calculus. As the fetus grows, it develops the capacity to feel pain and perhaps even to experience a degree of con-sciousness, but a calf, pig, or chicken has more developed interests than a fetus does. By the utilitarian moral standard, we should accord the life of a fetus no greater value than the life of a nonhuman animal at a similar stage of self-consciousness and capacity to feel pain.

Antiabortion advocates might argue that even before the fetus is sufficiently developed to have interests, it is at least potentially a being that can have interests. Does this potentiality not deserve respect? From a utilitarian standpoint, potential interests might seem to merit little if any consideration in comparison to the actual interests of more developed fetuses and human beings. But utilitarians do consider the potential interests of human beings who will live in the future. If these interests are considered, why should the interests of early fetuses not also be considered?

One important difference is that future generations will actually exist at some point in the future, but fetuses may never exist if a decision is made to have an abortion. Another difference is that utilitarians consider the interests of future generations in general, not the interests of particular individuals who may exist in the future. Thus, there are important differ-ences between the interests of individual fetuses, especially at very early stages, and the interests of future generations. Whether these differences are important enough to justify disregarding the interests of early fetuses is a matter of controversy.

If we disregard the interests of early fetuses, what specific conclusions should we arrive at regarding the morality of abortion from the utilitarian standpoint? Peter Singer has proposed that fetuses of less than 18 weeks are very unlikely to be capable of feeling anything at all because their nervous systems are insufficiently developed. Therefore, we cannot say they have any

---

[6] See page 5 for an earlier discussion of this topic.

interests to protect. Abortions during this period, Singer believes, should pose no moral problems. Between 18 weeks and birth, when the fetus certainly has a capacity to feel and may even be conscious, abortion should not be taken lightly. But even here the serious interests of the mother would ordinarily override the rudimentary interests of the fetus.

These same arguments apply to a newborn baby. A week-old baby is not a rational and self-conscious being. In fact, by the standards we have developed, the life of a newborn baby is of less value than the life of an adult pig, dog, or chimpanzee. Utilitarians might argue that killing newborn babies has some other antiutilitarian consequences, such as promoting a lower regard for human life that could increase the incidence of killing adults. But unless such arguments can be made, the utilitarian must conclude that infanticide can be justified, at least on some occasions. Again, these views contrast sharply with Hebrew-Christian morality. But the utilitarian argues that we should modify our views to bring them into line with what he believes to be the more plausible utilitarian standard.

Social Ethics

The general principle governing utilitarian social ethics is that equal consideration should be given to the preferences of everyone affected by social policies, with a view to achieving the greatest total satisfaction of those preferences. Three implications of this guideline are especially interesting.

First, most utilitarians have argued for democratic government as a means of achieving the utilitarian ideal of maximizing the satisfaction of preferences. The best way to ensure that the maximum number of preferences is satisfied is for each individual to exercise control over the government by means of the vote. Democracy also tends to encourage the development of an active, responsible character. Some utilitarians have found still another reason for preferring democracy to other forms of government. When citizens have the responsibility of deciding govern-mental policies, however indirectly, they tend to develop capacities of self-determination that are more conducive to self-realization than are the more docile and passive character traits fostered by nondemocratic polit-ical orders.

Second, utilitarians have favored the maximum degree of individual freedom, especially in the realm of ideas. In his important essay *On Liberty*, John Stuart Mill observes that one can easily assume that, when demo-cratic government has been established, the battle for individual liberty has been won. However, Mill argues, the majority may still be inclined to restrict the rights of dissenting minorities, especially when the ideas of minorities are highly unpopular. Mill believes that this is a mistake and that the rights of dissenting minorities can be defended on utilitarian grounds. He maintains that allowing individuals to pursue their own ideas and beliefs leads to the discovery of truth. In what some have called the "free marketplace of ideas," the best ideas will survive in the competition with other ideas. For example, science requires intellectual freedom so that ideas may be openly advanced and criticized to discover the truth. The same freedom is required in other areas, such as politics. The best way to conduct a society can be discovered only by allowing citizens the freedom to advance ideas and then allowing other citizens to expose their flaws.

Mill assumes that the discovery of truth leads to utility. Although he does not make any extended argument for this claim, we may assume his argument to be that knowledge of the consequences of actions provides the basis for a more effective pursuit of the utilitarian ideal. Thus, a utilitarian will support individual freedom, because individual freedom leads to the discovery of truth, and the discovery of truth promotes the greatest satisfaction of people's preferences.

Third, twentieth-century utilitarians have often argued for extensive welfare measures and at least a partial redistribution of wealth. Democracy and freedom for individual dissent are not enough to ensure maximum preference satisfaction. Equal opportunity does not compensate for the deleterious effects of a destructive family life. Perhaps even more important, it neglects the importance of genetic endowment. We know that early training has a great deal to do with emotional stability and how much effort individuals will expend to achieve their goals. We also know that IQ, physical health, and stamina, and probably many other traits, are primarily genetic. Therefore, even if equal opportunity is provided, those with more fortunate family and social backgrounds and more desirable genetic endowments will be in a better position to satisfy their interests. They will be able to pursue more interesting and lucrative careers, achieve greater social prestige, and otherwise enjoy a more comfortable and rewarding life. This restriction of these advantages to the fortunate few will probably not produce the greatest total satisfaction of interests.

Some utilitarians, including Peter Singer, have proposed that the utilitarian ideal would be realized more completely if society could adopt the famous Marxist slogan "From each according to his ability, to each according to his needs."[7] But Singer and most other utilitarians realize the

---

[7] Singer., p. 36.

practical difficulties in fully implementing this ideal. In this situation, the ideal utilitarian rule will not, in fact, produce the greatest utility, because it has little chance of being generally adopted owing to the natural selfishness of most human beings. If we do not pay a person more for being a computer programmer than for cleaning offices, she may not make the effort to get the advanced training needed for computer programming. And will not the failure to use the talents of many of the most gifted people fully result in less total preference satisfaction? Most of the advances in society are produced by the more talented members. If they have no incentive to use their talents, we might all be worse off.

These considerations have convinced many utilitarians that social policy must reward individuals for using their inherited abilities rather than strictly according to their needs. Therefore, we should, within certain limits, reward the more talented members of society for their special achievements. This recommendation illustrates the earlier guideline that a practice should not be implemented if it has little chance of success, regardless of how desirable it may be from a utilitarian standpoint. A less desirable rule that would actually be followed will produce more utility. Nevertheless, many utilitarians still feel that providing the basic necessities for all citizens, as the welfare state attempts to do, is required by their philosophy.

APPLYING UTILITARIAN THEORIES

We can now apply utilitarianism to some problems that require moral decision, using the methodology developed in the checklist.

Case 1: The Willowbrook School

Let us begin by considering the case presented at the beginning of this chapter.

1. The rule followed by the administrators of the Willowbrook School is not easy to formulate. Should we consider subjecting the population in general to a degree of pressure to participate in medical experiments, or should we confine the rule to inmates in public institutions? Should the rule mention that the children are retarded or that the risk is minimal and the chance of yielding valuable knowledge is great? The general guideline is that the morally relevant features must be included in the rule. From the utilitarian standpoint, the moral relevance is determined in part by whether the fact might affect the overall utility. But there are also other factors. As we have seen, the rule should be as general as possible and not include morally irrelevant factors.

Considering these factors, I have decided not to include the fact that the children are retarded because the decision would be made by the parents in either case. I have decided to include the fact that the children are in a public institution because the children are receiving benefits from the public. The state may thus have a right to expect something in return. The fact that the risk is minimal and that valuable knowledge may come from the experiments is important from a utilitarian standpoint because it is one indication that the benefit to others is likely to outweigh the potential harm to the children. The rule might be stated in the following way.

It is morally permissible to use mild coercion in getting inmates in public institutions to submit to medical experiments when the experiments promise substantial benefit to the general population (and perhaps the inmates themselves) and when risk is minimal.

2. The alternative rule should be the negation of this rule:

It is not morally permissible to use mild coercion in getting inmates in public institutions to submit to medical experiments when the experiments promise substantial benefit to the general population (and perhaps the inmates themselves) and when risk is minimal.

3. The audience of this rule would be the inmates of public institutions, the parents of the inmates (if the inmates are children), the administrators of the public institutions, the members of the medical profession who conduct such experiments, and anyone afflicted with the diseases that are the subject of the experiments. The general public is also affected, although to a lesser extent, in various ways that will be enumerated later.

4. The rule utilitarian approach requires that we distance ourselves from the particulars of the case at hand (except as illustrations) and consider the harms and benefits of a general policy represented by the two rules. The primary benefit of the policy described in the first rule is, of course, the valuable medical information that can be gained. The Willowbrook case illustrates the kind of knowledge that can result: confirmation of the value of gamma globulin, improvement of that serum, and increased knowledge of how the disease is transmitted. The information might benefit the inmates themselves (as it no doubt would in the Willowbrook case), and, if useful information is gained, it will certainly benefit the many people who would be afflicted in the future with the disease being investigated.

In a more indirect way, the information will benefit members of the general public, for they will have the assurance that more effective treatment would be available if they should get the disease. The members of the medical profession would benefit by the policy outlined in the first rule, for they would enjoy the satisfaction and professional advancement that results from being able to conduct medical experiments.

The effect on the administrators and the parents of the inmates (if the inmates are children) is more difficult to determine. However, they would have the satisfaction of knowing that their children, or the inmates of their institution, are participating in medical experiments that have the potential of conferring a benefit on humanity.

Finally, the inmates themselves might have some satisfaction in knowing that they are participating in experiments that have the potential of benefitting large numbers of people. (In the Willowbrook case, the retarded children would probably have little satisfaction from this knowledge.)

The inmates would experience most of the negative effects. They would be subject to the risks and possible pain and discomfort associated with the experiments. The parents and administrators would have to endure the anxiety associated with the knowledge that the experiments might result in harm or even death to their charges. They would also have to endure the bad publicity that would result from harm to the inmates. The members of the general public would also be negatively affected if they believed injustice had been done, perhaps wondering whether they might be subjected to a similar injustice if they were in a public institution. Finally, the medical profession might suffer a loss of prestige if the experiments were generally considered to be exploitative or otherwise immoral, even if these judgments had no utilitarian justification. The general public could also suffer harm as a result of diminished confidence in the medical profession.

5. Although some of the harms or potential harms (especially to the inmates) are real, the benefits of such policies would seem to outweigh those harms. The increase in scientific knowledge would benefit many future generations. This outcome would far overshadow the risk to the inmates, especially if the risk were controlled and relatively small. Therefore, the first rule has more in its favor from a utilitarian standpoint than the second rule and is morally obligatory.

6. Applying the first rule to the Willowbrook State School case, I shall conclude that the medical experiments were justified and in fact obligatory.

Case 2: The Morality of Whaling

Whales are mammals. Whale calves are fed and cared for by their mothers, and the bond between mother and child appears to persist beyond the period of lactation. Their nervous systems and the parts of the brain relating to the perception of pain are essentially similar to our own. Although some authorities say that the killing of a whale takes only five minutes, others say that it often takes much longer.

Whales are also social animals; they live in groups and relate to each other as individuals. Some species are monogamous, and, when one member of the family has been harpooned, other family members have been observed to wait offshore for days or even weeks for its return. Good scientific evidence backs up the ascription of a sophisticated emotional life to whales.

However, whalers in Japan and the Soviet Union (the two primary whaling countries) and other countries where whaling is permitted depend on whaling for their livelihood. Some whale products are quite useful to people. Whale oil is used to make soap and margarine, and whale meat is consumed by humans, livestock, and pets. Whales are also used for various commercial products, especially cosmetics.

So the question for the utilitarian is, If whaling can be controlled, to remove the threat of extinction, is it morally wrong to kill whales on a commercial basis?

1. The rule presupposed by the decision to kill whales on a commercial basis might be stated as follows:
    Whales should be killed for commercial use, as long as they are not threatened by extinction.
2. The rule presupposed by the decision not to kill whales on a commercial basis might be stated in the following way:
    Whales should not be killed for commercial use, regardless of whether they are threatened by extinction.
3. The relevant audience in this case includes the three groups affected by the possible decisions: those engaged in the whaling industry, those who use whaling products, and whales. If the second rule is generally followed, people in the whaling industry will lose their jobs. In Japan and the Soviet Union, this unemployment might involve a considerable hardship for a time, but the government could easily retain the affected workers, so their loss is not permanent. Because those who use whaling products can find substitutes, they stand to suffer no significant loss. Even if the price of certain products increases somewhat, monetary loss is relatively trivial in comparison with the whales' loss of life. The whales, of course, stand to suffer the more serious harm if the first rule is followed. Although humans probably outnumber whales, only the human beings affected by these two rules need to be considered. Furthermore, even whales who do not lose their lives may suffer the pain of separation from family members who have been harpooned.

4. It seems that a rule utilitarian analysis must conclude that the second rule would produce the greatest total utility, so it is morally obligatory. We have no reason to believe that such a rule could not realistically be followed because a number of nations have already discontinued whaling with no serious adverse consequences.
5. In this case, the rule is applied not to a particular situation but to a general practice. As the rule itself indicates, the conclusion must be that whales should not be killed for commercial use, even if they are not threatened by extinction.

Case 3: Reverse Discrimination

Allen Bakke, a white male, applied to the medical school at the University of California at Davis in both 1973 and 1974.[8] In both years Bakke's application was considered by the general admissions program, and he received an interview. His 1973 interview was with Dr. Theodore H. West, who described Bakke as "a very desirable applicant to [the] medical school." Despite a strong composite evaluation score of 468 out of 500, Bakke was rejected. His application had come late in the year, and no applicants with scores below 470 were accepted in the general admissions process after Bakke's application was completed. After his 1973 rejection, Bakke wrote to Dr. George H. Lowrey, associate dean and chairman of the admissions committee, protesting that the special admissions program operated as a racial and ethnic quota.

At the time Bakke was rejected, four slots were unfilled in the special admissions program for economically and educationally disadvantaged students. A total of sixteen slots in the freshman class of one hundred were reserved for students in the special admissions program. The students in the special admissions program did not have to meet the minimum 2.5 grade point average applied to regular students, and different standards were used in their general evaluation.

Bakke's 1974 application was completed early in the year. His composite score was 549 out of 600. Again Bakke's application was rejected. This year, as in the year before, applicants were admitted under the special admissions program with significantly lower composite evaluation scores as well as lower grade point averages and lower Medical College Admission Test scores. After the second rejection, Bakke filed a suit in the Superior Court of California.

---

[8] 483 U.S. 265; reprinted in James Sterba, *Morality in Practice* (Belmont, CA: Wadsworth, 1984), pp. 229–238.

The case eventually reached the U.S. Supreme Court, which rendered its decision on June 28, 1978. The justices were divided 4-4 on the principal issues in the case, with Justice Powell deciding with one group on one issue and with the other group on the second issue. On the one hand, the Court found that the special admissions program under which Allen Bakke was denied admission was unlawful and directed that Bakke be admitted. On the other hand, it found that institutions of higher learning could consider race as one factor in the admissions process.

From the standpoint of utilitarianism, are admissions policies like that of the University of California at Davis morally permissible, morally obligatory, or morally impermissible?

1. Any formulation of the rule under which the University of California at Davis was operating when it reserved 16 slots for disadvantaged students will be controversial, because the concept of a quota produces legal and moral problems. However, we shall formulate the rule as follows:

   A medical school may reserve a small percentage (less than 20 percent) of its openings for disadvantaged students.

2. The alternative rule would be this:

   A medical school may not reserve even a small percentage (less than 20 percent) of its openings for disadvantaged students.

3. The audience consists of the four groups affected by the rule and its alternative: the disadvantaged students who are candidates for the special admissions program; the students who are applying through the regular admissions program; the minority population in the country, consisting primarily of African Americans, Latinos, Asians, and Native Americans; and the general population.

   The disadvantaged students stand to benefit the most from the first rule, which gives them a greater chance of being admitted to medical schools. Not only are the admissions standards lower, but the students are competing for one slot out of 100, whereas the regular students are competing for one slot out of 84. The first rule has some negative effect on their interests because their fellow students may regard them as inferiors who could not make it under normal competitive conditions. Their future patients might also have less confidence in them than in physicians who were admitted in the regular admissions program.

   The regular students would suffer the most direct harm to their interests, because they would have less chance of admission to medical school. They would also find it more difficult to predict whether they

would be admitted because factors other than merit would be considered. This uncertainty could affect their ability to plan their lives. However, regular students would perhaps receive some benefit from a more diverse student population, composed in part of disadvantaged students.

The minority population would benefit if the disadvantaged students decided to serve in their communities. However, this outcome is not guaranteed. A more effective means of supplying physicians to serve in minority communities would be to select students who had demonstrated a prior commitment to this kind of work, regardless of their social or ethnic background. If the disadvantaged students did decide to serve in their own communities, the minority youth would benefit from the role models the physicians would provide.

It is difficult to determine how the interests of the general public would be affected by either the first or second rule. The general public might benefit from the decreased social unrest if minorities became convinced that the effects of past discrimination were being vigorously attacked. But this effect could well be counterbalanced by the feeling among the general population that many applicants were being unfairly treated.

4. We have extreme difficulty totaling up the harms and benefits to various interests and reaching a conclusion about which rule produces the greatest total utility. However, if the effects of past discrimination could be more quickly eliminated by policies of reverse discrimination, a good case can be made that the first rule is superior from a utilitarian standpoint. The bad effects of reverse discrimination would be temporary, and the good effects of eliminating the legacy of discrimination would be permanent.

    Keep in mind that, in making the utilitarian calculation, no abstract considerations of justice can be brought into the picture. Justice is important for the utilitarian only insofar as policies that are perceived to be just or unjust affect the interests of individuals.

5. Assuming that the first rule does produce greater total utility, we shall apply it to the Bakke case. We could then include that, from the utilitarian standpoint, the preferential admissions policy is obligatory.

EVALUATING UTILITARIANISM AS A MORAL THEORY

Now we are ready to evaluate utilitarianism according to our four criteria. Remember that every moral theory has points of vulnerability; no perfect moral theory exists. This lack of a perfect theory is a major reason that

several influential moral philosophies have evolved rather than one. As with the other theories, the following evaluations are my own, although they reflect the opinions of many moral philosophers.

Criterion 1: Consistency and Coherence

The form of utilitarianism we have described does not suffer from obvious internal incoherence. If the utilitarian is willing to define right actions as those that produce the greatest total utility or interest satisfaction, without arguing that some interests are inherently better than others, he cannot be charged with internal incoherence. The temptation to be inconsistent in applying the utilitarian moral standard arises when the utilitarian moral standard generates conclusions about conduct that conflict with our ordinary moral ideas.

Criterion 2: Justification

For a moral philosophy to be acceptable, it must give some reason to believe the moral standard is correct. We have also seen that a moral standard is not susceptible to strict proof because a moral standard cannot be derived from a higher moral standard, nor can it be derived in any direct or conclusive way from factual observation. What kind of justification, then, can be offered for the principle of utility? In a famous passage from Chapter 4 of *Utilitarianism,* John Stuart Mill presents some considerations that he hopes will convince his readers to accept the utilitarian doctrine. He starts by drawing an analogy between visibility and desirability, arguing that, just as the only proof that an object is visible is that people see it, so the only proof that anything is desirable is that people actually desire it. Then he points out that people do in fact desire happiness, so happiness must be desirable or good. Because each person's happiness is good for that person, the general happiness is a good to the aggregate of people.

If Mill intended his argument to be a "proof" of the utilitarian moral standard, he was certainly mistaken. Saying that something is "desirable" in the sense that it *is desired* by people has an entirely different meaning than saying that something is "desirable" in the sense that it *should be desired;* people may certainly desire what they should not desire. Another problem with Mill's argument, when taken as a proof, is that the fact that each person's happiness is a good for that person does not lead to the conclusion that promoting the general happiness is a moral obligation. People might be content to pursue their own happiness rather than the well-being of the majority. But these criticisms apply only if Mill was attempting to construct a strict proof, and his writings indicate that he was aware that the moral standard cannot be proven.

The most we can do, Mill may have believed, is show that the moral standard is a plausible one and that it commends itself to a rational person. Interpreted in this way, Mill's argument might be the following: People do desire their own happiness. This desire does not make happiness the right moral goal, but it does show that a morality based on happiness is solidly grounded in human nature. Such a morality is thus at least a possible candidate for a moral standard. If we combine this observation with the belief that a moral person has some obligation to others rather than merely to himself, we have some evidence to conclude that the happiness (or interest satisfaction) of others is a legitimate moral goal. Mill also believes that further evidence for the plausibility of the principle of utility can be derived from the fact that most of the moral beliefs we hold can be justified by the principle of utility.

Although these observations contain claims that can be questioned and certainly do not constitute a proof, they do lend plausibility to the standard of utility. If we believe that the institution of morality must be related to the human good, what more intrinsically plausible standard could we propose?

Criterion 3: Plausibility

One of the major problems with utilitarianism is that it appears to generate moral judgments that differ from our ordinary moral beliefs. We have already seen several moral issues in which this discrepancy arises. Another area in which these counterintuitive conclusions are generated is supererogatory acts—that is, acts that are "above and beyond the call of duty." We ordinarily distinguish between obligatory and supererogatory actions, but this distinction is difficult to make from the utilitarian standpoint because any action that produces more total utility than an alternative action is obligatory. Actions that we ordinarily consider supererogatory often produce more utility than any alternative, so the utilitarian is forced to reclassify them as obligatory.

Consider the following example.[9] Suppose your foolish neighbor confides that he is mortgaging everything he can to make a speculative investment that you are convinced will be disastrous for him and his family. If you expend enough time and effort, you believe, you can dissuade him

---

[9] For this example and a discussion of utilitarianism and its problems with supererogation and justice, see Alan Donagan, "Is There a Credible Utilitarianism?" in (ed.), *Contemporary Utilitarianism* Michael D. Bayles (New York: Doubleday, 1968), pp. 194–198.

from making the investment, whereas no one else can do so. The disaster you anticipate for him would be far greater than any inconvenience and embarrassment you would suffer in dissuading him. A utilitarian would argue that, on the whole, greater preference satisfaction would result if we adopt the rule that "Everyone who has adequate reason to believe that the course of action a neighbor proposes will be disastrous to that neighbor has the duty to dissuade that neighbor if he can do so without grave inconvenience or embarrassment." But are you morally obligated to follow such a rule? The question is not simply whether you ought to express your opinion to him; you should surely do so. But is it your duty to embark on a lengthy attempt to change his mind? The rule utilitarian must answer yes, but most of us would not.

Our moral intuitions may also seem to conflict with utilitarianism in the area of justice. When Jesus of Nazareth was killed, Caiphas, the Jewish high priest, justified the killing with the claim that Jesus' crucifixion, however unjust, would avert a greater disaster—possibly a rebellion against the Jewish authorities or a Roman persecution of the Jewish people. Consider the rule "Judges may not depart from the law, except if, by doing so, they can avert a major calamity to their nation or to the world." A rule utilitarian might object that such a rule would so discredit the judiciary that public life would be gravely injured, but such might not be the case. Some might even sleep better knowing that their judges would not be overscrupulous in applying the law during a national emergency. Thus, a rule utilitarian might be forced to admit that a miscarriage of justice is morally justified.

In the face of such objections, the utilitarian has two options: to reject ordinary beliefs as invalid because they conflict with utilitarian theory or to argue that utilitarian moral theory does not really conflict with ordinary beliefs. Most utilitarians have attempted to show that utilitarianism can account for our ordinary moral beliefs, especially those relating to supererogation and justice. Let us consider how the utilitarian might do this.

If she wants to argue that utilitarian theory can make a place for supererogatory actions, she might make the following argument. Praising those who perform supererogatory acts is in accordance with utility, but condemning those who fail to do so is not. The distinction between obligatory and supererogatory acts could be based on the differing abilities of people to perform unusual acts of bravery and self-sacrifice. The interest of morality is not served by requiring people to perform actions that are simply too far beyond their abilities because this overtaxing would only inspire contempt for morality in general. Moreover, people who attempt risky acts are likely to fail, thus creating negative utility. On the other hand, when supererogatory actions are performed, they should receive praise because they do contribute to the well-being of others. Whether this response is adequate is left for you to decide.

The problem of justice requires more sophisticated treatment. The utilitarian can certainly argue that, in general, rules requiring justice have greater utility; they inspire confidence in the judicial system and a sense of safety and well-being among the citizenry. However, if a serious conflict arises between two rules, a different approach may be necessary. For example, the utilitarian might argue that a conflict exists between the rule "Administer justice fairly" and the rule "Do what is necessary to save the nation from disaster." In such a case, the utilitarian would maintain, doing what leads to the greatest overall interest satisfaction in the particular situation is justifiable, so that in the case of Jesus, Caiphas was right to imply that one man's dying for the people was expedient. We must appeal, in other words, to act utilitarianism to resolve a conflict between two rules, when both are justified by utility. As before, you are left to decide whether this reply is adequate.

Criterion 4: Usefulness

A moral theory must provide a clear, workable method for resolving moral disputes, including disputes about which moral rule to adopt. The utilitarian decides on moral rules by determining their consequences for utility. But do we have the knowledge to trace the consequences of even a single action, much less the consequences of a general rule? Consider how a utilitarian would investigate the morality of premarital sexual relations. She would use the best available scientific data to determine the extent of possible negative consequences of the widespread practice of premarital sex, such as an increase in the number of pregnancies outside of marriage, a rise in the incidence of venereal disease, greater psychological disturbances, and the long-range effect on the stability of marriage. She would also have to investigate the advantages from a utilitarian standpoint of the widespread acceptance of the practice, such as the increased enjoyment of sex and a decrease in sexual frustration during the years when the sex drive is especially strong. She would also investigate the possibility that people would have a healthier, more relaxed attitude toward sex and that sexual adjustment in marriage might be improved.

How adequately can we determine these consequences, especially the long-range consequences, such as the effect on sexual adjustment and the stability of marriage? Without knowing these effects, the utilitarian cannot pass judgment on the morality of premarital sexual relationships from the utilitarian standpoint. She must either recommend that present practices be continued or that we experiment in new directions without fully knowing whether the results will be good or bad. Neither alternative is wholly satisfactory from the utilitarian standpoint. You will encounter problems like this one when you evaluate many practices from the utilitarian perspective.

In dealing with the problem of consequences, some utilitarians have admitted that they must assume what has been called the "ripples-in-the-pond postulate"; that is, they must assume that the important consequences of an action occur in relative proximity in time and place to the action itself. Just as the ripples produced by dropping a pebble in a pond are strongest near the point of impact, so the consequences of an action must be assumed to be most significant relatively near the action. But what if an action, such as adding minute amounts of a pollutant to the atmosphere, produces insignificant effects for centuries and then suddenly results in a catastrophe? Perhaps many other practices would have few negative consequences for a while but, after a few generations, would produce highly negative ones. What reason do we have for believing that the ripples-in-the-pond postulate is valid? And even if it is, can we calculate even the near-at-hand consequences of an action or rule?

The utilitarian's response is that we can at least have a rational opinion about the general consequences of many actions, and, if we have no opinion, perhaps we should hold to traditional moral rules. The standard of utility at least provides a method for evaluating some moral rules. The utilitarian may also argue that, if we do not know the consequences of adopting a given rule, we *should not* be able to pronounce on its morality. Furthermore, the problem of knowledge of consequences emphasizes again the importance of the social and physical sciences in utilitarian morality. Lack of knowledge about consequences is not so much a fault of utilitarian theory as it is a problem of the human condition, the utilitarian argues. Do you think this response is adequate?

CONCEPT SUMMARY

Because the utilitarian judges a rule by its consequences, any rules derived from the utilitarian moral standard must make assumptions about the consequences that will result from following the rules. If these assumptions are not accepted, different rules may be justified. Utilitarian personal ethics should be governed by the principle that the most effective way to contribute to the general welfare is usually to develop one's own abilities. Although utilitarianism may condone traditional moral views in some areas of personal ethics, it does not support the traditional prohibitions against suicide and euthanasia. Utilitarianism can also justify many of the common duties to others, such as the duties not to commit murder, theft, or fraud, but it does not support the prohibition of abortion.

In the area of social ethics, utilitarianism has been taken by its classical advocates to justify democracy and individual liberty. More recent exponents of utilitarianism have sometimes argued that greater utility will be produced if the state attempts to provide for the basic needs of all citizens, regardless of their financial resources. Special rewards, however, must still be given to the more talented members of society to induce them to make the maximum contribution.

Utilitarianism is an internally consistent moral philosophy. Mill's "proof" of utilitarianism fails as a proof, but it does give reason to believe that utilitarianism is a plausible moral philosophy. Utilitarianism leads to some counterintuitive moral judgments, especially regarding supererogation and justice. The utilitarian's ability to resolve moral problems is sometimes limited by our ignorance of the full consequences of the actions and general moral rules.

THE ETHICS OF RESPECT FOR PERSONS

On April 3, 1990, a baby girl was born to a couple that conceived the child to serve as a bone marrow donor for their daughter, Anissa, who was dying of leukemia. Abe and Mary Agola, who live in the Los Angeles suburb of Walnut, named the baby Marissa Eve. Fetal tests showed that the baby's marrow was compatible with Anissa's, and doctors said the transplant could occur in six months. There was a 70 to 80 percent chance that the transplant would cure Anissa.

Mr. Agola had to undergo a reversal of his vasectomy, and Mrs. Agola, who is in her mid-forties, had only a 73 percent chance of conception and a 23 percent chance of conceiving a child who would be a compatible donor.

Medical ethicists voiced qualms about creating one child to save another. The baby, they said, was not conceived "as an end in itself, but for a utilitarian purpose." The Agolas said they were hurt by such talk and that they would love the baby even if it proved to be an incompatible bone marrow donor for their stricken daughter.

Patricia Konrad, the couple's physician, said the bone marrow transplant would pose little risk for the baby. The procedure requires the infant to be put under general anesthesia to block pain while a needle is inserted into the hip bone to remove the marrow. Leukemia, a cancer of white blood cells, is typically treated by killing blood-producing cells with chemotherapy radiation and then transplanting compatible bone marrow into the patient. After waiting almost two years, the couple had failed to find a suitable living donor for Anissa. The odds of doing so are about 1 in 20,000. Mr. Agola told a reporter, "We just can't stand idly by and do nothing about it and wait for Anissa to die."[1]

Although we naturally sympathize with Mr. Agola, we may be troubled by the conditions under which Marissa was conceived. Was she merely

---

[1] "Conceived to Save Her Sister, a Child Is Born," *New York Times*, April 7, 1990, p. 8.

being "used" by her parents and her sister as a source of bone marrow? Was Marissa's dignity as a human being in her own right being disregarded in her conception? Would we want such a practice to become widespread?

Most of us consider these questions fundamental to the nature of morality; they certainly have been central to the Western ethical tradition. According to the Talmud, the whole law can be summarized in the statement "Do not do to your fellow what you hate to have done to you."[2] And in Matthew 7:12, Jesus says that the whole law and the prophets can be summarized in the saying "In everything do to others as you would have them do to you." The Greek and Roman Stoic philosophers also believed that all humans possess a divine "spark" that gives them a fundamental human dignity and equality.

Sometimes we express a closely related moral insight by distinguishing between things and persons: persons should not be treated as mere things or manipulated in a way that disregards their states as moral beings. Slavery is wrong, for example, because it treats people as commodities, regardless of the purposes they might have set for themselves. A slave owner can treat a human being like an object. Slavery fails to give proper respect to the personhood of the slave, and it is certainly not a condition we would want for ourselves.

We shall refer to this ethical tradition, whose central theme is that equal respect must be paid to the personhood of all human beings, as *the ethics of respect for persons.* It is an attempt to give a philosophical formulation to the basic ethical insights of the Hebrew-Christian and Stoic moral traditions. The ethics of respect for persons has been closely connected with Immanuel Kant (1724–1804), the greatest thinker of the German Enlightenment and one of the most important modern moral philosophers. Although my reliance on Kant is obvious, this account of the ethics of respect for persons should not be taken as a straightforward presentation of Kantian moral theory. It is nevertheless faithful to Kant's fundamental ideas and the structure of his moral philosophy.

We shall use two of Kant's formulations of the moral standard as the basis for our discussion, even though our interpretation of these standards will often differ from his. Kant himself believes that the two standards are equivalent, that they will always lead to the same conclusion regarding what is right or wrong. We have reasons to doubt this claim, so we shall stipulate that, for an action to be morally permissible by the ethics of respect for persons, it must pass both versions of the moral standard.

---

[2] Rabbi Dr. I. Epstein ed., *The Babylonian Talmud* (London: Soncino, 1948–52), p. 31a; quoted in Alan Donagan, *The Theory of Morality* (Chicago: University of Chicago Press, 1977), p. 57.

The version of the moral standard we will look at first is the universalization principle. We shall discuss a test for its proper application, which we shall call the self-defeating test. The second version of the moral standard is the means-ends principle. We shall consider two tests for its proper application: the negative test and the positive test. Let us examine these principles and tests in turn.

THE UNIVERSALIZATION PRINCIPLE AS A VERSION OF THE MORAL STANDARD

The idea that equal respect is due to all human beings is the basis for the universalization principle. We can formulate this principle as a moral standard of the ethics of respect for most persons in the following way:

> MS 1: An action is right if you can consent to everyone's adopting the moral rule presupposed by the action.

Like rule utilitarianism, this standard focuses on the evaluation of rules rather than individual actions. If we look only at actions, how can we determine whether our action is the same as the one we are willing to have others follow? Let us propose that we are willing to have others perform the same action if we are willing to have them adopt the moral rule that underlies our own action. This proposal assumes that every action involving moral choice does, in fact, presuppose a moral rule.[3]

To apply the universalization principle, we must first determine the moral rule presupposed by the action being evaluated. Suppose we are considering the possibility of obtaining some money by making a false promise to repay it. The rule presupposed by our action might be something like this:

> Everyone should obtain money by falsely promising to repay it.

Our second task is to decide whether we can consent to others' following the universalized rule. To do so, let us apply the self-defeating test.

The Self-Defeating Test

The question posed by the self-defeating test is this:

> Can I consent to others' acting simultaneously according to the same rule I use without undermining my own ability to act in accordance with it?

---

[3] My account of rules is in some ways like Kant's discussion of what he calls "maxims." But, again, I am not giving an exposition of Kant.

To determine whether I can consistently consent to others' acting according to the same rule I use, we must attempt to imagine realistically the conditions necessary for everyone to use this rule and the consequences that would normally follow if everyone did so simultaneously.[4] In the case of our current rule, the predictable result of everyone's performing the action in question would be that no one would lend money based on a promise to repay because everyone would assume (correctly) that such promises were lies. This result would undermine my ability to borrow money on the basis of a (false) promise to repay. Only if we postulated that people do not learn from experience could we consistently intend that others live by the same rule we adopted. So the rule is self-defeating.

Keep in mind that the self-defeating test assumes that we ask what would happen if I and others follow the rule simultaneously. Obviously, if I adopt my policy of dishonesty now and others do not adopt the policy until a year from now, I could get away with a lot of false promises in the meantime. The case would be different if others adopt my policy at the same time I do, and the policy would be self-defeating.

This conclusion about the morality of making false promises is not surprising; the self-defeating test would not be a very convincing test for morally permissible actions if it could not rule out false promising as immoral. Nevertheless, other examples seem to cause more trouble. Some people argue that the universalization principle runs into difficulties with respect to an occupation such as farming, because it is no more desirable that everyone grow food than that no one grow food. Consider the following abbreviated but acceptable formulation of the rule:

> Everyone should grow food.

I can certainly consistently intend that I and everyone else will grow food without fear of defeating my own rule. This state of affairs was once almost universal, and it still prevails in some parts of the world. But now consider the alternative rule:

> Everyone should not grow food.

I can certainly intend that I and all others will not grow food. This rule would lead to starvation, but starving people can refuse to do things as well as the best fed. So the rule is not self-defeating.

---

[4] See Onora Nell, *Acting on Principle: An Essay in Kantian Ethics* (New York: Columbia University Press, 1975), pp. 63–81. My version of the self-defeating test owes much to Nell's book, even though important differences exist. For an account of Kant's use of this same example that is probably closer to his intentions than either mine or Nell's, see Robert Paul Wolff, *The Autonomy of Reason: A Commentary on Kant's Groundwork of the Metaphysic of Morals* (New York: Harper & Row, 1973), pp. 165–169.

What shall we say, then, about the morality of growing food, because both the rule and its alternative can be universally followed? One scholar has proposed that, when both a rule and its alternative can be consistently universally adopted, acts in agreement with the rule or its alternative will both be classified as morally permissible; that is, they are neither required nor forbidden. In this case, we are neither required to grow food nor forbidden to grow food. Either action can be seen as morally acceptable behavior. This solution reflects the way we tend to think about such an issue and is generally consistent with the universalization principle.[5]

Another example illustrates an important aspect of the self-defeating test—namely, that a rule can be self-defeating if the *point* or *purpose* one has in mind is defeated with the action's universalization. We can illustrate this with an example having to do with whether we have an obligation to obey the civil authorities. First, consider the following rule:

Everyone should obey the civil authorities.

It seems clear that we can consistently and simultaneously consent to the universal adoption of this rule. We can without any problem accept the conditions required to carry out the intention, such as the general knowledge of and respect for law and authority. We can also accept the predictable results of successfully carrying out the rule, such as a safe, peaceful, and orderly society. This rule is not self-defeating. On the other hand, consider the alternative rule:

No one should obey the civil authorities.

We can argue that we cannot consistently and simultaneously consent to this rule, for the results would be general chaos; pursuit of any goal with reasonable prospect of security and success would be impossible. Although, in a narrow sense, continuing to disobey the civil authorities under these chaotic conditions might be possible, the *purpose* a person most likely has in mind by this disobedience (namely, gaining an advantage over her law-abiding fellows) would, no doubt, be undermined. Thus, the rule is self-defeating.

Many examples demonstrate how universalizing a rule covering a given action undermines the point of the action. Suppose you are considering cheating on your next quiz. You believe that everyone else could cheat as well as you, so your action could be universalized. This may be true, but the universalization of your action would undermine or at least seriously weaken the *purpose* you have in mind in cheating—namely, to make a better grade than your classmates. This example shows the importance of

---

[5] See Nell, *Acting on Principle*, p. 79.

considering the fullest consequences of the general acceptance of a rule. It also demonstrates that we have no completely mechanical way to determine whether a rule can be consistently and simultaneously adopted. Applying the universalization principle requires imagination and can sometimes be controversial. In the next section, we shall consider some of the problems in applying the universalization principle.

Guidelines for Applying the Universalization Principle

One problem in applying the self-defeating test has to do with how broad or narrow to make the rule to which you apply the self-defeating test. We know that more than one rule can be used to describe a given action, and the particular rule we see as underlying an action can make an enormous difference in our evaluation of the action.

Suppose I am scheduled for an important job interview and know that I would have a better chance at the job if I tell the interviewer that I intend to stay with the company for many years if I am hired. Actually, I have my eye on another position that is not available now, but I would take the more desirable position if it were offered. To get my first job, however, I lie about my intentions to stay with the company. Now, I might be able to universalize this action in the sense that others could lie too, but my point in lying would be undermined if every other interviewee lied too. However, I could still get around this problem by tailoring the rule to my own circumstances, as this rule illustrates:

> If my name is John Brown and I am interviewing for a job with ABC Chemical, and I really want to work for XYZ Chemical, I may lie about my intentions to stay with ABC Chemical if this is necessary to get the job.

This rule can satisfy the self-defeating test only because it applies to only one person. We can easily see in this case that the rule is inappropriate, but precise guidelines for how specific a rule can be without being too specific cannot be given. We can only say that the rules should not be too specific or too broad. This rule is too specific because it mentions particular places, times, and persons.

A rule that allows for no exceptions, however, is often too broad. Few of us would be willing to accept the consequences of a rule that says "Never lie." If an obviously crazed man comes into the room with a bloody knife in his hand and asks you for John Jones, I would probably think it morally justifiable to tell him a lie. We are much more likely to accept the consequences of a rule that allows lying in certain situations, such as "I can lie when it is necessary to save an innocent life." In other words, a rule must be specific enough to take into account the morally relevant facts.

Aside from these general guidelines, a person is alone in formulating the rule that seems most adequately to describe his or her own action or the action of another person. Because we know more about our own motivations and the circumstances of our own lives than about the motives and circumstances of another person, we are in a better position to formulate descriptions of our own actions than of the actions of others. So we must always be cautious in evaluating others' actions.

Another interesting class of examples is one in which neither the rules nor their alternatives can be consistently universalized. Consider the following rule:

Everyone should buy shoes but not sell them.

Here, I clearly cannot consent to the universal adoption of this rule because all purchases require simultaneous sales. But a similar conclusion follows when we consider the alternative rule:

No one should buy shoes, but everyone should sell them.

If both a rule and its alternative are not consistently universalizable, actions in accordance with the rule or its alternative would appear to be morally impermissible. Therefore, we shall assume that in such situations either a new rule must be formulated or the universalization principle gives no direction, and we should consider only the means-ends principle.

THE MEANS-END PRINCIPLE AS A VERSION OF THE MORAL STANDARD

A hypothetical person called John Whiteman is a racist of the old school: he believes that all blacks should be slaves. He would even be willing to be enslaved himself if he were found to have "black blood." Most of us would consider his view to be the very model of immorality, so we are more than a little disturbed to realize that Whiteman's position passes the test of the universalization principle. His viewpoint is not self-defeating, because everyone's holding this position and acting in accordance with it would not prohibit Whiteman from holding his views.

The fact that such a patently immoral action can pass the test of the universalization principle points out the inadequacy of this principle as a complete guide to morality. Relatively few actions are self-defeating, although the test is useful when it does apply. The universalization principle emphasizes the equality of all human beings, which is an important part of the ethics of respect for persons. It provides a minimal condition for morally acceptable rules. But the condition is not sufficient for a morally acceptable action, as this example shows. For this reason, we must consider another version of the moral standard of the ethics of respect for persons— the means-ends principle. The principle can be stated as follows:

> MS 2: Those actions are right that treat human beings, whether you or another person, as an end and not simply as a means.

What does it mean to treat someone as an end rather than a means? The answer to this question goes to the heart of the distinction between things and persons. Persons or moral agents have a capacity to formulate and carry out their own goals, whereas things have their purposes determined from the outside. A pencil sharpener, for example, was manufactured to perform a specific function, as was a coffee mug. Human beings, on the other hand, can determine their own purposes. This capacity of persons or moral agents to determine their own purposes is the basis of the means-ends principle. We shall say that "treating a person as an end" means respecting the conditions necessary for his or her effective functioning as a moral agent.

Before examining the conditions for the effective exercise of one's moral agency, however, we should ask what is meant by the reference to treating someone "simply as a means." This phrase implies that in some sense treating a person as a means is legitimate. In relating to other people in our day-to-day lives, we often do treat them as a means in the sense of being relatively unconcerned with their status as persons. When I go to the post office, I have no special interest in the aspirations of the postal worker who sells me stamps, other than a general positive attitude toward him or her. In one sense, I do treat him or her as a means to my end of obtaining stamps. But I do not treat him or her simply or merely as a means, because I do nothing to negate him or her status as a moral being.

Many social relationships involve the element of treating others as a means, but not solely as a means. I may treat my doctor as a means to recover from my illness, but I do not treat him simply as a means because I do not deny him his status as a person. Students treat their professors as a means to gaining knowledge and getting a degree, but they do not treat them simply as a means, because students do not obstruct the professors' humanity. Social relationships would be impossible if treating a person as a means were not permissible in this limited way.

Preliminary Concepts

The basic idea of the means-ends principle is simple, but its application is often difficult. To help you apply the principle, we shall discuss three issues: (1) the conditions of moral agency, (2) the principle of forfeiture, and (3) the principle of equality.[6]

The Conditions of Moral Agency   Two fundamental conditions are necessary for a person to act as a moral agent. The first is freedom or voluntariness, whereby a person controls or initiates his behavior by his unforced choices. The second condition is purposiveness or well-being, whereby a person sets goals for herself and has the abilities necessary for achieving them. Let us consider both of these conditions.

The condition of freedom or voluntariness naturally brings to mind the right to protection from violence and coercion. In acts of violence, such as robbery or rape, a person's freedom is diminished. The victim is acted on with direct physical or psychological compulsion and has no opportunity for consent. In acts of coercion, such as forced prostitution, a person gives his consent but has no real free choice in doing so. Deception also limits the freedom of others; in deception the person gives unforced consent, but only as a result of falsehoods or misrepresentations intentionally presented to him.

A person's freedom may be interfered with in other ways as well. Physical or mental illness, willful ignorance or self-deception, and obsessive submission to some dominating passion like drugs or alcohol can limit a person's voluntary action. Lack of knowledge is also a major impediment to free decisions.

The other condition necessary for moral agency is what we have called well-being—namely, the goods necessary for carrying out one's freely chosen purposes. If a person can choose goals but has no ability to carry them out, his moral agency is worth very little.

Several categories of goods are necessary for effective moral agency. Alan Gewirth has divided these goods into three categories. *Basic goods*—such as life, food, clothing, shelter, physical health, and emotional stability—are prerequisites of our purposive action. *Nonsubtractive goods* are abilities or conditions needed for maintaining undiminished one's level of purpose fulfillment. These goods include not being lied to, cheated, defamed, or insulted and not having one's promises broken or one's privacy invaded. We have already seen that breaking promises not only violates the self-defeating test but also tends to lower a person's capacity for action. Finally, *additive goods* are abilities and conditions needed for raising the level of purpose fulfillment. These goods include owning property, having a sense of well-being and self-respect, and being treated in a

---

[6] The following discussion relies heavily on Alan Gewirth, *Reason and Morality* (Chicago: University of Chicago Press, 1978), especially pp. 199–271, 338–354.

nondiscriminatory way. Additive goods also include the virtues of character—such as courage, temperance, and prudence—that enable people to pursue their goals more effectively. Other aspects of freedom and well-being also are important for one's being able to act as a moral agent. It is impossible to enumerate all aspects, but they will often be important in making moral decisions.

The Principle of Forfeiture   The means-ends principle requires that I treat everyone, myself and others alike, as ends and not mere means. The universalization principle also implies that everyone should live according to the same rules, which means that a person loses the right to be treated as an end if he does not treat others this way. Therefore, the ethics of respect for persons requires a principle of forfeiture, much as in natural law. The principle of forfeiture says that, if I treat others as mere means, I forfeit my rights to freedom and well-being. I do not necessarily forfeit all my rights, but in general my rights are forfeited in proportion to the rights of others that I trespass.

When the state punishes a criminal by putting him in prison or taking his life, he is deprived of some of the aspects of freedom and well-being necessary for his full functioning as a moral agent. Nevertheless, many believe that the punishment is justified because the criminal by his action has treated someone else as a mere means. Whether he has committed theft, fraud, rape, murder, or some other crime, he has done something to deprive others of their freedom or well-being. Punishment is a legitimate response to this action and does not violate the means-ends principle.

Criminal action is not the only way in which a person may forfeit some of his rights to be treated as an end and never as a mere means. If I slander or insult you, it might be appropriate for you to hit me or in some other way limit my freedom or well-being. When a businessperson or professional, through negligence, endangers the safety of her client or the general public, it may be appropriate to reprimand her or deprive her of her job, even if nothing worthy of legal action has been done.

Application of the principle of forfeiture is appropriate when a person either voluntarily or by implication enters into certain kinds of relationships. If you and I own two different stores that are competing for the same business and I eventually run you out of business, I am certainly harming your freedom and well-being. Still, I may be justified in running you out of business because one implicitly consents to this possibility when entering the competitive business environment.

The Principle of Equality   Another issue that you will frequently encounter in applying the means-ends principle is the problem of conflicting obligations. Recall the story of the two female counterspies who were in Britain during World War II. While they were there, the Allies learned that the Nazis knew their identity. If they were sent back, they would almost certainly be apprehended, tortured, and killed. What should have been done from the standpoint of the ethics of respect for persons?

The problem is that someone's freedom or well-being will be harmed regardless of which alternative is taken. If the counterspies are returned to the continent, they will suffer loss of freedom, physical violence, and death. If they are not returned, the Allied cause will lose a considerable advantage in the war, and probably many additional lives will be lost. Someone's freedom and well-being will be harmed with either alternative.

The idea of equal treatment implicit in the two moral standards again provides the fundamental guideline. The principle of equality says that, when someone's freedom or well-being must be violated, people should be treated equally unless reasons exist for them to be treated otherwise. Some additional criteria will be helpful in carrying out this principle: In treating everyone equally as an end, we must consider (1) how important the aspects of freedom and well-being are that are being threatened, (2) how severely these aspects will be limited, and (3) whether the aspects of freedom and well-being involved would be directly or indirectly violated.

If we applied these criteria to the case of the counterspies, we would probably come to the following conclusions: (1) The aspects of freedom and well-being involved are of the highest importance: ability to make a free decision and physical life itself. (2) The values of the women are seriously threatened; that is, they would suffer not simply harm to their freedom or well-being but loss of life and freedom altogether. Those who would be killed or injured because of the prolongation of the war would also suffer loss of life and freedom. (3) The threat to the women is obviously more direct and immediate than the threat to the Allied soldiers and civilians who would be harmed by the loss of access to the Nazi code.

Applying the principle of equality, we would probably conclude that returning the counterspies to the continent was morally wrong according to the ethics of respect for persons, primarily because their rights are more directly and severely violated. They were being used as mere means. If we are to justify returning them to Germany, we must use utilitarian considerations rather than arguments derived from the ethics of respect for persons.

Consider another example. Suppose a physician is asked by one of his or her patients to perform a sterilization. The physician believes sterilizations are morally impermissible, but no other physician practices in the rural area who could perform the procedure. In this case, someone's moral agency will be violated no matter what decision the physician makes: either the patient will have to go elsewhere to obtain the sterilization, or the physician will have to violate his or her conscience. How would one resolve the conflict problem by the principle of equality?

Using the three considerations suggested by the principle of equality, we can make the following observations: (1) Violation of conscience is a more serious violation of one's moral agency than going to another physician for the sterilization. (2) The physician's conscience will be directly violated, whereas the patient will presumably be able to obtain the sterilization elsewhere. (3) The threat to the physician's moral agency is more direct and immediate than the threat to the patient's moral agency. Therefore, the physician should not perform the sterilization.

We can use two tests to determine whether we are treating a person as an end and not as a mere means. The negative test asks whether a person's freedom or well-being is threatened by our actions. (Have we treated the person as a mere means?) The positive test asks whether we have assisted others in achieving their freedom and well-being. (Have we treated them as an end?) We shall see that the negative test is always applicable, whereas the positive test is only sometimes applicable. Therefore, we shall begin with the negative test.

The Negative Test

Our first inclination might be to argue that we should never override the rights of others, but the preceding considerations have shown us that sometimes we must. In situations involving criminal activity or a conflict of obligations, someone's freedom or well-being must be overridden. Keeping this point in mind, we shall formulate the question that constitutes the negative test of the means-ends principle:

> Does the action override my own or others' freedom or well-being?

As discussed in the previous section, this test is not always easy to apply. Let us consider several guidelines that will be useful in applying it.

First, the principle of forfeiture may be relevant. If John has violated another person's freedom or well-being, his freedom or well-being can justifiably be violated. When we imprison criminals, we violate their freedom and well-being, but we do so legitimately because the criminals have violated the freedom and well-being of others. This same consideration applies to corporate entities. When a corporation pollutes the environment in a way that violates the law, fines and other types of punishment imposed by the state violate the freedom and well-being of the corporation and its stockholders. But this violation is justified because the corporation has forfeited some of its rights by illegal conduct.

Second, sometimes it is impossible to avoid a situation where someone's freedom and well-being will be diminished. In such cases, we have a conflict problem that must be resolved by using the principle of equality to determine where the most serious violations of moral agency occur. For example, suppose Jane is a young engineer who finds that a certain pollutant that her plant is emitting poses a minor health risk to inhabitants of the surrounding area. The pollutant is not restricted by the government, and she wonders whether she should advise her superior to try to eliminate the pollutant. Remedying the problem will be expensive and probably make the plant less profitable, thereby forcing management to lay off some employees. What should she do?

It is not clear that the principle of forfeiture applies to the company and its stockholders, for the threat to health is not serious. But it certainly does not apply to the employees who will lose their jobs if the necessary antipollution devices are installed. Yet either the inhabitants in the surrounding area will suffer an impairment of their health, or some employees will lose their jobs. In such situations, a "balancing act" must be performed, just as in a utilitarian estimation of positive and negative utilities, except that we are balancing the violations of rights rather than positive and negative utilities. We must balance the infringements on the freedom and well-being of stockholders and employees against the infringements on the freedom and well-being of those who are adversely affected by the pollutants.

The Positive Test

The positive test of the means-ends principle requires that we do more than simply refrain from interfering with our rights to freedom and well-being and those of others. We also must positively contribute to others' status as moral agents, as well as our own. However, this obligation does not require that we devote our lives slavishly to helping others achieve a fuller state of self-realization. We would then be treating ourselves as a mere means to the good of others, which is forbidden by the means-ends principle itself. Therefore, each individual must determine when, where, and how this moral obligation is to be fulfilled with respect to others. So we will state the question posed by the positive test as follows:

> Does the action assist oneself (or others, in certain circumstances) in achieving one's own (or others') freedom and well-being?

To see how this test might be applied, let us begin with an example. Thirteen-year-old Jason Simmons has been diagnosed as having a ruptured appendix. His physician says he needs immediate surgery; however, Jason has been attending Christian Science services and has come to believe in healing through prayer. He does not want surgery, even though his parents do. Disregarding legal questions for the moment, should the physician defend the boy's right not to have surgery, or should she go along with his parents' request?

Applying the ethics of respect for persons, the rule presupposed by the position Jason has taken might be formulated as follows:

> People should be allowed to follow their own convictions, even if the result is their death.

The self-defeating test is not violated by this rule because Jason could pursue his course of action even if the rule presupposed by his action is universalized. His action would pass the negative test of the means-ends principle because he is not interfering in an illegitimate way with others' freedom or well-being. Although he would be interfering with his parents' desires to keep him alive, his action does not deny them an equal freedom to determine their own lives. Must we conclude, then, that it is morally impermissible for the physician to oppose Jason's request?

This case involves paternalism, which we may define as using coercion to get another person to do or refrain from doing something for his or her own good. In the usual version of paternalism, which we shall call strong paternalism, another person determines what is for my own good. *Strong paternalism* is clearly incompatible with the means-ends principle because it allows the freedom of other people to be overridden. Another kind of paternalism, called *weak paternalism,* says that paternalistic coercion can be used, but only to the extent necessary to preserve a person's freedom. Several circumstances—such as ignorance, intellectual immaturity, emotional disturbance, and social pressures—can decrease a person's ability to make a free, informed decision under these circumstances or to enable someone else to make a decision for that person. The use of paternalistic coercion, the weak paternalistic argues, actually protects the individual's long-term freedom.

Does the positive test of the means-ends principle apply in any way to weak paternalism? I believe it does. We have already seen that the central idea in the means-ends principle is the preservation of people's ability to act as moral agents. The basic thrust of the positive test, then, must be that in certain situations we have an obligation to actively promote the status of others as moral agents. Weak paternalism is simply the use of coercion to preserve that status when it is threatened. Therefore, weak paternalism can be justified by the positive test of the means-ends principle.

The key issue in this example for the ethics of respect for persons is whether Jason is making a genuinely free and informed decision. If he is, then living by the principles of Christian Science, even at the risk of losing his own life, represents his true goal. However, if Jason's decision is not genuinely free and informed, that choice does not represent his true goal. Several factors might prevent him from making a free and informed decision. For example, a thirteen-year-old boy may not be intellectually mature enough to evaluate the religious teachings on which he is basing his decision. Or he might be under undue emotional pressure from his peers or Christian Scientists whom he has come to respect. Or he may be rebelling against his parents in his decision.

To justify disregarding Jason's wishes, the physician must believe that he or she is actually assisting him in achieving greater long-range freedom. The physician must also feel that his or her special relationship as the boy's physician provides the proper occasion for the application of the means-ends principle. Because we can plausibly argue that a boy of Jason's age is not in a position to make a free and informed decision about such a serious issue and that the special patient-physician relationship does justify the obligation to help Jason realize his true goals, paternalistic action by the physician seems permissible.

There are at least two types of situations in which the positive test seems clearly applicable and one in which its application is more controversial.

First, the positive test should be applied when a special relationship of moral obligation exists between the people involved. The story about Jason illustrates two of the most important such relationships—namely, professional relationships and family relationships. Both parents and professionals have a special obligation to help others realize their goals. By voluntarily assuming a parental role, parents incur an obligation to help their children grow into autonomous moral agents. Similarly, by voluntarily assuming her role as a professional, a physician incurs an obligation to help her patients return to health, and a lawyer incurs an obligation to help her clients achieve justice in the legal system. The same obligation applies to other professionals and anyone who has assumed a relationship of special obligation to another person.

Second, the positive test should be applied when one person can help another in a significant way with relatively little sacrifice to himself. Being in a position to help another person in dire need produces an obligation in accordance with the positive test of the means-ends principle. Suppose John is fishing in his boat and suddenly becomes aware that someone is struggling in the water several hundred feet away. The person is shouting for help and obviously is in immediate danger of drowning. John could easily rescue him but does not do so, and the person drowns.

Most people would agree that John ought to have tried to rescue the drowning person. But why? John's behavior passes the self-defeating test, so if John's action is immoral by the ethics of respect for persons, it is because it violates the means-ends principle. It does not violate the negative test, but it does violate the positive test. John is in a position to help a person in extreme danger with relatively little cost to himself. John's relationship to the person (his being in a position to help) therefore imposes an obligation to aid the person in distress.

It is interesting to apply this same kind of reasoning to the question of famine relief. Does this same principle that we are obligated to help others in significant need when we can do so at relatively little cost to ourselves apply to people in other countries? Does distance or the fact that the starving people of Ethiopia live in another society negate our obligation to help them? Is any help we give to them supererogatory or obligatory?

Finally, some people believe that the very fact that people live in the same society justifies taxing the relatively wealthy to help the relatively less well off to have a more comfortable and satisfying life. Even if we have no special relationship to the needy (other than living in the same society with them), and if their need is not extreme, the obligation is valid, according to some advocates of the ethics of respect for persons. Whether this obligation exists and how far it extends are matters of considerable controversy. However, if this obligation exists, it must have limits; otherwise, the more gifted would be used as mere means to help the less fortunate. But we must keep in mind that the principle of equality requires that everyone be treated equally as an end, insofar as is possible. We shall return to this idea in discussing the social ethics of the morality of respect for persons.

We are now ready to summarize the steps in applying the ethics of respect for persons in a checklist. However, one further problem should be mentioned. If both the action and its alternative fail one or more of the tests, either action will ordinarily be considered morally permissible unless one of the actions violates the tests more flagrantly than the other. To settle this issue, do not use utilitarian considerations, but determine which action constitutes the least serious violation of the moral agency of others. The principles of forfeiture and equality will often be useful.

CHECKLIST FOR APPLYING THE ETHICS OF RESPECT FOR PERSONS

I. Determine the most appropriate rule presupposed by the action whose morality you are evaluating.

II. Apply the self-defeating test of the universalization principle, which asks whether others could act by the rule without undermining the possibility of your acting according to the rule and the conditions necessary to act according to the rule. Remember also that the rule must be universalized at the same time as the action being tested.

III. Apply the negative test of the means-ends principle, which asks whether the action overrides the freedom or well-being of oneself or others.

IV. If relevant, apply the positive test of the means-ends principle, which asks whether the action assists oneself (or others, in certain circumstances) in achieving one's own (or others') freedom and well-being.

V. Make a final decision on the morality of the action.

   A. If it passes the test of the universalization principle and the negative test of the means-ends principle (and the positive test where applicable), it is morally permissible.

   B. If it is morally permissible and its alternative violates the universalization principle or the negative test of the means-ends principle (or the positive test where applicable), it is morally obligatory.

   C. If it fails either the universalization principle or the negative test of the means-ends principle (or the positive test where applicable), it is morally impermissible.

   D. If both the original action and its alternative fail one or more of the tests, either action will ordinarily be considered morally permissible. Sometimes one alternative should be chosen because it does not violate the three tests as seriously as the other alternative does.

CONCEPT SUMMARY

The ethics of respect for persons takes as its central theme the equal dignity of all human beings. Our formulation of it is expressed in two moral principles.

The first principle, the universalization principle, states that an action is right if you can consent to everyone's adopting the moral rule presupposed by the action. The test for this principle involves asking whether the universalization of the rule would undermine the possibility of acting in accordance with the rule (the self-defeating test).

The means-ends principle says that an action is right that treats human beings, whether you or someone else, as ends and not simply as means. Two tests for the satisfaction of this principle are the negative test and the positive test. The negative test requires that an action not override people's freedom or well-being. The positive test requires that I promote my own freedom and well-being and help others, under certain conditions, to achieve theirs. The positive test is applicable in a special relationship, such as the relationship of a professional to her client or of parents to their children. It is also applicable when others are in dire need or perhaps when people are a part of a common social order.

In applying the means-ends principle, we must remember these two points: First, a person may forfeit some of his or her freedom or well-being by violating the freedom or well-being of others or by voluntarily entering into relationships that subject the person to such a possible forfeiture. Second, where everyone's freedom and well-being cannot be satisfied, all persons should be respected equally, insofar as possible.

THE PERSONAL AND SOCIAL ETHICS OF THE ETHICS OF RESPECT FOR PERSONS

We are now ready to look at the implications for personal and social ethics of the ethics of respect for persons. You will usually find that the means-ends principle provides the most helpful guidance, but both principles are sometimes useful.

Duties to Self

The most useful guideline here is the means-ends principle. You may be inclined to ask, "How can I treat myself as a mere means? Isn't the idea self-contradictory?" Yet a moment's reflection will show that we can indeed act in a way that diminishes or destroys the conditions we need to exist as effective goal-creating, goal-pursuing beings. A review of these conditions will suggest some of the duties we owe to ourselves according to the ethics of respect for persons.

The first condition is physical life itself. I have a duty under normal conditions not to destroy or impair my health or the physical integrity of my body. The question of suicide, however, is an especially interesting issue in the category of duties to self. It might seem that I have a duty never to kill myself because my death would destroy an essential condition for all further action. But perhaps my goals and values dictate that my life should end, in which case a conflict arises between my pursuit of my goals now and the conditions necessary for their pursuit in the future. Suppose I am dying of cancer, that for a few months I will be enduring great pain, and that in this condition I will lose my personal dignity. I will no longer be able to pursue, let alone realize, my goals. Under such circumstances, my freedom can take priority over my well-being. My wish to die should have priority over the fact that my death will nullify all possibilities of achieving any future goals.

This same obligation to preserve the condition of physical life also justifies self-defense in most circumstances. If someone threatens my life, I have the right and even the obligation to defend myself against this threat. The principle of forfeiture shows that I am not illegitimately overriding the goals of the one who attacks me.

The second condition is physical and mental well-being. I also have a duty under normal conditions to promote my physical and mental health. The positive test of the means-ends principle applies to duties to self because I have a special obligation to my own freedom and well-being. In most instances, increasing my general knowledge and education will also promote my abilities to pursue my goals. An interesting exercise might be for you to decide which virtues or traits of character would enhance your abilities to act as a purposive agent.

Duties to Others

Ordinary moral prohibitions against harming others—through such acts as murder, rape, theft, and physical assault—are easy to justify by the ethics of respect for persons. These acts directly override the freedom and well-being of others, so they violate the means-ends principle.

Our obligation to help others, especially when help can be given with relatively little cost to us, follows from the means-ends principle. We have already seen that failure to help others in distress violates the positive test of the means-ends principle, as long as giving the aid does not seriously jeopardize our own status as ends.

The means-ends principle provides especially useful and insightful tests in the area of sexual morality. Even our language about sexual relationships often sounds as though it was derived from the means-ends principle. Treating someone as a "mere sex object" is treating the individual as a thing rather than a person. If we treat someone as a mere means in a sexual relationship, we are not treating that person as a goal-creating, goal-pursuing agent. In rape, for example, a person uses violence or coercion to override the freedom of another to choose her own sexual partner.

However, by far the most common way of treating another person as a mere means in a sexual relationship is by some form of deception. The boy who tells his girlfriend "I love you" or "We'll get married if you get pregnant" without meaning it is depriving her of the ability to make an informed decision about a sexual relationship and is thereby treating her as a mere means. Seducing someone into a demeaning sexual relationship is also using that person as a mere means because it diminishes his self-esteem and reduces his ability to act effectively as a goal-pursuing agent.

Not all nonmarital sexual relationships are based on deception, nor are they all degrading. Suppose, for example, that two college students establish a sexual relationship based on mutual affection and pleasure, but neither is sure it is love. Each person knows the other's intentions, so no deception is present and the relationship is not demanding. They take proper precautions against pregnancy but have agreed that, if a pregnancy results, they will get married or at least will properly care for the child. What can we say about the morality of this relationship? The universal-ization principle does not pose a problem because the rule underlying the relationship can be universalized without being self-defeating. What, then, about the means-ends principle? Neither person is overriding the freedom of the other or diminishing the ability of the other to be an effective goal-pursuing agent. However, some would want to point out the likelihood of mutual self-deception when sexual passion is involved. Whatever we conclude about the morality of such relationships, clearly the ethics of respect for persons provides the basis for a positive, insightful approach to sexual morality.

Social Ethics

The principle that governs the social ethics of respect for persons is that social institutions should respect the freedom and well-being of others by following rules that are universally applied; that is, the state should treat all individuals equally as ends and not mere means. How is this task accomplished? We have seen that the means-ends principle has both a positive and a negative test. Both of those tests have important implications.

Let us first consider the negative aspect of the state's responsibility to its citizens. This function is what libertarians call the minimal state. It involves the state's protection of citizens' rights not to have their rights to freedom and well-being overridden by other citizens or the state itself. This protection is needed in several areas. First, the state must protect citizens against murder, theft, fraud, and physical violence. Without these protections, individuals do not have the conditions necessary to realize their purposes. Second, the liberty of individual conduct should extend to the economic sphere. Economic goals are central in many people's lives, and the right to pursue these goals should be protected as long as the rights of others are not seriously impaired. Third, the individual should have as much freedom as possible in the area of beliefs and lifestyle, including freedoms of speech, the press, religion, and assembly. Laws regulating controversial activities like polygamy or homosexuality can be justified only when the activity regulated poses a clear threat to the liberty of others.

The state also has positive obligations to its citizens. This function is what we shall call the *supportive state.*[7] The relationship of the state to its citizens and of citizens to one another requires that the positive test of the means-ends principle be applied, which in turn requires the state to promote its citizens' freedom and well-being. The state could not claim political authority without a commitment to the welfare of its citizens, and citizens have some obligation to one another by virtue of their living in the same society. Thus, the state should make some provision for the health, education, and general welfare of its citizens and give special support for those who, through no fault of their own, are not able to provide for themselves.

The question inevitably arises whether the positive obligation of the state can be fulfilled without violating the goals of other citizens. In taxing productive citizens to provide for the disadvantaged, is the state not using productive citizens as mere means? Is the state not limiting the moral agency of the advantaged to provide for the disadvantaged? The answer is that we must adopt our usual policy of dealing with conflicts produced by the application of the means-end principle. We must remember that the final obligation is to treat everyone equally as ends insofar as possible; we must try to produce a situation in which the least serious violations of the principle are produced. Thus, the advantaged must be taxed to provide benefits for other members of society, but the gifted should be allowed to keep most of the wealth they have earned. This requirement is made not to preserve incentive to productivity, as in utilitarian social ethics, but to avoid violating the status of the gifted as ends and not mere means to the good of others. You must determine just how these guidelines should be followed in practice.

---

[7] See ibid., pp. 312–327.

CONCEPT SUMMARY

We can act in ways that destroy the conditions necessary for our existence as effective moral agents. Therefore, we have a duty to preserve our life and health, pursue an education, and develop whatever abilities and character traits are important for advancing our status as individuals.

The negative duties to others that are a part of most moral philosophies—such as the duties not to commit murder, theft, or fraud—are justified by the universalization and means-ends principles. A duty to help others in distress is mandated by both principles, if carrying out this duty does not require us to treat ourselves as mere means to the ends of others. Respect for persons also provides many useful insights into sexual morality.

The principle that governs the social ethics of respect for persons states that social institutions should be designed to help citizens function as effective goal-pursuing agents. Thus, the state has an obligation to protect citizens from one another and to help the disadvantaged achieve their freedom and well-being.

APPLYING THE ETHICS OF RESPECT FOR PERSONS

Now let us apply the ethics of respect for persons to some problems that require moral decision, using the methodology outlined in the checklist.

Case 1: The Case of Baby Marissa

We shall begin by considering the case presented in the introduction to this chapter.

1. The rule presupposed by the Agolas in conceiving Marissa might be formulated in the following way:

   Parents may conceive children whose tissue is to be used in an attempt to save the life of another person, as long as the child is not harmed by the use of the tissue.

2. The self-defeating test asks whether the Agolas could conceive Marissa with the purpose of using her tissue in an attempt to save Anissa's life if other people felt free to do the same sort of thing when the occasion arose. The answer to this question is that the widespread acceptance of the practice would make it easier for the Agolas to do what they did. No doubt one of the most difficult aspects of the Agolas'

experience was having to endure the widespread criticism of their action. Therefore, we can conclude that if the rule were generally adopted, the Agolas would find it easier, not more difficult or impossible, to act in accordance with the rule themselves.

3. The negative test of the means-ends principle asks whether the action of the Agolas overrides their own freedom or well-being or the freedom and well-being of anyone else. It certainly does not override their freedom and well-being. They undertook the action out of their desire to save their daughter's life. The only other person whose freedom and well-being is threatened is Marissa herself. There is little question that Marissa would not have been conceived if the Agolas had not wanted to save Anissa. The fact that Mr. Agola had to undergo a reverse vasectomy indicates that the couple did not intend to have any more children. So in a sense it is clear that Marissa's conception came about primarily because the couple wanted to save Anissa's life. In this sense, Marissa was "used" to save the life of Anissa.

But at this point the distinction between being used as a means and being used as a mere means is significant. It is difficult to see how Marissa will be used as a mere means, because otherwise she would not have been conceived at all, and (more importantly) she will not be permanently harmed by the medical procedure. According to the Agolas' physician, she will not be harmed physically. The pain, if any, will be temporary. Presumably she will also not be harmed emotionally.

The only sense in which Marissa's life prospects might be damaged is by the knowledge, which she will inevitably acquire, that she was conceived in an attempt to save her sister's life. But if Marissa is shown the same love and care that Anissa has evidently been given—and the Agolas assure us that she will—there is no reason to believe that this will be a serious problem.

Critics of the Agolas' action might argue that if everyone adopted this rule, human life might be regarded with less respect. Perhaps our society might descend a "slippery slope" to a state in which children could be conceived for medical uses in circumstances where the child's life prospects would be seriously damaged by the medical procedures necessary to make use of their tissue. Or perhaps children could even be killed to be used for tissue and organ transplants.

The issue of how much weight this consideration should be given is not easy to decide. Certainly it is relevant in considering the long-term effects of the action. If the Agolas' action did contribute to other children being treated as mere means, this would be a relevant consideration. Here we have a factual issue that vitally affects our moral assessment of the Agolas' action. But this issue is difficult to settle, and in a liberal society, we have no good reason to believe that the Agolas' action would have such deleterious consequences. Therefore, we shall conclude that the negative test is not violated.

It may also be worthwhile to mention that children are often conceived by their parents with certain goals in mind other than simply producing another human being. Parents want heirs and descendants to carry on the family name or to obtain the social status that comes with having a family. Or they may want someone to support and care for them in old age. Peasants had children to help them tend the fields. Kings and queens conceived children to be heirs to the throne and ensure peace in the kingdom. If we do not believe these are examples of using children as mere means, we must ask whether any morally relevant difference exists that is significant enough to warrant placing the Agolas' action in a different category altogether.

4. The positive test of the means-ends principle is relevant because the Agolas are the parents of Marissa and Anissa and therefore have an obligation to promote their freedom and well-being. The question is whether the decision of the Agolas to conceive Marissa assists both Marissa and Anissa in achieving their freedom and well-being. Clearly the action is an attempt to assist Anissa, so the only question has to do with Marissa. Again, it should be recalled that she would never have been born apart from her parents' desire to help her sister, and there is every indication that she will be raised in an environment in which her moral agency will be fully respected. Therefore, we have no clear reason to believe that the positive test has been violated.

5. The rule passes both the universalization principle and the negative and positive tests of the means-ends principle. Therefore, the Agolas' action is permissible by the ethics of respect for persons. The alternative rule could be stated in the following way:

> Parents may not conceive children whose tissue is to be used in an attempt to save the life of another person, even when the child is not harmed by the use of the tissue.

This rule also passes the self-defeating test. If everyone adopted this rule, it would make it easier for the Agolas not to have attempted what they did. In fact, one of the most difficult aspects of their experience was the public disapproval.

The rule would not require the violation of Marissa's freedom and well-being, because following the rule would mean that she would never exist. Nor would it directly violate Anissa's freedom and well-being. The only question is whether it would violate the positive test. The Agolas' argument was that Marissa's conception was an attempt to save Anissa's life. "We just can't stand idly by and do nothing about it and wait for Anissa to die," Mr. Agola told reporters. Their argument, in fact, was that failure to conceive Marissa would have violated the positive test. However, there are questions as to how far one need go in fulfilling the positive test. A certain amount of discretion is permitted, and the unusual nature of the Agolas' action suggests that they might have refrained from doing it without violating the positive test. Therefore, we shall conclude that the positive test would not have been violated by this rule either.

Because both the first rule and its alternative are permissible, we shall assume that the Agolas' action was permissible but not obligatory by the ethics of respect for persons.

Case 2: Deceptive Psychological Testing

Dillard Johnson is a psychologist employed by the personnel department of a large corporation. One day his superior comes to him with a proposal: "Dillard, the company is worried about the possibility that some of our employees may try to form a union in the next year or two. We have always had good relationships with our employees, but we believe a union would change that. I want you to research the literature in your area and find out whether you can furnish us with a test for employees that will measure union sympathy. You should disguise the purpose of the test. Make it look like a test for new employment opportunities or something like that. Can you do this for us?"

Dillard knows he has a good chance to impress his boss with his value as a psychologist in the personnel department, but he has questions about the ethical propriety of complying with the assignment. What should he do?

1. The issue raised by Dillard's boss is one of obtaining information from people that may be used against them and in a manner that does not involve their knowledge or consent, but the moral issues raised would be somewhat different in other apparently similar cases. For example, if the test were for sexual orientation or political persuasion, it would be even more questionable because information about these aspects of an employee would not ordinarily be job related. An employer would have even less right to this information than to information about an employee's union sympathy. However, there is even a question whether the employer has a right to know about the union sympathies of his employers.

Because the issues raised may have to do with the type of information sought as well as the means of getting it, we shall formulate the
rule so that it applies to this particular action. The fact that Dillard is
a psychologist is also morally relevant because deceptive practices
of this sort might be permissible when done by other people even if
not permissible when done by a psychologist. Therefore, we shall
include this feature in the rule as well. A rule that takes into account
these morally relevant factors can be formulated as follows:

> Employers may ask psychologists to devise tests that measure the union
> sympathies of employees under conditions that deceive the employees as to what
> is being measured.

2. The self-defeating test asks whether a given employer (for example,
   Dillard's employer) could act in accordance with the rule if the rule
   described were a general practice. If it were generally known that
   psychological tests were deceptive, there might be much greater reluc-
   tance to take the tests. People who take psychological tests, knowing
   that they might serve a covert purpose, would probably attempt to
   determine what the real purpose of the test was. Even if the tests are
   well devised, their true purpose might become generally known after
   the tests are given a number of times. In addition, much more general
   distrust of psychologists might develop if it were widely known that
   they participated in this kind of deception.

   On the other hand, many people probably already believe that
   psychological tests often have a hidden purpose. And if a given
   test were used only a few times or in different areas, it is doubtful
   that its true purpose would be found out, so the rule might not
   be self-defeating if it were universalized. Therefore, we shall
   conclude that the rule could be universalized without being self-
   defeating.

3. The negative test of the means-ends principle asks whether directing
   psychologists to create such tests overrides the freedom or well-being
   of either the psychologists who are assigned the task of devising the
   test or the employees who take them. With respect to Dillard, the
   question is whether his professional integrity is compromised by
   the assignment to come up with the test. Many psychologists would
   believe that it is. But probably the clearest argument can be made
   from the employees' standpoint.

   Whether employees are required to take the tests or merely
   encouraged to do so under the (illusory) expectation of job advancement, both their freedom and well-being are diminished. By being

subjected to deception, they suffer an infringement on their freedom. By unknowingly divulging knowledge that could lead to their dismissal or job reassignment, they suffer an infringement on their well-being.

Dillard's boss might argue that Dillard and the employees implicitly consented to the kind of information gathering he is proposing when they became employees: Dillard to use his professional expertise to benefit the company and the employees to follow their superiors' instruction. Besides, it might be argued, the attempt to get the information that the company wants is legitimate from the standpoint of good management. However, it is doubtful that the doctrine of implicit consent can be extended to such deceptive activities, and knowledge of union sympathies, insofar as it is necessary at all, can be gained in less clandestine ways. Therefore, we shall conclude that the rule probably violates the negative test from Dillard's standpoint and certainly violates it from the employees' standpoint.

4. The question whether the positive test of the means-ends principle applies to the relationship of employers to employees is an interesting one. Certainly employers have an obligation not to violate the moral agency of their employees, but the extent of their positive obligation is more questionable. If the obligation does apply, the employer certainly violates it in this case. However, we shall give the employer the benefit of the doubt and hold that the positive test does not apply.

5. Because the negative test has been violated, we can conclude that the request of Dillard's boss is impermissible from the standpoint of the means-ends principle.

Now let us consider the alternative rule:

> Employers may not ask psychologists to devise tests that measure the union sympathies of employees under conditions that deceive the employees as to what is being measured.

This test passes the universalization principle: refraining from using such tests would not undermine others' ability to do the same thing. The only people whose freedom and well-being would be infringed by the alternative rules are the managers and stockholders of companies. They would be somewhat restricted in what they could ask their professional employees to do and might be restricted in the information they could obtain, or at least in the way they could get it. But in any case, applying the principle of equality seems to show that the infringement of the freedom and well-being of the psychologists and employees is more serious than the infringement of the freedom and well-being of managers and stockholders. Managers and stock-holders might be deprived of some useful information, but employees would suffer invasion of their privacy and possible loss of jobs, and psychologists would suffer violation of their professional integrity. We shall assume that the positive test is not relevant, but, if it is, the alternative rule would pass the test.

We shall conclude that the alternative rule is morally acceptable. Because the first rule is unacceptable, action in accordance with the alternative rule is morally obligatory.

Case 3: Surrogate Mothers

In a 7-0 opinion, the New Jersey Supreme Court ruled that commercial surrogate motherhood contracts are illegal. It nevertheless allowed custody of Melissa Elizabeth Stern, the child at the center of the Baby M case, to remain with her father, William Stern, and his wife, Elizabeth. In March 1987, almost a year before the decision of the New Jersey Supreme Court, Judge Harvey R. Sorkow of the State Superior Court of New Jersey had ruled in favor of Mrs. Stern, allowing her to adopt the baby, and against the baby's biological mother, Mary Beth Whitehead-Gould.

"We thus restore the surrogate as the mother of the child," the justices of the New Jersey Supreme Court said. "She is not only the natural mother, but also the legal mother, and is not to be penalized one iota because of the surrogate contract." The Court did allow the Sterns to retain tempo-rary custody of the child, perhaps reflecting their concern over testimony revealing that Gould-Whitehead's home life was not the best. Gould-Whitehead had divorced her husband of thirteen years and had married a twenty-six-year-old accountant who was the father of the child she was pregnant with at the time.

In a ninety-five-page opinion, the court found the contract between the Sterns and Whitehead-Gould violated the state's adoption laws be-cause it involved a payment for the child. A $10,000 fee was specified in the 1985 contract between the Sterns and Whitehead-Gould. "This is the sale of a child, or at the very least, the sale of a mother's right to her child, the only mitigating factor being that one of the purchasers is the father," the court said. "The surrogacy contract creates, it is based upon, principles that are directly contrary to the objectives of our laws," Chief Justice Wilentz wrote. "It guarantees the separation of a child from the mother; it looks to adoption regardless of suitability; it totally ignores the child; it takes a child from the mother regardless of her wishes and her maternal fitness, and it does all of this, it accomplishes all of its goals, through use of money."

The New Jersey Supreme Court did not prohibit women from freely becoming surrogates as volunteers, as long as no money was exchanged, and the surrogate mother had the right to revoke her decision.[8]

Is surrogate motherhood for money a violation of the ethics of respect for persons?

1. The rule presupposed by the contract between the Sterns and Whitehead-Gould might read as follows:

    People may make an irrevocable contract involving the payment of a fee, whereby a woman agrees to conceive a child by the sperm of a married male, as long as the contract is made without coercion and with full access to the relevant information, and the male and his legal wife can provide an adequate home for the child.

2. The rule would seem to pass the self-defeating test. No doubt a number of women, like Whitehead-Gould, would reverse themselves after making a contract to be a surrogate mother and decide they wanted to keep their child. Perhaps their anguish at having to comply with the contract would deter many women from making such a contract in the first place. If all women were to be deterred for this reason, then the universalization of the rule would indeed be self-defeating. It is highly doubtful, however, that this situation would arise, so the rule does not seem to be self-defeating.
3. The negative test of the means-ends principle requires that the freedom and well-being of anyone affected by the rule should not be overridden; in this case, the freedom and well-being of the surrogate mother and the fetus are most at peril, but the freedom and well-being of the Sterns must also be considered.

    Whitehead-Gould reversed herself on whether she wanted to keep her child, but the fact that a person is prohibited from reversing herself on a decision that was freely made does not seem to be a violation of the means-ends principle. As long as there is one free and informed decision, a person's moral agency has been preserved. Information is not sufficient to determine whether Whitehead-Gould's decision was not fully free and informed, but we have no reason to believe it was not.

    Chief Justice Wilentz argued that a surrogate mother contract bypasses the usual requirement that the adopting parents should have to prove themselves qualified to raise the child in a competent manner. However, the court itself did not consistently follow this

---

[8] Robert Hanley, "Surrogate Deals for Mothers Held Illegal in New Jersey," *New York Times*, February 4, 1988, p. A1.

argument because it allowed surrogate mother contracts as long as no money was involved.

A more interesting fact is that parents who conceive their children in the normal way are already exempt from these requirements, so the question raised is whether surrogate motherhood is more like adoption or normal parenthood. The truth is, of course, that it has analogies and disanalogies with each. Like normal parenthood, the conception involves the father's sperm; like adoption, the conception involves the egg of the mother who gives up the baby. The fact that there is an exchange of homes for the baby and that the biological mother does not raise the child is also analogous to adoption. Perhaps the analogies with adoption are more extensive, so that the failure to provide safeguards for the child is a problem, but even here laws could be enacted to ensure that the parents who are to raise the child should pass the same criteria as adopting parents. The court itself seemed to recognize this possibility when, according to the *New York Times* report, it virtually invited the New Jersey legislature to enact new laws governing surrogate motherhood.

One might argue that in some sense the baby is being "used" as a means to promoting the wealth of the surrogate mother and the happiness of the new parents, but the child is not being used as a mere means unless its freedom and well-being are overridden. If the baby is properly raised, there is no reason to believe the child is being used as a mere means in this sense.

4. The positive test of the means-ends principle is relevant because parents do have an obligation to promote the well-being of their children. This obligation would apply to both the Sterns and Whitehead-Gould. It is difficult to see that the surrogate mother is promoting the freedom or well-being of the fetus in any special way. On the other hand, she is not overriding its freedom and well-being as long as the child is placed in an adequate home. The parents who receive the child would promote the child's freedom and well-being by properly raising it. Therefore, the positive test is passed, or at least not violated.

5. The alternative rule can be stated as follows:

People may not make an irrevocable contract involving the payment of a fee, whereby a woman agrees to conceive a child by the sperm of a married male, even if the contract is made without coercion and with full access to relevant information, and the male and his legal wife can provide an adequate home for the child.

This rule also passes the self-defeating test because everyone could consistently follow it. It does not pass the negative test of the means-ends principle because it denies the freedom of parents like the Sterns and potential surrogate mothers like Whitehead-Gould to enter into such contracts. This rule might be thought of as promoting the freedom and well-being of the fetus because it does not allow conception for the purpose of supplying other people with children. But we have already seen that there is no reason to believe the freedom and well-being of the child need protection, as long as parents who receive the child are capable of providing an adequate home for it.

Because the first rule passes all of the tests and the second rule does not, we must conclude that giving legal permission to engage in contracts for surrogate motherhood is morally obligatory.

Case 4: Buying and Selling Blood

Plasma International had a problem. Headquartered in Tampa, Florida, it had profited from the world's need for whole blood and plasma by buying blood in the southeastern United States and selling it at a reasonable price. Most of its donors, however, were people who used the money to buy wine. When several cases of hepatitis were reported in the users of Plasma International's blood, the company began looking for a new source.

Using a team of medical consultants, Plasma International found the ideal donors in the West African nation of Burami. The company negotiated agreements with several tribal chieftains and was able to buy blood for beads and trinkets. The cost of buying the blood amounted to about 15 cents a pint, but the same pint was sold for about $25.

When the story of Plasma International became public, it provoked a storm of criticism. How can Plasma International justify exploiting the ignorant tribespeople? How can it buy blood so cheap and then sell it to people who are sick or injured and must have the blood at any price?

Sol Levin, a former stockbroker in Tampa and one of the founders of the company, failed to see what was wrong, and we might imagine his argument. He was providing a needed service: supplying uncontaminated plasma and whole blood at market prices. He was giving the African tribespeople what they wanted for their blood. Otherwise, they would not have had the opportunity to exchange their blood for anything. Furthermore, there was no indication that substandard procedures were used to collect the blood or that the tribespeople were harmed medically by the donation. Finally, the blood recipients were paying reasonable prices by market standards.[9]

---

[9] This case was prepared by T. W. Zimmer and P. L. Preston, Florida Atlantic University, from eds. *Business and Society* Robert D. Hay, Edmund R. Gray, and James E. Gates (Cincinnati, OH: South-Western, 1976). Used with permission.

This example raises several moral questions, but one such question focuses on the relationship of Plasma International to the African donors. Was the purchase of the blood at these low prices justifiable by the morality of respect for persons?

1. The methods used to extract the blood were evidently safe, which should be made a part of the rule. Otherwise another set of morally relevant considerations would be introduced. In cultures that do not have the same tradition of individualism that is prevalent in the West, tribal chieftains often make decisions for the entire tribe. Seemingly the only way to apply the ethics of respect for persons to people in such cultures is to assume that when a person's representative gives consent, he gives his consent. With these considerations in mind, the rule presupposed by the practice of Plasma International might be stated in this way:

    A firm may buy blood from donors at prices that allow it to enjoy an unusual profit margin on the resale of the blood, even though the donors are not aware that they could sell the blood for more, as long as safe methods of blood extraction are used and the donors or their representatives give consent.

2. The practice of Plasma International provoked a considerable protest in Tampa. If similar practices were widespread, it stands to reason that the objections would be much more vehement, so much so that action might be taken to prevent them. Therefore, we have some reason to think that the practice might be self-defeating if it were widely employed. However, this conclusion is not certain, so we must conclude that there is only a probable violation of the self-defeating test.

3. The negative test of the means-ends principle asks whether the action of Plasma International overrides the freedom or well-being of the donors. The donors' well-being was not overridden in any obvious way. Because the methods they used were safe, their health was not being threatened. Furthermore, the donors, as far as it can be determined, were not coerced into making the decision to give blood. Even if their tribal chieftain in effect made the decision for them, in a nonindividualistic culture this must be considered a noncoerced decision. Nevertheless, it is probably not fully informed, in the sense that the chief and the donors may not have realized that the price for which they were selling their blood was so far under the market price. Even though the action of the chief and his tribespeople was not coerced, therefore, it was not fully informed and therefore not completely free. So we

must conclude that there was a violation of the negative test, although not a severe one.

4. The positive test of the means-ends principle asks whether the practice of Plasma International, as described in the rule, assists the donors in achieving their freedom and well-being. The well-being of the tribespeople is promoted in some way by the fact that they are given something for their blood. However, it is not clear that the relationship between buyer and seller is one in which either side has an obligation to promote the freedom or well-being of the other. So we shall conclude that this test is not relevant.

5. The alternative version of the rule might be stated as follows:

> A firm may not buy blood from donors at prices that allow it to enjoy an unusual profit margin on the resale of the blood if the donors are not aware that they could sell the blood for more, even though safe methods of blood extraction are used and the donors or their representatives give consent.

This rule does not violate the self-defeating test of the universalization principle: if every firm followed such a rule, there would be no problem with Plasma International's following it. It does not violate the negative test of the means-ends principle because it would not allow firms to take advantage of ignorant people by buying blood at below-market prices. Finally, if the positive test is not applicable in the first rule, it is not applicable in this one, either.

Because the first rule fails to pass the negative test of the means-ends principle, and because the second rule passes all of the tests, we must conclude that Plasma International's practice was impermissible from the standpoint of the ethics of respect for persons.

Two final comments should be made. First, the first rule violates the self-defeating test and the negative test of the means-ends principle in a relatively innocuous manner. It is not entirely clear that a universalization of the rule would be self-defeating. Although the donors may not be fully informed that they are selling their blood at below-market prices, the decision to sell a pint (or even several pints) of blood was probably not a decision with far-reaching consequences on their lives. It is important to see that some cases should probably be considered borderline, and this may be one of them. In fact, perhaps the considerations from the standpoint of the ethics of respect for persons could be legitimately overridden from a utilitarian perspective. Second, the morality of selling blood to people under conditions of great need has not been considered. The moral problems raised by selling blood might be more serious than the ones raised by buying it.

EVALUATING THE ETHICS OF RESPECT FOR PERSONS AS A MORAL THEORY

Now we are ready to evaluate the ethics of respect for persons with our four criteria. Remember that a subjective element is always present in evaluating moral theories. The following evaluations are my own, although they reflect widely held positions among moral philosophers. These evaluations are for your own consideration rather than for uncritical acceptance.

Criterion 1: Consistency and Coherence

The fact that this moral philosophy has two moral standards rather than one might be considered a type of incoherence. The fact that the two standards sometimes yield different conclusions might be considered a type of inconsistency. But the stipulation that an action must pass the tests of both standards before it is considered morally acceptable rules out these problems. Besides, the two moral standards taken together express a common moral theme—namely, the equal respect due all persons.

Another possible source of incoherence is the two principles used in applying the means-ends principle. These principles are (1) that a person can forfeit his rights to freedom and well-being by violating the rights of others and (2) that the rights of others should be respected equally. If they are not derivable from the theory itself, a problem of coherence arises. But because both of these principles can be derived from the idea of equality embodied in the universalization principle, they do not create an incoherence in the theory.

Criterion 2: Justification

Evaluating the justifications of the two moral standards of the ethics of respect for persons presents special difficulties. Kant's arguments are too complex and controversial to be discussed here. We shall therefore evaluate arguments by contemporary writers who advocate principles at least analogous to the universalization principle and the means-ends principle, beginning with a consideration of the universalization principle.

The universalization principle is primarily a requirement of equality. It states that everyone must be able to adopt the rule underlying an action. The idea underlying this requirement is that rules applicable to me must be applicable to others in similar situations. If the rules cannot be universally applied without undermining my own ability to use them, then I must not act in accordance with them, either. But in what sense must I be willing for others to adopt the same rules of behavior I adopt? In other words, how would I justify the universalization principle?

One answer to this question is that the force behind the universalization principle is derived from the nature of morality itself. Some philosophers have maintained that the plausibility of the principle is derived from the term *moral*. To see the force of this claim, consider the case discussed in Chapter 4 of John Zimmerman, an attorney whose physician discovers an aneurism in his adversary's client. Suppose Zimmerman refuses to reveal the information and the boy dies. Suppose, also, that a few months later his own daughter is in an accident, and the attorney for the other side discovers information about his daughter's medical condition that could save her life if he revealed it. Instead, he conceals the information, and Zimmerman's daughter dies. When Zimmerman discovers what the lawyer has done, he is enraged and tries in every way possible to have the attorney disbarred or otherwise punished. He calls the lawyer's conduct immoral, an outrage to society, and a disgrace to the legal profession.

Most of us would say that, by this reaction, Zimmerman has conceded that his own conduct in concealing similar information was immoral. But suppose Zimmerman insists that his conduct was not immoral, even though he admits that the only significant difference between the two cases is that in this case he is related to the deceased person. At this point, we would probably severely criticize Zimmerman's behavior. One way of stating our criticism would be to say that Zimmerman does not know how to use the words *moral* and *immoral*. If he is going to use moral language correctly, he must apply the same rules to himself that he applies to others.

How could Zimmerman respond to this agreement? On the one hand, he could deny that he is violating the rule that governs the use of the words *moral* and *immoral*. He could say that he is just an ethical egoist who is unwilling to universalize his egoism. And surely one would want to call such egoism either *moral* or *immoral*, not *amoral* as one would have to do if egoism were outside the boundaries of morality altogether. On the other hand, Zimmerman could say that, although his position may not be *moral* in the proper sense of that term, he does not care. "Why should I be moral if it is contrary to my self-interest?" he might ask. At this point, we must then show why a person should govern his actions by moral principles. We shall not pursue this issue further here. The justification of the universalization principle is a complex issue that still provokes controversy. But the implausibility of Zimmerman's replies to criticism of his behavior indicates that the universalization principle is deeply rooted in our moral thinking.

The justification of the means-ends principle is, if anything, more controversial.[10] One of the most plausible arguments is that refusal to respect the essential nature of personhood in oneself or others involves a contradiction. The first step in exposing this contradiction is to maintain that if we cannot be personal agents without having our freedom and well-being respected, we will necessarily claim the right to have these aspects of our personhood respected. This claim is not merely a matter of the intellect but primarily embodied in our action. That is, we must act as if we have the rights to the freedom and well-being we need to accomplish our purposes. But if the implicit assumptions of our action are based on nothing more than the fact that we are moral agents, we are forced by the constraints of consistency to acknowledge that any other person who is a moral agent like ourselves has exactly the same rights. To deny this respect to other agents while claiming it for ourselves is inconsistent.

Even though this argument is impressive, we can still ask how the fact that we implicitly claim certain rights by our action justifies the claim. And perhaps there are no implicit moral claims behind certain types of action; perhaps we just act in our self-interest. A successful justification of the means-ends principle must answer these questions.

Criterion 3: Plausibility

Many people, especially those strongly influenced by traditional moral ideas, would maintain that the ethics of respect for persons is more compatible with their previously held moral beliefs than with utilitarianism or egoism. They might well hold that respect for persons is closer to their moral beliefs than natural law is, although the version of the theory presented here may not suggest traditional positions on such issues as premarital sex or suicide.

Perhaps the most general criticism of the ethics of respect for persons, from the standpoint of agreement or disagreement with our previously held moral beliefs, is that the theory does not sufficiently account for an

---

[10] One of the most interesting attempts to justify a principle like the means-ends principle is Alan Gewirth's *Reason and Morality*. I am indebted to his book for the basic ideas presented here, although this particular version is my own and differs in important aspects from Gewirth's. I am also indebted to Henry Veatch's review of Gewirth's book in *Ethics* 89 (July 1979) for my presentation and criticism of these ideas. For other discussions of this issue, see Marcus Singer, "On Gewirth's Derivation of the Principle of Generic Consistency," in *Ethics* 95, No. 2 (January 1985), pp. 297–301; and Alan Gewirth, "From the Prudential to the Moral: Reply to Singer" in *Ethics* 95, No. 2 (January 1985), pp. 302–304. For some of the most recent discussions of Gewirth's philosophy, see Deryck Beyleveld, *The Dialectical Necessity of Morality* (Chicago: University of Chicago Press, 1991), and Michael Boylan, ed., *Gewirth: Critical Essays on Action, Rationality, and Community* (Lanham, MD: Rowman & Littlefield, 1999).

action's consequences. In many issues of public policy, for example, utilitarian considerations seem relevant. Sometimes it seems justifiable to sacrifice some innocent lives to save the lives of a larger number of people. If killing some civilians is necessary to end a war and ultimately save many more lives, is it wrong to do so? Is it wrong to adopt policies that increase unemployment somewhat but reduce the inflation rate? It sometimes seems morally permissible, if not obligatory, to engage in an action that involves wrongs to individuals because the overall consequences justify it.

Criterion 4: Usefulness

Applying the ethics of respect for persons can be difficult for three reasons. First, the rule describing an action can be stated in many different ways, which means that different conclusions will be drawn depending on which rule is used. Usually this problem is not too severe because the most adequate rule is reasonably obvious. However, the rule sometimes must be stated in an ambiguous or open-ended way to be acceptable. At other times, the proper rule may be difficult to determine, and the way in which the rule is stated may decisively influence the outcome of the ethical analysis. When these problems arise, they diminish the usefulness of the theory in providing a clear indication of what should be done.

Consider the case of the physician who does not believe in sterilization but who is asked to perform a sterilization on a man for whom she is the only available physician. We would probably not want to consider a rule that reads, "Physicians should always follow their patients' wishes." Nor would we want to consider a rule that states, "Physicians should always follow their own consciences, even if it means denying their patients' wishes." Perhaps a better rule is the following: "Physicians should always follow their patients' wishes, even if it involves violating the physician's own strongly held moral beliefs, as long as a patient's request is within the bounds of ordinary morality." This rule is still open-ended, because the phrase "within the bounds of ordinary morality" has various interpretations. But there does not appear to be any way to eliminate the open-ended character of a rule covering this situation.

A second difficulty is that we sometimes find it hard to determine whether an action passes the tests of the two moral standards. Sometimes the self-defeating test is hard to apply. For example, suppose we are attempting to determine whether the self-defeating test is passed by a rule allowing physicians to lie to their patients when the physician believes it is for the patients' good. If it were generally accepted that physicians will sometimes lie to their patients, would patients no longer trust physicians? If patients generally lost confidence in the word of physicians because this rule was followed, then physicians could still lie to their patients, but they could not achieve the purpose they had in lying. The rule would thus be self-defeating. However, physicians' lying in such special circumstances as the rule describes might not be enough to undermine a general confidence in the word of physicians, so the rule would not be self-defeating. At any rate, the application of the self-defeating test of the universalization principle sometimes depends on factual assumptions about the consequences of actions that are often little more than speculation.

We have also seen that the means-ends principle is difficult to apply in many ethical controversies. It is not always easy to determine how the negative test applies or whether the positive test is relevant.

A third problem with this theory is that we sometimes find that both an action and its alternative have difficulties with one or more of the tests. The sterilization case mentioned previously might well be one in which both the rule and its alternative would violate the negative test of the means-ends principle. The rule requiring physicians to honor patients' wishes would violate the moral agency of physicians, and the alternative rule requiring physicians to honor their own consciences would violate the moral agency of patients. In such situations, we are forced to make a judgment as to which violations are more serious, and this judgment makes the solution to the problem controversial. Any moral theory will yield ambiguous conclusions in some instances, so this state of affairs is not a refutation of the ethics of respect for persons. Nevertheless, this limitation, which should be noted in any evaluation, is especially prominent in respect-for-persons morality.

CONCEPT SUMMARY

The ethics of respect for persons has no obvious inconsistencies. An argument for the universalization principle is that the universalization principle is required by the meaning of the word *moral,* but some people might argue that an action guide need not meet the requirements of morality. An argument for the means-ends principle is that as agents, we necessarily claim that our purposes and the conditions necessary for their realization should be respected. If we make this claim simply because we are agents, we must respect an equal claim on the part of other agents. But the fact that we make a claim to certain rights does not necessarily mean the claim is valid, and we may not necessarily even have to make this claim.

The ethics of respect for persons is generally consistent with most people's prior moral beliefs, although its lack of emphasis on consequences leads to some conclusions that many people find implausible. However, respect-for-persons morality sometimes cannot produce a clear resolution of moral dilemmas. Possible problems are that the rule describing an action can be stated in more than one way, it is difficult to know whether an action passes the tests of the two moral standards, and the action and its alternative are equally justifiable or unjustifiable.

VIRTUE ETHICS

Entil Corporation permits its employees to borrow company tools. Al House took full advantage of the privilege, even ordering unneeded tools for his unit so that he could use them in his home workshop. Michael Green, Al's subordinate, alerted Al's boss to Al's abuse of company policy, and the boss reprimanded Al. Enraged that somebody had "ratted" on him, Al called each of his subordinates into his office and asked who had complained to his superior. When Al questioned Michael, Michael denied any knowledge of what took place. Later, Michael went into Al's office and said that he had complained to Al's superior. Explaining his action to his wife, he said, "I just got tired of looking in the mirror and saying to myself, 'You are a coward and a liar.'"[1]

W. Lynn Beason is an engineer who often serves as a consultant or expert witness in his field of specialization, window safety. He became interested in this as an area of research as a graduate student when the town in which he lived was hit by a tornado. He saw there were design problems with windows, and he decided to try to clear them up. Now he regards himself as a public safety advocate. Eschewing the label of "crusader," he says he simply uses the public interest as a guidepost when undertaking his work, especially as an expert witness. Noting that some engineers he knows operate as "guns for hire" when serving as expert witnesses, Beason is very uncomfortable with this. Instead, he says to a potential client that he will look at their case and do his best to understand it. He then tells the potential client how he assesses the case. If they want him to testify, he will do it. If they do not want him, he expects the client to pay him for his time. Beason says, "I tell that to everybody, you know, because that's very comfortable."

---

[1] This is a modification of Case 4, "Borrowed Tools," in Charles E. Harris, Jr., Michael S. Pritchard, and Michael J. Rabins, *Engineering Ethics: Concepts and Cases*, 2nd ed. (Belmont, CA: Wadsworth, 2000), p. 289.

This does not mean that Lynn Beason's life as an expert witness is easy. What he says on the witness stand is not necessarily welcomed by all sides. Perhaps his greatest challenge was the threat of a lawsuit for more than one million dollars for allegedly making false statements in questioning someone's window safety testing methods. Instead of backing off, he filed a countersuit and continued his campaign. Eventually, his adversary withdrew its suit against him. Undaunted by the unpleasantness (and potential costliness) of all this, Beason remains dedicated to his cause. He describes himself as a very stubborn, persistent person.

Reflecting on his approach to his work, Beason says, "I would like to feel good about what I do, okay, and you know, you can do lots of things and not feel bad about what you do, but I would like to feel good about what I do."[2]

These two cases illustrate a different way of thinking about ethical problems than the ones we have so far considered. Michael was not so much disturbed because he had broken a moral rule against honesty as he was troubled by the damage to his self-image that his lying had caused. He did not like *who he was* when he looked at himself in the mirror and saw a liar and a coward. Ethics, for Michael, was not so much a matter of following rules as it was being a certain kind of person or having a certain type of character.

Similarly, in committing himself to public safety, even at the risk of personal loss, Lynn Beason probably did not think of himself as following a moral rule. There is no moral rule that requires a person to assume unusual risks for the sake of the public good. Rather, Mr. Beason had a certain ideal of what it means to be a good professional, and he wanted to live up to that ideal. He wanted to think of himself as a person dedicated to the welfare of the public.

The approach to ethics pictured in these two cases is different in important ways from the rule- or principle-oriented theories we have so far considered. The emphasis is on character rather than action as such, although it can provide direction for behavior. This type of ethics usually goes under the name of *virtue ethics* or *aretaic ethics*. *Arete* is the Greek term for "excellence" or, as it is often translated, "virtue." A *virtue* is a character trait that inclines us to act in a way that is morally desirable. A *vice*, by contrast, is a character trait or tendency that inclines to act in a way that is morally undesirable.

Virtue ethics has a long history. Perhaps the most important figure in the virtue ethics tradition is Aristotle, whose *Nicomachean Ethics* is the

---

[2] See Case 54, "Window Safety," in *Engineering Ethics: Concepts and Cases*, 2nd ed., op. cit., pp. 351–352.

most important work in ancient moral philosophy. Much traditional Christian morality, and to some extent Christian morality today, is formulated in the terms of the ethics of virtue. For many Christian writers, the three primary "theological virtues" are faith, hope, and charity. At various times in the history of Western philosophy, such as the eighteenth century, the ethics of virtue or excellence has been prominent. Some contemporary feminist writers have also developed their ethical ideas by way of a discussion of the virtues, especially the virtue of care. We shall focus on Aristotle and feminist virtue ethics.

What is Virtue Ethics?

As with rule ethics, we can construct a moral standard for the ethics of virtue:

> MS: An action is right if and only if it is what a virtuous person would do in the circumstances.

The contrast with rule ethics is immediately apparent. Instead of determining what is right by looking to rules, we determine what is right by deciding what a person of exemplary character would do. Virtue ethicists believe that the virtue orientation reveals some aspects of common morality that are not apparent from the standpoint of a rule-oriented ethics and that there are distinct advantages to basing ethics on character, rather than rules and principles. Several of these advantages deserve mention here.

First, virtue ethics seems less abstract and is at least sometimes closer to the way we actually think about troubling moral issues. Instead of asking whether euthanasia, for example, is right or wrong, we might be more inclined to ask whether a courageous person or a person who cares about his family could end his own life. Similarly, we might ask whether a caring or loving son or daughter could participate in the ending of the life of a parent. Whatever answer we come to, virtue ethicists would claim the issue would have been debated in a more concrete and realistic manner.

A second advantage is that virtue ethics often seems more appropriate as a basis for morally evaluating people. When we judge people, we do not do so in terms of moral rules. Rather, we do so in terms of their virtues—or their vices. We say they are honest, compassionate, or loyal, or that they are liars or thieves. We have already seen how the language of virtues and vices seemed to be the most appropriate language for describing the characters and ethical situations of Michael Green and Lynn Beason.

Third, virtue ethics provides a better way than rule ethics of under-standing why people perform heroic deeds that go above and beyond the call of duty, that is, actions that are supererogatory. We have already shown that at least one version of rule ethics, namely utilitarianism, finds it difficult to provide a satisfactory understanding of supererogatory actions at all. For utilitarians, at least on some accounts, actions are permissible, impermissible, or required, but never supererogatory. Virtue ethics, by contrast, can readily account for supererogatory actions: we act in a noble or heroic way because this is the kind of person we want to be and these are the ideals we want to follow. Mr. Beason decided to engage in actions that some would call supererogatory. It is reasonable to think that he came to this decision, not by meditating on moral rules, but by thinking about what kind of professional he wanted to be. He aspired to be a professional who was strongly committed to public safety, even at the risk of personal sacrifice. Other engineers might have decided differently.

Fourth, decisions about what kinds of character and lifestyles we want to endorse are not matters of deciding which moral rules we will obey, but which virtues we shall emphasize. Do I want to be a scientist, where self-discipline is at a premium, or a social worker, where care and empathy are more important? Or perhaps I want to be a firefighter or soldier, where courage and loyalty are necessary. When we look at the ethics of Aristotle and the ethics of care, which picture of the ideal person seems more appealing? Or perhaps we find a combination of these two ideals more appealing. For these kinds of moral deliberations, the ethics of virtue is far more helpful than an ethics of rules. Before we can consider these issues further, we must take a more extensive look at the nature of virtue or excellence.

WHAT IS A VIRTUE?

We have already said that a virtue is a character trait that inclines us to act in a way that is morally desirable. This definition, however, does not tell us much about what a virtue is or how it functions in moral philosophy, so the following comments about virtue—and conversely about vice—should be useful.

First, a virtue is what some modern virtue theorists call a "disposition." A disposition is a character trait, which manifests itself in a motivation to do certain sorts of things when the appropriate circumstance arises. A person who has the virtue or character trait of courage acts courageously when the need for courage arises.

Second, because it is a trait of character, a virtue—or its corresponding vice—is necessarily stable and abiding. Being courageous one time in your life is not enough to make you a courageous person; you must show courage in many situations. As Aristotle says, ". . . one swallow does not make a spring, nor does one day. . ."[3] You cannot be courageous for an hour and a coward the rest of your life and still be a courageous person. Similarly with the vices: being dishonest one time does not make you a dishonest person; being regularly dishonest does.

Third, because it is a stable part of a person's character, a virtue (or its corresponding vice) is hard to change, once established. We are not necessarily virtuous by nature; perhaps we are more naturally inclined to pursue pleasure and avoid pain. As the expression "second nature" implies, however, training can at least make the virtues a second nature, even if they are not a first nature. So a person of genuinely good character—even if this good character is a second nature and the result of training—will just naturally or spontaneously do the right thing. Such a person has come to want to do the right thing and do it without thinking. For this reason, virtue ethicists hold that moral education should begin early in life, when the child is naturally more pliable and open to training in the right direction. Moral education should take place in the home and at school, and in the public arena as well.

Fourth, virtues and vices have to do with feeling or emotion. The good person takes genuine pleasure in being good. It gives her a sense of satisfaction to be honest, compassionate, or brave. She feels like she is being true to herself. Ultimately, for Aristotle and many virtue theorists, there is an aesthetic element here. We look at ourselves or others when they are compassionate, honest, or loyal and we find it pleasing and even "beautiful." We like what we see. When Michael Green looked at himself, he did not like what he saw.

Think of two students who are attending a symphony concert, one because he is required to do it in order to fulfill a requirement for a music appreciation class and the other because he genuinely enjoys classical music. Only the latter is a real lover of classical music. Similarly, only people who act nobly because it gives them pleasure are good in the fullest sense of the term. A person who refrains from excessive drinking or eating because he knows he should may be what Aristotle calls "continent," but does not really exhibit the virtue of temperance. Only the person who takes pleasure in refraining from binges of drinking or eating displays

---

[3] Aristotle, *Nicomachean Ethics*, trans. By Terence Irwin (Indianapolis, IN: Hackett, 1985), 1098a20. Hereafter we shall refer to this work as *NE*. The numbers used are the standard references to this work and are the same in any edition.

genuine virtue. Aristotle seems to hedge sometimes on this issue. Perhaps a genuinely courageous person does not have to enjoy standing his or her ground in battle when his or her life is in danger, but at least the person must not be distressed by it.[4] Nevertheless, Aristotle seems to believe that our attitudes toward courses of conduct are never emotionally neutral. A man of the right character will not only act nobly but have a positive feeling about it.

We have seen that the moral standard of virtue ethics asks what a virtuous person would do in a given situation. In order to apply this moral standard, we must get some feeling for what it is like to be a person of a certain sort, to be a person with a certain character trait or set of character traits. How is this done? Novelists, playwrights, biographers, and others in the literary tradition can help by telling stories about people who act nobly and virtuously. One can think of Plutarch's *The Lives of the Noble Grecians and Romans* as an example. In the Christian tradition, the lives of the saints and many of the stories in the Bible come to mind. For philosophers, painting word pictures is the more appropriate mode. Through such word pictures, we can learn what a person would do in given situation. Let us call these pictures of ideal virtuous people *virtue portraits*. One of the most interesting such pictures of the noble and virtuous life is given by Aristotle.

ARISTOTLE'S PORTRAIT OF THE VIRTUOUS PERSON

The Magnanimous Man and the Golden Mean

In one of his most vivid pictures of the kind of person he considers admirable, Aristotle describes what is often translated as the "great-souled" or "magnanimous" man.[5] Since Aristotle thinks only males can attain this state of excellence and since some of his descriptions explicitly apply to males, we shall retain his gender orientation, despite the moral objections we might have to it.

The magnanimous man, for Aristotle, "thinks himself worthy of great things and is really worthy of them." He knows, in other words, that he is a superior person, and his superiority is based on the fact that he exhibits the virtues to an unusual degree. If a person thinks he is superior and is not, he is vain; but the genuinely superior person knows he ranks above

---

[4] *NE*, 1146b7–8.

[5] *NE* 1123b35–1125b25.

the average person, so his opinion of himself is not an indication of vanity. This does not mean, however, that the magnanimous man comports himself in an arrogant and haughty manner to those who are inferior to him, for that would be vulgar. Even with those who are his equal or superior, he is not fawning or obsequious, for that would also be beneath his dignity. As a mark of his own sense of dignity and self-worth, the magnanimous man likes to confer benefits on others, but is reluctant to accept them. He renders aid willingly, but is reluctant to ask for help. He is also not emotionally repressed or full of resentment or envy toward others, and he is not afraid to express both love and hate.

The magnanimous man has a certain detached attitude toward fortune. He will have a "moderate attitude to riches and power and every sort of good and bad fortune, however it turns out." He has learned to be "neither excessively pleased by good fortune nor excessively distressed by ill fortune. . ."[6] He even has the same attitude toward danger and death. Although he does not face dangers for a small cause, he is willing to face danger for a worthy cause, even at the risk of death, for "he does not think life at all costs is worthwhile."[7] Finally, the magnanimous man tends to have slow movements, a deep voice, and calm speech, for he is not in a hurry, and he is not perturbed by most of the events of life. As we might say today, it takes a very stressful or dramatic situation to "get him going."

In other places in the *Nicomachean Ethics*, Aristotle mentions other character traits that he admires and that fit well with his description of the magnanimous man: pride, ambition, good temper, friendliness, truthfulness, and a ready wit. Notice that we would not call some of these characteristics moral virtues at all, but rather psychological traits. Aristotle does not distinguish in the way we do between moral and non-moral traits, but we shall be concerned primarily with the moral virtues.

Many have criticized this virtue portrait and have found it unappealing or even offensive. Yet most of us have probably met people—both men and women—who fit this description in a general way. They have a certain aristocratic bearing and nobility about them that is not arrogant. We recognize a certain "presence" in their personality that seems to command respect; we know that they are "different" from most of the rest of us.

Aristotle tells us something else about his portrait of the ideal person which is often misunderstood, namely that the virtues of the ideal person are "means" between undesirable character traits. Each virtue is, according to Aristotle, located on a scale of a given emotion, and the virtue is in fact a

---

[6] *NE*, 1124a15.

[7] *NE*, 1124b5.

mean between two extremes. Consider this example. Good temper is located on the anger scale, on one end being the vice of irascibility and at the other end being the vice of undue passivity. This does not mean, however, that one's emotions should always be "moderate" and that it is always wrong to get really angry. Rather, our response to a situation should always be proportionate or appropriate to the situation. Sometimes it is entirely proper to be outraged, as when we encounter the use of torture or the abuse of children. On the other hand, it is proper to be only a little miffed when a person is carelessly inconsiderate of us, as when they forget to invite us to a party. To be outraged and to boil in anger over such a trivial insult is not a proportionate response to the situation.

Here is another example. The virtue associated with the proper relation to physical pleasures, such as food, drink, and sex, is self-control. The emotional scale in this case is precisely the desire for these sorts of pleasures. The excess is gluttony, drunkenness, or sexual addiction. The deficiency is a disorder in which one does not eat sufficiently, has an excessive aversion to drinking (which is more than a simple decision to avoid all alcohol), or is a sexual prude. Again, however, it is important to keep in mind that adhering to the mean is not necessarily the same as "moderation," as we ordinarily understand this term. Jane might have a glass or wine before meals, while Jill might drink only once a year, but get really drunk when she does. We might be inclined to call Jane's practice an illustration of the mean and not Jill's, but both practices could be considered different ways of following a mean. Jane's practice might be more appropriate to her lifestyle and Jill's to hers, but neither shows an addiction to alcohol. As we have seen, the mean is better described as a philosophy of "appropriateness" than "moderation."

To take another example, Aristotle has great admiration for courage or bravery, especially in battle. While no one would doubt that courage is a virtue, however, Aristotle has problems in determining the mean with respect to it. Aristotle's analysis relates it to the emotion of fear: a brave person has the right amount of fear at the right time and place, and for the right reason. A coward will have too much fear and the rash or foolhardy person will have too little fear. But perhaps it is better to describe the rash or foolhardy person as just overconfident in the face of danger, rather than lacking in fear, thus introducing a different emotional scale.[8] In any case, the admirable person will display courage or bravery in an appropriate or proportionate way in any given situation.

---

[8] *NE*, 1115a5–1117a5.

With regard to justice, Aristotle thinks there are two senses. In the more general sense, justice refers to the whole of the virtuous life. In this sense, a person who lives virtuously lives justly. What we might call special justice is different. In this narrower sense, justice is a mean insofar as it consists of a state of affairs which is intermediate between A having too much or B having too much. The goods with which Aristotle is especially concerned in discussing justice are money and honor. The just state is one in which every person has his rightful share of money and honor, whatever that might be in an individual case.

These observations help to explain what Aristotle had in mind when he said that the mean was "relative to us."[9] To follow a mean is to pursue that course of action between excess and deficiency which is appropriate to us in our circumstances. Deciding what that mean is requires reason and intelligence, or, perhaps better, "practical wisdom."[10] Such practical wisdom develops with age, and the young cannot be expected to have it to the same degree.

Love and Friendship, Happiness, and Luck

So far Aristotle has given a portrait of the virtuous man that looks something like this. While conscious that he is a superior person and never fawning to others, the virtuous person finds it vulgar to lord it over those who are not as morally advanced as he is. He values his own independence and finds it easier to give favors than accept them. He is open in the expression of his emotions, whether it is love or anger and hostility. He possesses enough wisdom in practical matters so that he can manifest the virtues in a way that is appropriate to the situation and his own personality and lifestyle. For example, he can enjoy pleasure without being enslaved to it, and he can be courageous without being cowardly or foolhardy.

We have argued that such a person need not be thought of as vain, but he still might appear somewhat aloof and solitary. No account of Aristotle's virtue portrait should be allowed to leave this impression, for Aristotle spends a great deal of time talking about what is designated by the Greek term *philia*, which is usually translated as "friendship." Sometimes "friendship" may be the best translation of *philia*, as when Aristotle describes two people who enjoy doing philosophy or hunting or playing games together.[11] But *philia* also designates many relationships that we would ordinarily not

---

[9] *NE*, 1106a30.

[10] *NE*, 1040a25–1040b30.

[11] NE 1171b32–11712a8.

describe as "friendships," such as the love of mother and child, the relationship of husband and wife, or relationships that have a passionate sexual aspect. This suggests for one scholar, Martha Nussbaum, that *philia* is sometimes more appropriately translated as "love."[12] In Nusbaum's interpretation of Aristotle, the most important type of love for him is one in which "each partner loves the other for what that other most deeply is in him or herself..."[13] Aristotle also says that a friend is "another yourself,"[14] implying that what is deepest in our friends is also a part of us.

Friendship is "the greatest external good."[15] Humans are naturally social beings who want to live together. Living together with friends is therefore a major source of happiness. Some friends are friends for utility, such as a business partner. Others are friends for pleasure, such as a person we enjoy being around because of his ready wit. But the best kind of friend is a friend for virtue—one whose presence, because of his own virtues, encourages the highest and best of which we are capable.[16] Friends of this type are an inestimable boon, not only to virtue, but also to happiness. Aristotle gives what some might consider a surprising picture of what friends do together:

> Some friends drink together, others play dice, while others do gymnastics and go hunting or do philosophy. They spend their days together on whichever pursuit in life they like the most; for since they want to live with their friends, they share the actions in which they find their common life.[17]

For Aristotle, the virtuous person is, or usually is, happy. Aristotle claims that we all seek happiness, which is one translation of the Greek term *eudaimonia*, a term that is sometimes also translated as "flourishing." In fact, happiness is flourishing in accordance with virtue. But Aristotle has enough of the tragic sense of life to know that sometimes happiness is not within our ability to attain. Sometimes the external circumstances of life keep us from enjoying the happiness that we might otherwise have. Friendship and love are important to the happy life, but sometimes we are not lucky enough to find the kinds of people we need for love and friendship. Whether we have the other virtues and the wisdom to manifest

---

[12] Martha Nussbaum, *The Fragility of Goodness* (New York: Cambridge University Press, 1986), p. 354.

[13] Ibid, p. 356.

[14] *NE*, 1169b5.

[15] *NE*, 1169b10.

[16] *NE*, 1170b25–1171a5.

[17] *NE*, 1127a–1127a5.

them in the proper proportion also depends to a great extent on early training, but some of us are not lucky enough to be born in homes where that training is given. Whether we have the wisdom and emotional stability to manifest the virtues in the right proportion in a given situation requires intelligence and emotional stability, and, here again, some are not fortunate enough to possess these qualities. And sometimes sickness or natural disasters or other circumstances are such that few of us, including Aristotle himself, could live up to the ideal that Aristotle proposes. Thus an element of luck is involved in attaining the happy life, and even, to some extent, in being a good person.

FEMINISM AND THE ETHICS OF CARE

Ethics in a Different Voice

Aristotle's virtue portrait was associated with the upper-class Athenian gentleman, but the picture seems to fit many other groups as well. The aristocratic ideal during the Victorian age in England also has seemed to many to be reminiscent of Aristotle's ideal. In the tradition of Western society, the virtues Aristotle praised also have a distinctly "masculine" and especially military cast. Indeed, they are stereotypically "masculine" virtues: independence, domination, courage or bravery, self-control, loyalty and so forth.[18]

While these virtues are virtues indeed and worthy of our admiration, it should come as no surprise that representatives of the feminist movement have found Aristotle's list of virtues incomplete at best. Since the late eighteenth century, some women have protested the excessively male orientation of Western culture and philosophy, of which Aristotle is a prime example. In 1792, Mary Wollstonecraft published *A Vindication of the Rights of Women*, in which she argued that the notion of women as naturally oriented toward pleasure-seeking and feeling and submissiveness is false. She believed that the quickest way for women to assume a more prominent place in society is for them to adopt the character traits associated with masculinity, that is, the sorts of traits that Aristotle praised. This is especially the case with rationality, because it is rationality, not feeling, that distinguishes humans from animals.

Writing a century later, John Stuart Mill, in *On the Subjection of Women*, argued that virtue is gender neutral and that society should not

---

[18] I have found Rosemarie Tong's *Feminine and Feminist Ethics* (Belmont, CA: Wadsworth, 1982) useful in writing this section.

set up any moral standards for women that are different from those of men. Women have been brought up to believe that their appropriate set of character traits is different from that of men. Women are probably no less selfish than men, but women are taught to be selfish with respect to the interests of their families, whereas society at least does not discourage the pursuit of individual self-interest in men.

In the twentieth century the interest in feminine and feminist themes has increased enormously.[19] One book, however, has been especially influential in philosophical ethics. In 1982 psychologist Carol Gilligan published *In a Different Voice: Psychological Theory and Women's Development*.[20] In the book she argued, unlike some earlier feminist writers, that women are indeed more likely to have certain character traits than men and to approach moral dilemmas in a different way from men, but that these character traits and this characteristically feminine approach are at least as valuable as, and perhaps superior to, approaches associated with men. She emphasized even in the introduction, however, that men as well as women could display these character traits and this approach to moral reasoning.[21] So we shall be more concerned with this different approach to virtue and ethical reasoning, rather than the question of whether and to what extent it is associated with a particular gender.

Gilligan believes that psychology confirms certain general differences between boys and girls. In a word, this difference is that "boys in their games are more concerned with rules while girls are more concerned with relationships."[22] As a part of this difference, boys tend to be concerned with asserting rights, while girls are more concerned with caring for others and finding a way to preserve relationships. One very well-known case, used on a test for measuring moral development constructed by Gilligan's teacher, Lawrence Kohlberg, illustrates the supposed differences between males and females. In the case, Heinz cannot afford to buy a drug which he needs to save his wife's life. What should Heinz do? Should he steal the drug to save his wife? Jake and Amy, both in the same sixth-grade class at school, answer the question quite differently, even though they did not

---

[19] In general the term *feminine* has been used to refer to characteristics that may be especially associated with women, whereas *feminist* connotes a more critical and polemical stance, in which the rights prerogatives of women are asserted. This is a more aggressive stance which argues for equal treatment of women in all areas. We shall in general use the term *feminist* to refer to the philosophical literature discussed in this chapter.

[20] Carol Gilligan, *In a Different Voice: Psychological Theory and Women's Development* (Cambridge, MA: Harvard University Press, 1982).

[21] Ibid, p. 2.

[22] Ibid, p. 16.

share the stereotypical "male" and "female" academic interests. (Jake was interested in literature and Amy in mathematics and science.) Jake says that Heinz should steal the drug, because the right to life is greater than the right to property. Amy, instead of weighing abstract rights in order to determine which right should have the priority, was more concerned with preserving the relationship between Heinz and his wife:

> If he stole the drug, he might save his wife then, but if he did, he might have to go to jail, and then his wife might get sicker again, and he couldn't get more of the drug, and it might not be good. So they should really just talk it out and find some other way to make the money.[23]

Amy's reply has had enormous influence on feminist ethics. Notice that there is no reference here to abstract principles, such as justice or fairness or rights. Rather the focus is on how Heinz can best care for his wife in the long run. The way to do this is to "just talk it out" and find some creative way to preserve the relationship, assure care for Heinz's wife, and keep Heinz out of jail. The moral dilemma is a conflict of responsibilities, not a conflict of rights, and the goal is to include everyone in the solution.

This approach to ethics illustrates what has come to be called the *ethics of care*, which is the principal virtue in much feminist ethics. The concept of care, as it is ordinarily used, has two components. On the one hand, it connotes solicitude, nurturing, and compassion. On the other hand, it suggests a certain anxiety, worry, or concern about something. It is the first component that is of central importance in the ethics of care, but the second may play some role as well. Amy showed care in her concern for the welfare of both Heinz and his wife, and the focus was on healing. The ethics of care takes into account all of those involved in a situation, so the concern for family and community and human relationships is strong. Interdependence is valued over independence and autonomy. In addition, many have associated the ethics of care with gentleness, supportiveness, and intuitive understanding and sensitivity.

An Ethics of Relationships

Gilligan's emphasis on the virtue of caring has been developed by several writers, one of the most important of whom is Nel Noddings. For Noddings, the ethics of care is one type of relational ethics:

> A relation... is any pairing or connection of individuals characterized by some affective awareness of each. It is an encounter or series of encounters in which the involved parties feel something toward each other. Relations

---

[23] Ibid, p. 28.

may involve love or hate, anger or sorrow, admiration or envy, or, of course, they may reveal mixed affects—one party feeling, say, love and the other revulsion. I am most interested in the caring relation, but I am also interested in how we develop other kinds of relations and what we might do, in particular, to discourage the making of rivals and enemies.[24]

Noddings develops this relational ethics of caring in terms of several key ideas. First, in relational ethics, instead of judging our own action solely by whether it conforms to a rule or principle, we evaluate our action, at least partly, on the basis of others' response to it. The response of others includes both their feeling and their action.

A second characteristic of Noddings' ethics of care is that it is built on a foundation of what she calls *natural caring*. "In situations where we act on behalf of others because we want to do so, we are acting in accord with natural caring."[25] As with many feminist ethicists, Noddings finds the paradigm of natural caring in the care of a mother for her child, but this is by no means the only example. Fathers can care for their children and their wives, and both men and women can exemplify caring in many other ways, such as their solicitude for their ageing parents.

Upon this foundation of natural caring, Noddings holds, we build a superstructure of *ethical caring*. Noddings believes that we can train ourselves to be caring even when we may not be so inclined, taking advantage of our natural tendencies toward empathy (understanding and sharing the feelings of another) and sympathy (a feeling of pity or sorrow for someone else's misfortune).

> There are times when the plight of another triggers in us both the empathetic "I must" characteristic of the caring response and a self-regarding "I do not want to." In these moments we must draw on our memories of caring moments. We use these memories to sustain or to summon the empathic feeling—the "I must"—that activates a caring response to the other.[26]

A third characteristic of Noddings' ethics of care is her insistence that ethical caring is not somehow higher or more admirable than natural caring. For some philosophers, such as Kant, an action motivated by natural feelings of care and concern is not as morally praiseworthy as an action motivated by a conviction that I *should* care for others out of a sense of duty. But such an attitude tends to separate our biological nature and

---

[24] Nel Noddings, *Women and Evil* (Berkeley: University of California Press, 1989), p. 184.

[25] Ibid., pp. 184–185.

[26] Ibid., p. 185.

our natural human inclinations from the more purely "ethical." The dualism between the body and emotion on the one hand and the "ethical" and "rational" on the other is typical of much of the ethics Noddings criticizes.

Finally, Noddings holds that the major obstacle to an ethics of caring is anything that tends to separate us from others. While this may be obvious, its importance requires that it be explicitly stated. Much of Noddings' ethical discussion is an analysis of how we construct barriers between ourselves and others, and how this obscures moral insight and paves the way for unethical conduct. We separate ourselves from others by treating them as "the enemy," "the competition," the "non-believer"—in other words, those who are not "not-me" or "not-us." The "not-me" and "not-us" refer to the two major forms that separation can take. The first form is individualism, where we see ourselves in opposition to others, whether it is business competition or war or simply a failure to take into account the feelings and interests of others. The second form is group exclusivity, in which a group or even a society sees those outside as unworthy of full ethical consideration. She calls this approach to others "separatist thinking."

VIRTUE PLURALISM

Aristotle and Noddings give very different virtue portraits. The magnanimous man appears to exhibit separatist thinking, in that he recognizes his superiority to and difference from most people. He exhibits the military virtues of courage or bravery, as well as justice. While he prizes friendship, his friends are members of a rather exclusive group, and friendship is based on reciprocal benefit, not sympathy, caring, and the desire to nurture and help. The caring person, on the other hand, has an empathetic understanding, which promotes communication, nurturing, and healing of animosities. The attitude of domination or at least superiority is replaced by a concern for equality and harmony.

We must be careful, however, not to overemphasize the differences between the two virtue portraits. Aristotle accords great importance to friendship, as we have seen, and he believes that we cannot be fully human apart from a community. Even though the magnanimous man recognizes his superiority to most other people, he finds it vulgar and unbecoming to lord it over them in an ostentatious way. He is generous to the appropriate degree, and he avoids vanity and boastfulness. Most of the virtues, furthermore, would probably find recognition by both writers. Honesty, loyalty, and self-control, for example, would probably find recognition in both camps.

The virtue portraits of Aristotle and Gilligan and Noddings do not exhaust the list. Various virtues and sets of virtues can be emphasized to form different pictures of the ideal person, although these two portraits are two of the major alternatives. Furthermore, in resolving many moral issues, it may not be necessary or even useful to refer to an overall virtue portrait. The more comprehensive attitude toward the virtues, then, may be what we can call *virtue pluralism*, namely the view that there is no single valid account of the virtues or the ideal virtuous person. In elaborating this account, a general listing and classification of the virtues is useful. It is in this spirit that the following list of virtues is offered. We shall see, as we proceed, that the list is not complete.

GROUP I: THE VIRTUES OF CONSCIENTIOUSNESS WITH RESPECT TO OTHERS

Fairness or Justice
Honesty
Gratitude
Trustworthiness
Obedience
Loyalty
Honor
Discretion

GROUP II: THE VIRTUES OF BENEVOLENCE

Caring
Kindness
Empathy
Sympathy
Forgiveness
Mercifulness

GROUP III: THE VIRTUES OF SELF-DISCIPLINE

Courage
Temperance or Self-Control
Patience
Humility (absence of arrogance)
Prudence
Integrity (acting consistently with the virtues and moral principles one values)

GROUP IV: THE VIRTUES OF SELF-ASSERTION AND SELF-DEVELOPMENT

Pride (healthy self-esteem)
Ambition
Perseverance

Independence of thought and action
Competitiveness

The first two groups are oriented toward others and the second two toward oneself. Groups I and III are somewhat negative, having to do with fulfilling obligations and disciplining oneself. Groups II and IV are more positive in nature, having to do with benefiting others and promoting one's own self-realization. Group I for the most part contains virtues for which Aristotle had especially high regard, although courage or bravery is in Group III. Group II contains virtues that are especially emphasized by feminist ethicists.

Virtue pluralism, however, raises two questions. The first question is, "Which virtues should I cultivate?" In answering this question, I will want to look at my own character and circumstances and determine my own capacities. I may also want to look at my chosen career. For example, we can refer to "professional virtues" as those especially important in professional life. A physician may want to emphasize the virtues of care and empathy, whereas an attorney may want to emphasize a strong sense of justice, as well as courage and loyalty to his client.

The second question is, "How shall I resolve conflicts of virtues?" We are sometimes pulled in different directions by different virtuous tendencies. I may not be able to show both mercy and fairness or both honesty and kindness in a situation of moral choice. Unfortunately, just as some situations do not permit the honoring of conflicting rules, some situations do not permit the honoring of conflicting virtues. It is up to me to determine in a given situation which virtue should take priority. How do I make this decision? One way of answering this question would be to have a hierarchy of virtues, just as we suggested a hierarchy of rights. If we had a hierarchy of virtues, such that some virtues take priority over others, we could refer to this scale in deciding between competing virtues in a choice situation. Unfortunately, such a hierarchy seems more difficult to create than a hierarchy of rights. Aristotle would place great value on justice, and some feminist writers would place special value on caring, but we must leave it to what Aristotle called "practical wisdom" to determine what virtues should take priority in a situation of moral choice.

CHECKLIST FOR APPLYING VIRTUE ETHICS

I.   Determine the alternative actions that are possible in the situation.
II. Determine the virtues and vices that correspond to these courses of action.

III. Evaluate the actions in terms of whether they appear to be grounded, either directly or indirectly, in the virtues appropriate to a morally worthy person in that situation.

    A. If the choice is between actions that manifest virtues and actions that manifest vices, select those actions that manifest the virtues.

    B. If the choice is between two or more actions that manifest different virtues, select the action that represents the most desirable virtues in the situation.

CONCEPT SUMMARY

The moral standard of virtue ethics says that an action is right if and only if it is what a virtuous person would do in the circumstances. Some ethicists believe virtue ethics has certain advantages over rule ethics, such as being more relevant to practical moral decisions, more appropriate for evaluating people (as opposed to actions), and more appropriate for evaluating lifestyles. A virtue is a disposition to do certain sorts of things when the appropriate circumstances arise. Virtues are states of character that are relatively stable and difficult to change. They also have an emotional component. As part of this emotional component, a truly virtuous person takes pleasure in being virtuous.

Aristotle's picture of the virtuous person emphasizes the values of military life and virtues that have often been associated with an aristocratic upper class. The virtues are "means" between extremes, but this must not be interpreted as necessarily a doctrine of moderation. Sometimes, for example, it is appropriate to get very angry, but anger should be appropriate to the situation. The virtuous person is usually happy, but happiness depends upon external factors, such as the existence of appropriate friends, a home environment appropriate for early training, and so forth. Such factors are to some extent beyond our control, so Aristotle recognizes a tragic element in human life.

Psychologist Carol Gilligan found that girls seem to use a different set of considerations in handling a moral dilemma. They are concerned with caring for others and for nurturing relationships, rather than applying rules and concepts of rights. Nel Noddings has developed these ideas, emphasizing that ethical caring is built on our natural tendency to care. She believes that "separatist thinking," which places barriers between an individual and others or one group and another group, should be replaced by a kind of thinking that attempts to consider the concerns and feelings of all of those affected by an ethical decision. Virtue pluralism recognizes that different people can emphasize different virtues and that there may not be any way to establish one virtue or set of virtues as superior overall.

THE VIRTUES AND PERSONAL AND SOCIAL ETHICS

Duties to Self

Aristotle's ethics places great emphasis on a person's duties to himself. The magnanimous man is clearly concerned with his self-image, and some would say that he is too self-absorbed. Nevertheless, the magnanimous man must apply himself to developing the virtues in himself that he can admire. Since happiness is activity in accordance with the virtues, this is understandable. A care-oriented ethicist will also have self-interested concerns, but for somewhat different reasons. An ethics oriented toward nurturing relationships and community must learn to cultivate both sides of the caring relationship, and that implies concern with self as well as others.

For both Aristotle and advocates of the ethics of care, then, one has an obligation to develop a virtuous character. While the virtues are best learned early in life, we have little control over our earliest training. So, as we mature, we have an obligation to nurture our own character development. In addition to developing the virtues that are praised by Aristotle or Noddings, it would seem that we also have an obligation to develop those virtues that would support our own chosen vocation and lifestyle. An aspiring physician should promote the virtues of care and nurturing, and an aspiring military officer should pay special attention to the virtues of courage and loyalty.

For virtue ethics, an important part of our obligation to ourselves is developing our abilities to apply the virtues in particular situations. Aristotle calls this ability "practical wisdom," and he recognizes that perception of the individual circumstances is important in knowing how to find the mean in a particular set of circumstances. For care ethics, we must be sensitive and empathetic enough to understand the feelings and interests of all of those involved in a moral dilemma. We must know how to encourage people to "talk it out," as Amy said, and come to a consensus, if possible, about what to do in a situation of moral choice.

Many of the virtues that Aristotle praised are compatible with an ethics of care as well, even though in some instances they would take a somewhat different form. It may take a great deal of courage to be caring, as when Quaker medical personnel risk death to rescue fallen soldiers. We can easily think of ways in which the ethics of care could incorporate some of the other characteristically Aristotelian virtues.

Because virtue ethics places such importance on developing those character traits that make one a virtuous person, it is, at least in part, an ethics of
self-realization. This is especially true of the ethics of Aristotle, but it is true to
some extent of the ethics of care as well. As we have pointed out, one must
cultivate both sides of the dyadic caring relationship, and this implies concern
for oneself. Philosopher David Norton formulates the chief moral imperative
of a self-actualization ethics in this way: "It is every person's primary responsibility first to discover the *daimon* [the principle of self-actualization] within
him and thereafter to live in accordance with it."[27] Like Aristotle, Norton
believes that self-actualization is a project for a lifetime. Norton's focus on self-
actualization leads to an emphasis on the virtues appropriate to the four stages
of development: childhood, adolescence, maturity, and old age.[28] The most
prominent feature of childhood is dependence on others, and the corresponding virtue of childhood is *receptivity* to the instructions of elders. Adolescence
is the time when individuals free themselves from the supervision of parents
and other adults and find their own mode of self-actualization. The characteristic virtue of adolescence is *openness* to new values and experiences. In
maturity, a person finds his or her own path to self-actualization, so the virtue
of maturity is *fidelity* to one's self-development. Old age is characterized by the
completion of life; the virtue appropriate to old age is *acceptance* of the life
one has lived. Notice that these virtues are not on our earlier list of virtues, and
they could well be added.

Duties to Others

We are obligated to manifest the virtues in our relationships with others.
We should be honest, fair, loyal, caring, and so forth. In addition, we have
an obligation to promote the development of the virtues in others, at least
in those with whom we have a special relationship. For example, parents
must promote the moral development of their children. The use of stories,
important in all moral education, is especially important in the moral
education of children. Stories about George Washington or "honest Abe"
Lincoln or stories about the saints have always been vehicles for moral
education.

Virtue ethicists have long recognized that friendship plays a special
role in the good life and in the development of virtue. Following the
inspiration of Aristotle, one writer defines friendship as "the mutually
acknowledged and reciprocal exchange of goodwill and affection that exists
among individuals who share an interest in each other on the basis of

---

[27] David L. Norton, *Personal Destinies* (Princeton, NJ: Princeton University Press, 1976), p. 16.

[28] Ibid., chap. 6.

virtue, pleasure, or utility."[29] Our own individual form of self-development is aided and sustained by our relationships with others. As this definition points out, friendship is not only an inestimable aid to pleasure and utility (achieving our goals), but also a promoter of virtue. We can be more honest or courageous or compassionate because our friends admire those qualities in us and we admire those qualities in them. So one of the best means of promoting the virtues in others is by means of friendship.

Social Ethics

Aristotle's political philosophy is contained in his *Politics*, a book that was intended to be read in conjunction with the *Nicomachean Ethics*. In the *Politics* Aristotle inquires into the purpose of the state and finds, not surprisingly, that the purpose of the state is to promote human happiness. Since the happy life is the virtuous life, the state must promote the virtues in its citizens. The first thing to remember here is that without the state (or the social order in the larger sense, which is what the Greek term *polis* implies), at least many of the virtues would not be possible at all. One cannot be generous if he lives on an island by himself, and certainly, friendship is not possible apart from other humans whom one can have as friends. The second thing to keep in mind is that the state promotes virtue in a more positive way through moral education, which is perhaps the most important job of rulers. For Noddings moral education is equally important.

If we consider the development of virtue to be a form of self-actualization, we can ask what kind of state best promotes self-actualization. David Norton believes the political order most conducive to self-actualization is what he calls "developmental democracy," where the "paramount function of government is to provide the necessary but non-self-suppliable conditions for optimizing opportunities of individual self-discovery and self-development."[30]

These conditions, Norton believes, are different for different stages in a person's life. Children need education; adolescents need the opportunity for new experiences; adults need meaningful work; the elderly need physical security. Citizens should have rights to those conditions necessary for self-realization. Some of these rights are "negative," such as the right to protection against physical violence, forcible intrusion into one's property or person, and fraud. Other rights, however, are "positive," such as the

---

[29] Nancy Sherman, *The Fabric of Character* (Oxford: Clarendon Press, 1989), p. 124. See *NE*, VIII.2.

[30] David Norton, *Democracy and Moral Development* (Berkeley: University of California Press, 1991), p. 44.

rights to the necessities of life, education, and the variety of experiences that a person needs to make crucial decisions about the course of one's life. If Norton is correct, a virtue ethics cannot be developed independently of a doctrine of rights.

Perhaps the most obvious contribution that democracy can make to the development of character and virtue is the part it can play in promoting independence of thought and self-reliance. A citizen of a democracy, having a say as she does in government, must learn to think for herself, examine the facts, and be able to come to independent decisions about what policies the state should adopt. There are other virtues a good citizen of a democracy must possess. He should develop a sense of fairness and an ability to consider the opinions of others. The give-and-take of public discussion of issues should develop these traits. Finally, public discussion presupposes honesty, for the validity of public debate depends on the participants' being honest in the presentation of their views.

Concept Summary

Aristotle's magnanimous man is clearly concerned with his own moral perfection, and a care ethicist must develop those virtues, such as compassion and empathy, which enable him or her to exhibit care and cultivate relationships. A virtue ethicist will also need to develop those skills necessary to apply the virtues in particular situations. Norton describes the cultivation of the self at the various phases of a person's development, from childhood to maturity. We also have an obligation to promote the maturation of others in the virtues. For Aristotle, friendship, one of the greatest sources of happiness, would not be possible if one could not have virtuous friends.

In social ethics, virtue ethics looks for a social system that provides the most favorable conditions for the development of the virtues. Norton finds a form of democracy the most favorable system for such development, and he calls this social system "developmental democracy." The term suggests that the system promotes self-actualization and the cultivation of the virtues. Democracy also promotes independence of thought and other virtues necessary for participation in democratic life.

Applying Virtue Ethics

We can now apply virtue ethics to some cases involving moral decision, following the methodology outlined in the checklist. The first and fourth cases will be analyzed from the standpoint of the ethics of care, the second case from the standpoint of virtue pluralism, and the third and fifth cases from the standpoint of Aristotle's virtue ethics.

Case 1: Abortion

Mrs. Plass is seven months pregnant. She is considering an abortion, because she has decided that she does not want to have another child. She is twenty-nine years old and does not want to have a college-age child when she is in her fifties. She has been thinking about this decision for three months, but has just now decided that she wants to have an abortion. She has also just won a free cruise in the Caribbean, and she will miss it if she does not have the abortion. Is it morally permissible for her to have an abortion?

We shall look at this case from the standpoint of the ethics of care.[31]

1. The first step is to determine the alternative actions that are possible in the situation. In this case, Mrs. Plass can either decide to have the abortion or not to have the abortion.
2. Mrs. Plass must then determine the virtues and vices that correspond to these two options. Because we are focusing on the ethics of care, we shall take care as the relevant virtue and non-caring as the relevant vice. Rather than approaching the issue from the standpoint of the abstract rights of the fetus to life or the mother to privacy, we shall look at the situation through the language of relations. Looking at the fetus, the primary consideration is the ability of the fetus to call forth our desire to care for it.[32] We must also consider the caring relationships of the mother and other members of the family.
3. As Noddings points out, the embryo does not have the ability to call forth a strong desire to care; we do not hold funerals for lost embryos. On the other hand, a newborn infant has the ability to call forth a strong desire to care. The status of the fetus is between these two extremes. Rather than deriving our assessment of our relationship to the fetus from our assessment of its moral standing, Noddings believes that we should assess the moral standing of the fetus from our assessment of our relationship to it. "A creature that can respond to us in ways that call forth our desire to care is one to which we shall accord something like moral standing."[33] By this

---

[31] Many of the ideas in this case analysis come from Nell Noddings, *Women and Evil* (Berkeley, CA: University of California Press, 1989), especially pp. 142–154.

[32] Ibid., p. 151.

[33] Ibid., p. 151.

criterion, early abortions are morally permissible, and later abortions are generally less so.

However, in addition to the ability of the fetus to call forth a desire to care, we must also consider the mother and other members of the family and the extent to which they exhibit the ethics of care. Mrs. Plass does not seem to have a caring attitude toward the child, although we have said that at three months its ability to elicit a caring relationship is limited. Still, her concern seems to be exclusively with her own needs, and this is troublesome from the standpoint of the ethics of care. It seems, in fact, that her attitude is selfish and self-centered. We are not told anything about the father, other possible children, grandparents, and others whose relationship is important from the standpoint of the ethics of care. It is clear, however, that from the standpoint of the ethics of care, the decision whether to have an abortion should be made in a way that involves them. A caring person would have to make the decision in this way.

In the light of these considerations, the decision of Mrs. Plass to have an abortion for such trivial and self-centered reasons is at least morally problematic from the standpoint of the ethics of care, if not morally impermissible.

Case 2: Animal Rights

Mr. Myerson is considering investing in a farm to raise claves for veal. The calves will be housed in cages that prevent them from moving, to insure that the veal will be tender. Before deciding whether to invest, he visits the farm. He finds that the animals are clearly uncomfortable and appear to have developed physically in abnormal ways. Attendants at the farm say the animals show signs of unhappiness and depression. Should Mr. Myerson make the investment? We shall also look at this case from the standpoint of the ethics of care.

1. Mr. Myerson must first determine the alternative actions that are possible in the situation. We shall say that the alternatives are to make the investment or not to make the investment.
2. Mr. Myerson must first decide whether the ethics of care applies to our attitudes toward animals. Because empathy is an important aspect of caring, and because it would be very difficult not to experience empathy with animals, we must assume that the ethics of care applies to animals. Most people would probably think that a person who does not show sympathy and compassion toward animals, could not show it to humans either.

3. Now we must evaluate the two courses of action in terms of whether they appear to be grounded, either directly or indirectly, in the virtues appropriate to a morally worthy person. In evaluating the actions, Mr. Myerson will have to choose between the virtues of kindness, sympathy, and caring and the virtues of prudence and ambition. From the standpoint of the ethics of care, the first three virtues are the most important, and they seem incompatible with this kind of cage farming. Therefore, Mr. Myerson should not make the investment.

Case 3: The Job vs. Conscience

Gerald Wahr is scheduled to complete his degree in chemical engineering in June. He anticipated returning to the family farm to help with its operation.[34] In early May, his father became seriously ill, and Gerald is now convinced that the only way to save the family farm is to take a job in engineering. Most of his fellow seniors have already taken jobs, and the interviewing season is over. The only employment opportunity Gerald finds is with Pro-Growth Pesticides. The family farm is an organic farm, however, and Gerald's father has always strongly opposed the use of pesticides. Gerald himself has become convinced that pesticides harm the environment generally and farm products in particular. Gerald also knows he will be asked about his views on pesticides. What should he do? Let us look at this issue from the standpoint of Aristotelian virtue ethics.

1. Gerald must first determine the alternative actions that are possible in the situation. He thinks of three possibilities. (a) He could refuse to interview for the job, (b) interview but answer questions about his views on pesticides honestly, or (c) interview and misrepresent his views on pesticides in order to get the job.
2. In determining the virtues and vices that correspond to these courses of action, Gerald might come up with the following analysis. (a) If he refuses to interview for the job, he will continue to be an honest person and he will also maintain his integrity. That is, he will continue to be a person who acts consistently with his principles. He may, however, not manifest proper loyalty to his family, because he would fail to help them keep the farm. He would show loyalty to the family ideals, however. (b) If he interviews for the job but answers questions about his views on

---

[34] This case is an adaptation of one in Michael S. Pritchard, *Teaching Engineering Ethics: A Case Study Approach*, National Science Foundation, Grant No. DIR-8820837, pp. 244–263.

pesticides honestly, he will preserve his honesty, but may compromise his integrity by applying for (and possibly getting) a job that would be inconsistent with his principles. He will preserve his loyalty to his family, however, at least in the sense of helping them keep the farm. (c) If he interviews for the job and misrepresents his views on pesticides, he will manifest loyalty to his family, but fail to be honest or a person of integrity.

3. Now we must evaluate the alternatives open to Gerald in terms of whether they are grounded, either directly or indirectly, in the virtues appropriate to a morally worthy person. How should he evaluate these three options? He will fail to properly manifest at least one of the virtues he prizes no matter what he does. Options (a) and (b) will violate only one of the virtues, while (c) will violate two. Option (c), furthermore, seems to more directly manifest the vices of dishonesty and lack of integrity. While (c) seems to be the least desirable, the choice between (a) and (b) is more difficult. If he can find another job opportunity, clearly option (a) is the most desirable. If this possibility is not open to him, it may depend upon what kind of person Gerald most wants to be: a loyal person or a person with integrity. From the standpoint of Aristotle's virtue portrait, the magnanimous man would probably want to be consistent with his own values even more than he would want to be loyal. Integrity seems more fundamental to the magnanimous man's self-image than loyalty. From this perspective, Gerald should refuse the interview.

Case 4: The Patient Wants to Die

A 36-year-old accountant, whom we shall call Charles Johnson, married and the father of three young children, is diagnosed as having immunoblastic lymphadenopathy, a fatal malignant tumor of the lymph nodes. He has been receiving a variety of treatments, yet his condition has steadily worsened. Charles knows that all surgical and medical measures have been exhausted. He suffers daily from excruciating nerve-root pain; he must take addicting doses of narcotics but still is not free from pain. The expenses of his treatment are rapidly exhausting his family's financial resources. Charles' wife and family are beginning to withdraw from him emotionally, in anticipation of his inevitable death. Having reconciled himself to his death, he asks the doctor for the means of killing himself to end his pain, the suffering of his family, and the depletion of the funds that are so important for his family's well-being. Is it morally permissible for the physician to acquiesce in this request?[35] We shall look at this question from the standpoint of the ethics of care.

1. For the purposes of this analysis, the options of the physician are to assist the patient or not to assist the patient in ending his life.
2. We are considering only the implications of the virtue of care here, so the question is: Which option best fulfills or manifests the ethics of care?
3. From the standpoint of the ethics of care, which emphasizes relationships, this case gives evidence of developing into a tragic situation. Not only is Charles in great pain, but his family is breaking the bonds of love just at the time when he needs their support the most. Noddings' advice is appropriate: "When someone is suffering and wishes to die, all affected parties should take part in the decision."[36] The psychological pain of separation from those he loves the most should not be added to Charles' physical pain. Only discussion will reveal whether there is a stable and well-thought-out preference for death. The decision to die should be made, not just by Charles, but by the entire family. The group decision would unite the family, whereas the individual decision by Charles alone will only separate him from his family and make his death more painful for everyone.

Case 5: Perilous Pursuit

James is walking in a nightclub district and is suddenly accosted by some thugs who take his billfold and run down a dark alley. He sees that they drop the billfold but have taken his money. He retrieves his billfold, but hesitates before running after them. Should he continue to pursue them down the dark alley or let them go?

1. The alternative actions here are to pursue the robbers or let them go.
2. If we think of this situation as involving a dilemma with regard to courage, we should keep in mind that courage is a mean between cowardice and rashness. In this case the question would be whether James' running after the thugs and attempting to retrieve his money would exemplify courage or rashness.
3. As Aristotle points out, determining what to do in a particular circumstance requires practical wisdom. Of course, it also requires as much detailed knowledge of the situation as possible. Let us

---

[35] This case was supplied by Harry. S. Lipscomb, M.D. Used with permission.

[36] Noddings, *Women and Evil*, p. 132.

suppose that James saw a knife flashing in the dark and that the alley is dark indeed. Let us further suppose that he only had $50 in his billfold and it was money he could well afford to lose. In such circumstances, running after the thugs would probably exemplify rashness more than courage.

EVALUATING VIRTUE ETHICS

Criterion 1: Coherence and Consistency

Virtue ethics has no set of principles, so one cannot say the theory is incoherent because its principles are incompatible with each other. It is true, however, that a person may not be able to embody all of the virtues in an equally developed state in his life. A person who is especially courageous may not be as temperate in his daily life as a less courageous person. Care and the associated virtues of empathy and interconnectedness may be associated with a different psychological type than those virtues associated with the magnanimous or great-souled man, who prizes his independence. But this opposition can be overdrawn; even the magnanimous man can display care and concern for his friends and those he considers his inferiors. Certainly, however, different virtues may give rise to different moral judgments, as Case 3 illustrates; but different rules can also lead to different moral judgments, so virtue ethics does not seem to have any special difficulties with the first criterion.

Criterion 2: Justification of the Moral Standard

There are at lest two ways we might justify the moral standard of virtue ethics. First, if virtues could always be correlated with moral rules and the moral rules are themselves justified, we could provide a foundation for the virtues. Unfortunately, virtues cannot always be correlated with moral rules. Consider the following list of virtues and correlative moral rules.

Virtue	Moral Rule
Honesty	Act honestly
Courage	Act courageously
Compassion	Help those who need help, when appropriate
Gratitude	Express gratitude to our benefactors

The first two virtues can be expressed reasonably adequately by the corresponding rule. With the second and third virtues, however, the correspondence is more problematic. Cultivating the virtue of compassion requires us to have a certain inner attitude of concern toward others, especially those who are suffering. Merely obeying a rule cannot fulfill this requirement. This is even more true of the virtue of gratitude. We can perform apparent acts of gratitude without the motive, but genuine gratitude is constituted by the motive of gratitude, for "what constitutes an act of gratitude is the motive from which it is done."[37] Ungrateful people can fulfill the rule as well as grateful people, so that the virtue of gratitude is not equivalent to the moral rule.

Thus, although there is always a moral rule corresponding to a virtue, the two might not always be equivalent. In the absence of this equivalence, it is difficult to see how the virtues can be justified by an appeal to moral rules.

A second way virtues could be justified is by an argument that they are necessary for human flourishing or well-being. A virtue ethicist might argue that people cannot be happy or develop their potentialities without cultivating the virtues. We cannot achieve our potential without being courageous, honest, self-disciplined, and so forth. Further, we cannot achieve our full potential apart from life in a society where these virtues are honored and cultivated by others.

This argument has obvious limitations. It may be that achieving any personal goal requires the development of some virtues, but not necessarily all. The composer Richard Wagner may have been creative and self-disciplined, but he was not humble or compassionate. Others are humble and compassionate, but lack self-discipline. Still others achieve other goals by dishonesty and ruthlessness. People probably need to have some virtue to flourish, but they need not have all of them. It is not clear, therefore, how far this approach can go in justifying the virtues. We must also assume, of course, that self-realization is a worthy goal. Given these problems, the best justification of virtue ethics may be that it gives a plausible account of some areas of moral reasoning in common morality.

Criterion 3: Plausibility of Moral Judgments

Most people would regard the virtues listed in the four groups as morally praiseworthy. We have also pointed out that some areas of moral thinking in common morality, such as, for example, considering whether to do

---

[37] Walter Schaller, "Are Virtues No More Than Dispositions to Obey Moral Rules?" in Louis J. Pojman, *Ethical Theory* (Belmont: CA: Wadsworth, 1998), p. 391. Reprinted from *Philosophia* 20 (July 1990), pp. 1–2.

something that is above and beyond the call of duty, are best accounted for by virtue ethics. It is true that when the virtues conflict in concrete situations, we can disagree with the way an individual resolves the conflict. This would be a criticism of an individual's resolution of the conflict, however, but not of virtue ethics as such. Therefore, we can say that virtue ethics rates rather high by the criterion of plausibility.

Criterion 4: Usefulness in Resolving Ethical Conflicts

Virtue ethics may not rate as high as some versions of rule ethics by the criterion of usefulness. We have seen that there is no agreed-upon hierarchy of the virtues, so virtue ethics does not provide clear guidelines for resolving conflicts between virtues in specific situations. The virtue ethicist believes that a person who has developed moral character will usually do the right thing, but we have already pointed out that people who manifest different virtues or whose virtues are developed to different degrees might not always come to the same conclusion. Therefore, virtue ethics might not be helpful in resolving some ethical conflicts. We have already pointed out, however, that it may prove more useful than rule ethics in some decision situations where considerations of virtue appear to be paramount and in decisions about supererogatory acts and about character formation and lifestyle.

CONCEPT SUMMARY

Virtue ethics has no principles that can conflict, and so does not suffer from any obvious incoherence, nor does it necessarily give rise to inconsistent moral judgments.

Virtue ethics can be justified by appealing to the corresponding rules or by an argument that one must be virtuous to flourish. Both of these justifications, however, are subject to criticism. The correlation of moral rules and virtues does not show that they are equivalent, and this still leaves open the question of how the moral rules are themselves justified. Although some virtues may be necessary to any significant form of self-realization or flourishing, all the virtues are not.

Most of us would agree that the virtues are desirable, so we can say that virtue ethics rates high by the standard of plausibility. Virtue ethics does not give as much guidance as one would like in resolving conflicts between virtues in specific situations, however, even though it is useful in understanding some decisions where considerations of virtue appear to be paramount, and in decisions about supererogatory acts and about character formation and lifestyle.

APPLYING THE MORAL THEORIES

Our evaluations of moral theories do not allow us to say that one moral theory is clearly more rationally defensible and a better account of common morality than all the others. Nevertheless, the following points, directed primarily toward the application of the four rule-oriented theories, should be kept in mind.

First, we have shown that argument about moral principles and theories is possible. If our aim is to pursue rationality in ethics, we cannot say just anything we please in ethics. Even if complete agreement on the proper moral principles is unlikely, ethics is still a rational activity. There are constraints on what moral principles can be defended.

Second, the moral theories tend to come to similar conclusions in many areas. All of the theories would agree that murder, lying, theft, slavery, rape, assault, slander, and fraud, for example, are wrong. Even the egoist would probably prefer to live in a society in which these acts were forbidden, provided others would agree to the prohibitions. The four theories converge, then, on a core area of morality.

This convergence is obscured by the types of cases usually discussed in ethics texts, including this one. The cases presented for analysis, in both the text and Appendix II, are usually the more difficult and controversial ones, not the core cases on which most people (and most moral theories) would agree. For example, no cases pose the question of whether murdering a parent to collect an inheritance is morally permissible. All of the theories (with the possible exception of act egoism) would agree that it is not morally permissible. On the other hand, there might be cases that ask the question of whether it is wrong to administer a lethal dose of an analgesic to a person who is suffering from terminal cancer, is in great pain, and wants to die. These latter cases are the kinds that are morally troublesome and intellectually interesting. However, exclusive focus on them can convey the false impression that all moral evaluations are difficult and controversial.

Third, some theories do come out better in our rankings than the others do. Using the criteria for evaluation we developed, utilitarianism and the ethics of respect for persons seem to be more acceptable theories, all things considered. Virtue ethics is perhaps most useful in certain situations. Remember that virtue ethics focuses on persons rather than actions.

This conclusion about the general superiority of utilitarianism and the ethics of respect for persons is widely accepted among moral philosophers. Thus, although a single theory has not yet gained universal acceptance, utilitarianism and the ethics of respect for persons are widely thought to be the most rationally defensible moral theories. So the moral principles that are justified by these theories would be the most rationally defensible moral principles.

Fourth, moral philosophers have reached some degree of consensus about what should be done when utilitarianism and the ethics of respect for persons disagree. In general, the ethics of respect for persons should prevail except when utilitarian considerations are very strong, or the infringements on the proper consideration due individuals is minimal. Thus, killing a person and using his organs to save the lives of several other people would not be morally permissible, even though greater overall utility might be produced. But suppose a small number of people are carriers of a plague that will kill 99 percent of the people who contract it. Suppose further that these individuals became carriers of the plague through no fault of their own and that they will not themselves die of it. Suppose that, because of unusual conditions, such as those that would prevail after a nuclear war, it is not possible to isolate the individuals from other humans. Would it be permissible to kill them to prevent massive deaths? Many moralists would say yes, even though the disease carriers have done nothing worthy of death and would not die of the plague themselves. After making these points, however, we must still concede that morality has a place for personal judgment and even personal commitment. Moral theory can provide enormous insight into moral problems and their solutions. Even apart from resolving moral controversies, it can help us understand more clearly the moral issues at stake in a controversy.

In analyzing the cases in Appendix II, you should keep several things in mind. First, you must decide which moral theories to use. Although it might be desirable to use all of the theories in analyzing every case, sometimes some theories will obviously be more relevant than others.

Second, you will have to decide what factual issues are raised by a case. Sometimes a so-called "moral" controversy turns out to be a disagreement over the facts and not a disagreement over moral principles at all. When the factual disagreement is resolved, the controversy ends. For example, a disagreement about whether an engineer should object to a new chemical process that results in emitting a substance from a smokestack might depend entirely on whether the substance is harmful to people or the environment.

The case descriptions will not always present all the facts you need to resolve the issue. If you were in an actual situation, you would be able to investigate the issue and perhaps resolve the factual uncertainty. Because you do not have this option here, you will have to make certain factual assumptions and clearly state what they are. As we all know, however, investigation will not always resolve factual uncertainties. If you have reason to believe that investigation would not resolve a question about the facts, it is better to attempt to decide how the ethical issue should be resolved in the face of factual uncertainty.

Third, in analyzing cases, you should always watch for issues involving the meanings of crucial terms. Sometimes a so-called "moral" controversy is actually a disagreement over the meanings of certain terms and whether the terms apply in a given situation. Once these debates are settled, there may be no further disagreement. Two people might disagree about the definition of *lie* or *breaking confidentiality* or whether using another's intellectual property is extensive enough to be called "theft." Most people agree that lying, breaking confidentiality, and stealing are wrong, at least under most circumstances, so the question hinges on the problems in applying the moral principles involving lying, breaking confidentiality, and stealing. If two people disagree over the definition of a "lie," for example, they may also disagree over whether a statement is really a lie, and so over whether the moral principle "Don't lie" is relevant.

Fourth, keep in mind that deciding whether a principle applies (a relevance problem, in our terminology) is not always sufficient to resolve a moral issue. Sometimes more than one moral principle is relevant in a situation, producing a conflict problem. The circumstances may be such that, even though a course of action may involve lying, breaking confidentiality, or stealing, for example, it still might be the right thing to do. Suppose a physician believes that breaking patient-physician confidentiality is justified to expose a case of child abuse. In this case, he believes that the moral principle requiring us to protect the innocent overrides the moral principle requiring us to keep confidentiality.

Fifth, in attempting to resolve the cases in Appendix II in which there is a conflict problem, remember to look for creative middle-way solutions. That is, if the competing moral considerations seem roughly equally important, look for solutions that attempt to do justice to all of the competing considerations. For example, Martin Luther King, Jr., developed a policy of nonviolent resistance. The policy enabled him to resist injustice but to do so in a way that did not involve violence (at least on his part) and he accepted the legal consequences of breaking the law. Thus, he was able to honor his desire both to promote social justice and to do so in a way that respected the basic institutions of the United States. Of course, if one obligation is far more important than the other, the creative middle-way solution is inappropriate. The more important obligation must be honored at the expense of the less important one.

Sixth, it is worth emphasizing again that in some cases rational people can disagree over both which moral theory is most appropriate and what conclusions a given moral theory yields. Moral theory has its limits. It cannot provide automatic answers in all moral problems, nor can it take the place of the morally sensitive and discerning individual. Moral theory is not a dictatorial master but a helpful guide in the moral life.

CASES FOR ANALYSIS

Case 1: A Lawyer's Dilemma

In July 1973, Robert Garrow, a 38-year-old mechanic from Syracuse, New York, killed four persons, apparently at random.[1] The four were camping in the Adirondack Mountains. In early August, following a vigorous manhunt, Garrow was captured by state police and indicted for the murder of a student from Schenectady. At the time of the arrest, no evidence connected Garrow to the other deaths; in fact, two of the people were not even known to be dead. One was a young Illinois woman, the other a Syracuse high school girl listed as a runaway. The body of the third, a camping companion of the Illinois woman, was found on July 20, before Garrow's capture. The court appointed two Syracuse lawyers, Francis R. Belge and Frank H. Armani, to defend Garrow.

Some weeks later, during discussions with his two lawyers, Garrow told them that he had raped and killed a woman in a mine shaft. Belge and Armani located the mine shaft and the body of the Illinois woman but did not take their discovery to the police. The body was finally discovered four months later by two children playing in the mine. In September, the lawyers found the second body by following Garrow's directions. This discovery, too, went unrecorded; the girl's body was uncovered by a student in December.

The Illinois woman's father read that Belge and Armani were defending a man accused of killing a camper in the Adirondacks. Knowing that his daughter's companion had also been found dead there, he journeyed to Syracuse to talk to the lawyers. He asked whether they knew anything about his daughter, but they denied having any knowledge that would help him. Belge and Armani maintained their silence until the following June. Then, to try to show that he was insane, Garrow made statements from the witness stand that implicated him in the other three murders. At a press conference the next day, Belge and Armani outlined for the first time the sequence of events.

The local community was outraged. The lawyers, however, believed they had honored the letter and spirit of their professional duty in a tough case. "We both,

---

[1] Reported in several sources, including "Slayer's Two Lawyers Kept Secret of Two More Killings," *New York Times*, June 20, 1974, p. 1.

knowing how the parents feel, wanted to advise them where the bodies were," Belge said, "but since it was a privileged communication, we could not reveal any information that was given to us in confidence."

Their silence was based on the legal code that admonishes the lawyer to "preserve the confidence and secrets of a client." The lawyer-client "privilege" against disclosure of confidences is one of the oldest and most iron-clad in the law. If the defendant has no duty to confess his guilt or complicity in a crime, it can make no sense to assert that his lawyer has such a duty. Otherwise, the argument goes, the accused will tell his lawyer at best a deficient version of the facts, and the lawyer cannot as effectively defend the client. This argument frequently seems unconvincing; it certainly did to the people of Syracuse. Should the lawyers have revealed the whereabouts of the Illinois woman's body to her father?

Case 2: The Use of Cadavers for Crash Testing

Germany's Heidelberg University used more than two hundred corpses, including those of eight children, in automobile crash tests.[2] The university claimed it received relatives' permission. The research ministry of Baden-Wuertemberg (the state in which the university is located) ordered the university to document these permissions. The revelation of these tests drew immediate protests in Germany. Rudolph Hammerschmidt, spokesman for the Roman Catholic German Bishops' Conference, objected, "Even the dead possess human dignity. This research should be done with mannequins." ADAC, Germany's largest automobile club, issued a statement saying, "In an age when experiments on animals are being put into question, such tests must be carried out on dummies and not on children's cadavers."

German law permits the use of cadavers for research if relatives grant permission. In the crash tests, the bodies are strapped into cars that are smashed into other cars, walls, and barriers. The impact on humans is measured with cameras and electronic sensors. Heidelberg's Dr. Reiner Mattern, head of the forensic pathology department, indicated that children's cadavers had not been tested since 1989 but that testing of adult cadavers is continuing. He added that the tests have saved lives, including those of children.

Clarence Ditlow, head of the Center for Auto Safety, a public advocacy group in Washington, D.C., reported that tests with cadavers were conducted by at least two research teams in the United States during the 1980s, including Detroit's Wayne State University. Ditlow said that the center advocates three criteria for such testing: (1) prior consent by the deceased person, (2) informed consent of the family, and (3) assurance that the data sought by the tests cannot be gained from using dummies.

---

[2] This case is based on Terrence Petty, "Use of Corpses in Auto-Crash Tests Outrages Germans," *Kalamazoo Gazette,* November 24, 1993, p. A3. The case was prepared by Michael S. Pritchard and originally printed in Charles E. Harris, Jr., Michael S. Pritchard, and Michael J. Rabins, *Engineering Ethics: Concepts and Cases* (Belmont, CA: Wadsworth, 1995), pp. 183–184. Used with permission.

Robert Wartner, a Wayne State spokesman, said the university's Bioengineering Center conducted tests as apart of a study by the federal government's Centers for Disease Control. However, he added, "Cadavers are used only when alternatives could not produce useful safety research."

Time magazine (December 6, 1993, p. 70) reported that German parents were initially upset when asked whether their children's bodies could be used in auto crashes. However, nearly all, said *Time*, granted permission when they were told that data from the tests are "vital for constructing more than 120 types of instrumented dummies, ranging in size from infants to adults, that can simulate dozens of human reactions in a crash." In addition, despite a 75 percent increase in the number of cars on the road over the last twenty years, the fatality rate decreased more than 50 percent. "Much of that improvement," *Time* said, "is due to the introduction of such devices as seat belts, air bags, safer windshields and stronger doors—all of which were developed with the aid of crash dummies." Is the use of cadavers in crash testing morally justified?

Case 3: Highway Safety Improvements

Tom Byrne, a young civil engineer, is assigned the task of spending $25,000 for highway improvements.[3] Option A is to spend the money for improvements at an urban intersection, which 24,000 vehicles use each day. The intersection averages two fatalities and six injuries each year at the intersection. Option B is to spend the money for improvements at a rural intersection, which 6,000 vehicles use each day. The intersection averages one fatality and two injuries each year. Government figures at the time placed a value of $235,000 on each human life and $11,200 on each injury. Byrne sees that he will prevent more deaths and accidents by choosing option A. He also sees that the chance of a person's getting killed or injured is greater at the rural intersection. Which option should he choose?

Case 4: The TV Antenna

Marsha Johnston works for Antenna Engineering, which has designed the antennas and a thousand-foot TV antenna tower for a local TV station.[4] The tower has been put in place, except for the last section containing the antenna baskets. Because the antenna baskets are attached to the top section, it cannot be lifted in the same way as the other sections. To hold the last section away from the tower as it is hoisted so that the antenna baskets will not be damaged, the construction workers, none of whom are engineers, bolt some lifting arms to the section. These arms, which extend beyond the edge of the

---

[3] This case is based on one developed by James Taylor of Notre Dame University.

[4] This case is a modification of a real case. It is described in more detail in R. W. Flumerfelt, C. E. Harris, M. J. Rabins, and C. H. Samson, eds., *Introducing Ethics Case Studies into Required Undergraduate Engineering Courses*, final report to the National Science Foundation on Grant No. DIR-9012252, November 1992, pp. 231–261.

tower section, would allow the section to be held far enough away from the tower to prevent damage to the antenna baskets. Not being confident that this method of lifting the final section is sound from an engineering standpoint, the construction workers call Johnston, asking, "Can you look at our proposal for lifting the last section to be sure it is safe?"

Johnston calls her boss, Bill Mason, the president of the design firm, to relay the request. His response was emphatic:

> No way! If we are involved in construction in any way and there is an accident, we are liable. Our contract was only to design the tower and the baskets. We have no responsibility for construction. We tried to be the nice guys once before and ended up being sued for $250,000. We are a small company and cannot afford to lose our insurance.

Johnston knows enough about the contractor's proposed way of lifting the last section to suspect that it is indeed unsafe and that there is a real possibility that the section could fall, killing the construction workers who will be riding the section to the top of the tower. Unfortunately, she also knows that Mason's fears for the welfare of his company are legitimate and that she will probably lose her job if she gives the contractors any advice. What should she do?

Case 5: Violent Lyrics

A rap CD contains lyrics that appear to advocate violence against women. The lyrics suggest that women are sexually excited by being slapped and receiving other forms of physical and verbal abuse. The lyrics also suggest that men can take a woman's protest as a way of actually giving consent to sexual intercourse and that rape is a myth. In response to criticism, members of the rap group respond that they have a right to advocate their views and that they sincerely believe males in our society need to reclaim their masculinity.

Critics of the group argue that the group encourages rape and abuse of women. Defenders of the group either agree with the group's philosophy or argue that freedom of expression should override other considerations. Which side has the stronger moral argument?

Case 6: An Unusual Request

James Harrison is a 17-year-old high school senior and an honors student. He has been studying the world population problem and is convinced that the explosive growth of the human population must be stopped. In an attempt to do his part to slow population growth, he asks his local physician for a vasectomy. His physician refuses, arguing that Harrison is not mature enough to make such a decision. Harrison argues that people his age are not prevented from climbing mountains, racing cars, engaging in risky sexual practices, and doing many other things that can affect their lives in even more serious ways. Therefore, he should be allowed to have a vasectomy if he wants one. Was his physician morally justified in her decision?

Case 7: Should the Physician Tell?

While 75-year-old Ethel Morgan is undergoing a routine hernia operation, the surgeon discovers that she has one undescended testicle. The surgeon informs Morgan's family physician, who orders a genetic analysis. The analysis shows that she is genetically male. The family physician knows that Morgan was never able to have children and that she has one adopted daughter. He also knows that she is happily married and that both she and her husband would be deeply disturbed if they knew about the undescended testicle and the genetic analysis. Should the physician reveal the information? Should he have ordered the genetic tests? What if Morgan were 21 instead of 75?

Case 8: Killing Pain

Mike Brown has terminal throat cancer, which produces excruciating pain. His physician knows that the analgesic necessary to eliminate the pain will itself be life shortening. The physician believes that such practices are wrong. Should she administer the analgesic anyhow, because her patient requests it?

Case 9: Amish Schools

Zachary Yoder wants his children to attend Amish schools rather than the public schools in Pennsylvania. Others argue that the Amish schools are inferior in quality and will make it virtually impossible for the children to leave the Amish community because they will not have a sufficient education to find jobs elsewhere. They also maintain that the children cannot gain sufficient information about the larger American society from Amish schools, so the children cannot make an informed decision as to whether to leave or stay in the Amish community. Thus, the free choice of the children cannot be preserved if they attend Amish schools.

Yoder argues that if his children go to public schools, they would not have a sufficient knowledge of Amish culture to make an intelligent and genuinely free choice about whether to remain a part of it. He also states that they will be alienated from their culture by peer pressures and the influence of secular American society. Finally, he says that he has the right to determine the education of his children. Members of the local school board are considering going to court to force Yoder to send his children to the public schools. Would they be morally justified in doing this?

Case 10: How Far Should Friendship Go?

Shawn and Kevin, two young men in their mid-twenties, have been close friends since they met during their college years.[5] They share numerous similar interests and greatly enjoy each other's company. Kevin gratefully acknowledges to himself

---

[5] This is a modified version of a case prepared by Professor Robert F. Ladenson. Used with permission.

that Shawn has been a fine friend in every respect that counts. Shawn has listened patiently to Kevin when he needed encouragement or advice, lent his car when Kevin's broke down, helped him move his belongings from one apartment to another, and put up Kevin's relatives when there was no room in Kevin's apartment. The friendship has not been one-sided, however. Kevin has provided similar kinds of support and encouragement.

Shawn has written a number of short stories and poems, and he has been working on his first novel for the past two years. Several weeks ago, he learned about a small house in a quiet semi-rural area that he believes would provide an ideal working environment. He asked Kevin to loan him $5,000 for the down payment on the house. Even though Kevin supports Shawn's literary endeavors, the request takes him by surprise, since monetary affairs have not played a significant role in their relationship.

Kevin works as a project manager for a large engineering firm and can afford to loan the money to Shawn, but he is not sure how Shawn can afford to repay the loan on his salary as manager of a small bookstore. Kevin does not feel that he has any strict obligation to loan Shawn the money, but he wonders what he will think of himself if he does not. Will he be the kind of "friend" he thinks he should be? How should he think about this issue?

Case 11: Taking Care of Your Own

Louise Lax, 25 years old and married for four years, has just discovered that she has a genetically based disease and that she has a 50 percent chance of passing it on to any offspring. She and her husband have not had any children, but they very much want to have a family, even if she is not alive to care for them until maturity. She wants to take the risk of having a child. However, the state has just passed a new law stating that if a woman gives birth to a defective child after learning that she or her husband is a carrier of this disease, the husband and wife must pay for the upkeep of the child. Such children cannot usually be cared for at home. If the parents cannot pay for the child's care, usually about $40,000 a year, the state will take over, but the parents will have part of their salary deducted to pay for the child's care. This arrangement will continue throughout the parents' lives until the debt is paid, even if the child dies. The Laxes argue that this arrangement is unfair and unjustly punishes them, just because they happen to be carriers of a disease. Would such a law be morally justifiable?

Case 12: Firecrackers in New York

The use of firecrackers is a prominent ritual in many traditional celebrations of the Chinese New Year.[6] For several years, however, the administration of New

---

[6] This is a modified version of a case prepared by Professor Robert F. Ladenson. Used with permission.

York City has refused to allow the setting off of firecrackers in Chinese New Year celebrations. Citing safety considerations, a spokesperson for the Mayor's office note an Associated Press report of a firecracker storage area in China that caught fire, resulting in the deaths of 47 people.

Opponents of the Mayor's policy say they simply want to be allowed to use firecrackers in specially designated areas under close city supervision They point out that such procedures are used in large public fireworks displays on the Fourth of July, which to their knowledge, has not resulted in any deaths or serious injuries. They also emphasize the enormous cultural significance for many of the Chinese people living in New York City of celebrating the Chinese New Year in a traditional manner that includes using firecrackers.

In February 1998, Mr. Wang Jian, a 28-year-old former U.S. Marine, set off a string of firecrackers on the steps of New York City's City Hall. Immediately thereafter, he walked down the steps and allowed himself to be handcuffed by police officers who arrested him. Mr. Wang faced up to a year in prison and a fine of $1,000. "I did it to make a political statement," said Mr. Wang. "I wanted the politicians to know that the Chinese will stand up for what they believe in."

Upon his release Mr. Wang received a hero's welcome from many residents of New York's Chinatown. Restaurant owners in New York's Chinatown offered Mr. Wang free meals, local businessmen offered to contribute money toward his legal defense, and even police officers showed deference to him.

Some members of the Chinese community in New York, however, were critical of Mr. Wang's action. Mr. Richard Hsueh, President of Chinese American Voice, a radio station in Flushing, expressed the opinion that Mr. Wang went too far in expressing his point. Mr. Wang said that before setting off the firecrackers on the steps of New York's City Hall, he made sure that the steps were empty. Was his action morally justified?

Case 13: E-Mail Exposure

Every e-mail system has a designated "postmaster," to whom undeliverable mail is forwarded. The postmaster is supposed to either send the mail (which might have an incorrect address) to the proper person or return it to the sender. In a business or governmental organization, the postmaster is usually a department head or other administrator. Although it is against the policies of most organizations in the state, postmasters sometimes read the messages before delivering or returning them.

A program has recently been invented that will automatically return undeliverable e-mail to the sender without forwarding it to a postmaster, so that the confidentiality of the messages is better protected. Unfortunately, the program is rather expensive and would be a considerable burden to small organizations. Many organizations would probably dispense with e-mail altogether before installing the software. Ben Rosen, a state legislator, is nevertheless proposing a law that would make installation of the program mandatory on all e-mail systems in the state. Would such a proposal be morally justifiable or even required?

Case 14: Compensation in Canada

In October 1999, the government of Canada agreed to pay $2.3 billion to 230,000 federal workers, both current and retired, in the form of back pay with interest, to conform with the principle of "equal pay for work of equal value" embodied in Canada's Human Rights Act.[7] The drafters of this law, enacted more than 20 years ago, noted that the vast majority of women in the workforce in Canada were clustered in a small number of "women's" jobs, such as office worker, nurse, or waitress.

Women in these jobs, the drafters noted, usually receive less pay than men in predominantly male jobs, which, despite their higher salaries, are comparable to the predominantly female jobs in terms of factors such as the mental or physical demands of the job, working conditions, or educational prerequisites. For example, a chief librarian made $35,050 while a dairy herd improvement manager made $38,766. A computer operations supervisor made $20,193, while a forestry project supervisor made $26,947. A typist made $10,531, while a sailor made $14,097. In all of these instances the predominantly female and the predominantly male jobs were determined to have comparable point levels.

The settlement has drawn strong criticism. Critics argue that the determinations of "equal" jobs is arbitrary and that it will increase taxes, already the highest in the Group of Seven industrialized nations. Defenders of the settlement argue that even if the lower wages for predominantly female jobs reflect going market salary rates, these rates themselves reflect pervasive discrimination against women in the workforce. Is the settlement morally justified?

Case 15: MP3 Files

MP3 audio files enable users to exchange compact disk recordings digitally over the Internet.[8] Music lovers use MP3s to search for rare recordings. People also can use them to copy an entire compact disk and transmit it to anyone at no cost. Recently the Recording Industry Association of America (RIAA) has undertaken a major effort to combat copyright violations. The RIAA sends letters to colleges and universities whenever its researchers discover on-campus servers offering copyrighted music. According to Frank Creighton, an RIAA Senior Vice President, the Association has found that about 70 percent of the infringing sites were on university campuses.

In the fall of 1999 network administrators at Carnegie Mellon University, without prior warning, checked the public folders of 250 student computers connected to the University's network, and found 71 students whose files

---

[7] This is a modified version of a case prepared by Professor Robert F. Ladenson. Used with permission.

[8] This is a modified version of a case prepared by Professor Robert F. Ladenson. Used with permission.

contained illegally copied MP3s. The students lost their in-room Internet connections for the rest of the semester, which meant they had to use a university computer lab to gain access to the Internet. All the students were given a right to appeal their penalties, and students who attended a 90-minute class on copyright had their penalties reduced by one month.

Under the Digital Millennium Act, which Congress passed in 1999, online service providers, such as universities, can avoid liability if they take certain steps specified in the Act. These include, in cases when the university has been informed of an infringement, shutting off access to the infringing material and notifying the user who posted it, so that he or she can take up the matter with the copyright holder.

Supporters of the Digital Millennium Act argue that theft of intellectual property is as wrong as any other type of theft. Is the law and its enforcement justified on college campuses?

Case 16: Selling Super-Kill

Super-Kill has been banned in this country, but Longwise Corporation still manufactures the product for overseas sales, especially to Third World countries. Critics point out that Super-Kill has been proven harmful to humans and the environment. They argue that it is morally wrong for Longwise to sell a product overseas that it knows is harmful and that in many cases may be sold to unsuspecting customers.

Longwise CEO Rayford Hamilton argues that Super-Kill is a very effective insecticide and can be manufactured much more cheaply than other products that could be sold to Third World countries. Many farmers can thus buy Super-Kill when they cannot afford alternative products. Furthermore, using the chemical does increase crop yields, thus reducing malnutrition and starvation. Hamilton argues that more good is produced in foreign countries by selling the DDT abroad than by not selling it, to say nothing of the good produced in this country by the increased jobs and profits. Finally, other countries are also manufacturing Super-Kill, and they will sell the product if Longwise does not. Should Longwise be prevented from selling Super-Kill overseas?

Case 17: Who Owns Them?

Country X, located in Latin America, has recently adopted a policy of strictly limiting the collection of biological specimens, both plant and animal, within its borders.[9] Under the new regulations individual scientists and companies must apply for permits that, in one case, cost $600,000 and can take more than three years to obtain. Formerly Country X had no policy in regard to collection of

---

[9] This is a modified version of a case prepared by Professor Robert F. Ladenson. Used with permission.

biological specimens for research by foreign scientists. During the 1950s and 1960s a major American drug company, using plants found in the jungles of Country X, developed two drugs that turned out to be effective for treating certain types of cancer. Country X did not share at all in the company's profit.

John R, a scientist with the National Institute of Health in Washington, D.C., believes that experimentation with another native plant of Country X could lead to a significant breakthrough in treatment of other kinds of cancers. He has been waiting for Country X to process his permit application for two and a half years now, and fears the plant may become extinct by the time he obtains permission to collect it.

Other nations, which, like Country X, historically did not restrain the collecting of biological specimens within their borders, have begun to impose restrictions. One driving factor in this regard is the perception of many nations that genetic engineering has significantly increased the potential for commercial use of genes. For example, researchers at the University of Wisconsin have isolated a substance 2,000 times sweeter than sugar from a West African berry. If a table sweetener is developed from this substance it would be produced, in all likelihood, in genetically modified bacteria, which would eliminate the need to use the berry. Another driving factor in the new restrictive policies of several nations is the patenting of genetically modified plants and animals in the United States, which has been allowed since 1980 under a major decision of the U.S. Supreme Court. Some nations take the stance that if, for example, a company genetically engineers a seed taken from a farmer's field, patents the engineered seed, and makes a profit, then, in all fairness, the company should pay substantially for the original seed.

Critics of the attempts of countries to exert control over the biological specimens in their country complain that the present rules adopted in many countries are much too restrictive and that some countries overestimate the value of their raw genetic resources. Citizens of these countries also underestimate the cost of developing a product from this raw material. They point out that in developing a drug or other product, a company may have to spend as much as $500 million. Are countries justified in exerting control over their biological specimens in their country? What limits should there be on these controls?

Case 18: A Plant Closing

American Textile and National Textile have recently merged. Managers of the new conglomerate have decided to close several of the most inefficient plants, and their attention has naturally turned to the Hoppersville operation. A mainstay in the local community for more than 75 years, the plant is hopelessly outdated. It is not only less efficient than the newer plants, but the older equipment also poses many more hazards for workers. The older machines produce more noise and are less safe to operate. They also throw off a lot of particles that produce much lower air quality than can be achieved in the newer plants.

Employees of the plant, 50 percent of whom are within seven years of retirement, have organized to protest any plans to close the plant. They argue that the plant still generates a profit, even though not as great a profit as some of the newer facilities do. Employees know that the plant cannot be economically brought up to state-of-the-art manufacturing, but they are willing to work under present conditions. They argue that the company has an obligation to the employees and the community to keep the plant open, at least for another decade, when most of the longtime employees will have reached retirement age. What should the managers do?

Case 19: Carrying Ideas from Company A to Company B

While an employee of Company A, Joel Morelli developed a computer program that he thought would enable a firm to keep track of large inventories more efficiently. It turned out that the program was not as useful as Morelli had thought, and the company never marketed the product or patented it. Company A was a small firm that had close but informal relations with its employees, so that it did not require its employees to sign an agreement that employees must not take "intellectual property" developed at company A to a new employer.

Two years later, Morelli moved to company B. He quickly found that a modification of the program he had developed at company A would enable company B to keep track of its own inventory more effectively than any other program, so he began using it in his own work. Company B does not intend to market the product. Was Morelli's action "theft"? Was it wrong?

Case 20: Executive Compensation

Chief executive officers in American companies earn 160 times more than the average American employee, whereas similar executives in Japanese companies earn only 16 times more than the average Japanese employee.[10] The American executives might argue that these salaries are justified to attract qualified people to the high-stress positions. "If highly qualified people occupy these positions," the argument goes, "everyone will benefit: even the lowest-paid worker will be better off than he or she would be otherwise, because there will be more and better-paying jobs." Others argue that corporations have the moral right to allocate the resources as they wish, and so there is no moral problem, even if the previously mentioned claim is invalid. What are the moral and factual issues in the debate over justified executive salaries?

Case 21: Billing for Medical Services

Physicians can "fudge" on insurance claims in various ways. For example, physicians can code the removal of a mole as a larger procedure ("upcoding") or break down surgeries into smaller procedures and charge for each procedure individually.

---

[10] Jill Abramson and Christopher J. Chipello, "High Pay of CEO's Traveling with Bush Touches a Nerve in Asia," *Wall Street Journal*, December 30, 1991, p. A1.

Often these practices are clear cases of insurance fraud, but sometimes the considerations are more complex.

Sophia Jackson has been Dr. Kaufmann's patient for more than 25 years. Her financial situation is precarious, but she comes in regularly for removal of moles. Ordinary mole removals are not covered by her health insurance, but they are covered if they are coded as necessary to "rule out cancer." Kaufmann does not believe the moles he has removed during the past year were cancerous, but he also knows that Jackson worries about them incessantly. To relieve her of anxiety and not jeopardize her finances, he routinely "upcodes" the procedures as necessary to "rule out cancer." Is this ethically permissible?

Case 22: Bloggers and Media Responsibility

On September 8, 2004, Dan Rather produced documents on an episode of 60 Minutes II that purported to prove that then-President G. W. Bush was a "slacker" who used his dad's influence to avoid military service in the early 1970s. Several days later, Rather and CBS admitted that the documents had not been authenticated and were, in fact, fakes. Within three months of the incident, Rather announced that he was resigning from his CBS News anchor post, a position he had held for 24 years.

On January 27, 2005, CNN's chief news executive, Eason Jordan, was alleged to have remarked at a conference that U.S. soldiers were targeting journalists in Iraq. Within two weeks, Jordan resigned from his job of 23 years.

A relatively new technology—weblog publishing (or "blogging")—has been cited as one of the primary causes of the resignation of these prominent newsmen. Blogging (publishing news and opinions using a personal computer) has become a prominent and powerful force in our society. The inexpensive and easy-to-use technology has enabled thousands of individuals to publish their thoughts online and be read worldwide. Often, numerous bloggers will assemble around a common cause and use their collective voice to raise public awareness of an issue or push for change. In the above instances, a significant number of bloggers, disturbed by the apparent carelessness of Rather and Jordan, instigated an online campaign calling for them to resign. Many believe that this campaign was a significant factor in both resignations.

The value of blogging is controversial. On the one hand, the advent of blogging technology has the potential to positively affect the quality of news reporting. Ambitious and resourceful bloggers are able to check the facts reported by the mainstream media and hold journalists accountable for the stories they report. The threat of public condemnation is enough to cause journalists to think twice when reporting controversial news, making sure to substantiate their stories. The benefits to the public are increased accuracy in news reporting and the exposure of fraudulent reporting.

On the other hand, blogging also has negative potential. To begin with, bloggers are themselves unaccountable; the worst that can happen to bloggers who falsely report news items or broadcast controversial or false opinions is that they will lose readership. In addition, there are no qualifications to become a blogger; anyone can become a news blogger, even people who are not trained as journalists or have no expertise in any of the fields on which they report. Finally, bloggers do not have the same extensive fact-gathering resources available to paid journalists; hence, their reporting may be less than fully informed. The potential consequences of blogger influence are the ruined careers of respected journalists and the dissemination of poorly informed opinions. Given these potential benefits and consequences, should attempts be made to restrict blogger influence or hold bloggers accountable for their reporting? Would such actions be morally justified? Are bloggers justified in holding professional journalists to account?

Case 23: Dissent and Repression

The 2004 Republican National Convention was supposed to be a pivotal moment in George W. Bush's campaign for re-election. In the months leading up to the convention, Bush found himself in a tight race with rival Sen. John Kerry. He had suffered several damaging political losses over his foreign policy initiatives, and polls showed that popular support for the incumbent was waning among American voters. Further, the country was becoming increasingly divided over the American invasion of Iraq and the ongoing conflict with Iraqi insurgents. To keep the country unified and to show support for the American troops in Iraq and Afghanistan, Bush knew it would be important to present a positive message at the RNC.

However, many Americans opposed Bush's Iraq policy, in addition to a number of his domestic policies, including those on Social Security and taxation. Thus, the convention was likely to attract many protests. These protests could not only damage the public's perception of Bush, but they also had the potential to divide the country further during a time of war, just as had happened at the time of the 1968 presidential election during the Vietnam War.

During the convention, many protestors were arrested by New York City police on charges of "disturbing the peace" or "hindering governmental operations." However, not only were protestors arrested; several innocent bystanders were also detained. Many were taken to a place called Pier 57 in Manhattan along the Hudson River, which was leased during the convention by the Republican National Committee. Pier 57 was once a garage for buses, but during the convention, it became a detention center for political dissidents. Detainees were reportedly held without charge or access to lawyers or medical attention. The building was contaminated with asbestos and chemical spills and there were signs warning entrants to wear face masks. Numerous detainees reported having to sleep on an oil-stained concrete floor, and many contracted skin rashes. The message was clear: at a time when the country needed unity, dissent would not be tolerated.

Is dissent ever morally unjustified? Is drepression of dissent ever morally justified? To what extent should the individual's right to freedom of speech be given priority over the common good?

Case 24: Google Print and Copyright Infringement

In October 2004, Google announced the launch of an ambitious project called Google Print. The project aims to make the complete text of all the books in the world fully searchable using digital indexing technology. To further this goal, Google has contracted with five of the world's greatest libraries to scan and digitize their entire collections. The project, says product manager Adam Smith, will enable publishers "to introduce their work to countless readers around the world...We are really excited about...the good it will do for the world."

However, the project is not without its critics, many of whom feel that scanning copyrighted books and making them available to view free of charge violates copyright laws. To alleviate this concern, Google has taken several steps. First, it has stated that, while all pages of a book will be searchable, not all pages will be able to be read by users. The number of pages available to read will be determined by the book's copyright status. Further, additional pages will only be made available at the request of the publisher. Finally, the publisher has the option of contacting Google and notifying them that they would like to exempt certain books from the scanning process. However, if the publisher does not contact Google, Google will go ahead and scan the books found on the shelves of the five libraries.

Despite Google's attempt to respect the rights of copyright holders, some still object to the project. One major complaint has been that Google has shifted the burden of responsibility to avoid copyright infringement from the user to the copyright holder. "We think they have to stop this entirely," said Patricia Schroeder, president of the Association of American Publishers.[11] "Google's procedure shifts the responsibility for preventing infringement to the copyright owner rather than the user, turning every principle of copyright law on its ear."[12] But Google's Adam Smith claims that the project is "legal under the principles of fair use" because it only permits users to read books in their entirety if the copyright has expired or if the publisher agrees to make the full text available to read online.[13]

There are certainly arguments in support of Google's project. First, Google Print will make information available to people who might not otherwise be able to access this information, which would enable people to gain necessary knowledge and create a more educated population. Second, the digital index will make it much easier for people to find relevant sources based on word searches, which will increase the speed with which research can be conducted. Third, Google claims that the project will enable publishers to track market value of a book according to the number of times a book is viewed by users. This would enable

---

[11] Yuki Noguchi, "Google Delays Book Scanning," *Washington Post*, August 13, 2005.

[12] Margaret Kane, "Google Pauses Library Project," CNET News.com, August 12, 2005, http://news.com.com/Google+pauses+library+project/2100-1025_3-5830035.html.

[13] Eric Auchard, "Google Pauses on Book Search After Copyright Flap," Reuters, August 12, 2005.

publishers to better service their market according to the needs of consumers. Finally, Google has said that publishers will be able to advertise their product on the search program, as well as link users to other sites where users will readily be able to purchase their books, thereby increasing their revenue.

There are also arguments against the Google project. First, by making copyright works available for viewing, Google Print could create a disincentive to buy books, for many books will be available free of charge online. Second, by copying books without the explicit authorization of copyright holders, Google Print could undermine the institution of copyright law. A compromised copyright law would certainly inhibit the process of creating new copyright works, because writers could not be certain that they will be rewarded for their work.

Is Google morally justified in creating digital copies of copyright works and making them available to users free of charge?

Case 25: Judith Miller and Freedom of the Press

On July 7, 2005, *New York Times* reporter Judith Miller was sent to jail to serve out a sentence for contempt of court. Miller was charged with civil contempt for refusing to testify before a federal grand jury investigating a leak naming Valerie Plame as a covert CIA agent. The Plame affair began nearly 2 years earlier, when former U.S. ambassador Joseph Wilson wrote an op-ed in the *New York Times* criticizing President Bush and the Iraq War. To discredit Wilson, a federal official informed several reporters that Wilson's wife, Valerie Plame, was a covert CIA operative. Miller was one of the reporters who received the information, but she never printed a story on the matter at the time. Revelation of the leak sparked a federal investigation into the identity of the informant. Miller was subpoenaed to testify before a grand jury, but refused to identify the informant. According to Miller, "If journalists cannot be trusted to keep confidences, then journalists cannot function and there cannot be a free press."

This case highlights an acute tension pertaining to freedom of the press. On the one hand, a free press is an important means to uncovering corruption in high places, such as powerful corporations or among government officials. In many instances, exposing government or corporate wrongdoing requires an inside informant. However, if journalists are known to expose their informants, few whistle-blowers would be willing to come forward. Thus, generally speaking, it is socially beneficial for journalists to keep their confidences so that the threat of public exposure inhibits high level corruption.

On the other hand, the wrongdoing in this instance was leaking the information, which made the federal official who was the informant a criminal. Under Section 421 of the Intelligence Identities Protection Act, "Whoever...intentionally discloses any information identifying [a] covert agent to any individual not authorized to receive classified information" is subject to prosecution under the law. Thus, if Miller testified to the identity of the informant, she would be exposing governmental corruption.

Miller faced a dilemma: protect her source and ensure her ability to gain the confidence of future inside sources, thereby enabling her to uncover future scandals, or identify her source and expose government wrongdoing now but forfeit her ability to gain the confidence of informants in the future. Which action is the more morally justified? When should the freedom of the press to protect anonymous sources be infringed?

Case 26: Religion, Society, and Same-Sex Marriage

Since 2002, same-sex marriage has been a controversial issue in the United States, and it was a significant issue between Sen. John Kerry and George W. Bush during the 2004 U.S. Presidential Election. Indeed, many attribute Bush's victory in 2004 to his ability to gain the support of a large number of social conservatives, in part because of his opposition to same-sex marriage legislation.

Many commentators on the issue believe that the debate hinges on the basis of the definition of "marriage." Supporters of same-sex marriage tend to define marriage as a legal contract. There are 1,049 laws in which "rights, benefits, and privileges" are tied to marital status.[14] Thus, marriage entitles citizens to a variety of civil benefits to which persons as equals are equally entitled. Further, the 14th Amendment includes an equal protection clause, which provides people equal protection of the laws. Thus, if marriage is a civil right, to deny people the right to marry because of sexual orientation is to deny them equality under the law.

Opponents of same-sex marriage, often conservative Christians, tend to define marriage in religious terms, as the union of a man and a woman sanctioned by God. Many argue that same-sex marriage defies this traditional definition of marriage, in addition to sanctioning an "aberrant" or "immoral" sexual relationship. Further, they argue that same-sex marriage will lead to the breakdown of the family, which is upheld as the primary social unit. However, those who support same-sex rights argue that the Christian perspective should not be included in the debate about the definition of marriage since the United States upholds the principle of the separation of church and state.

Is marriage simply a civil right, or is the state morally justified in denying same-sex marriage rights based on religious reasons? Does the separation of church and state require that religious beliefs be left out during public debate about moral issues? Does it require religious people to remain politically inactive?

Case 27: Religious Freedom and Public Education in France

On October 20, 2004, two French Muslim schoolgirls—Dounia and Khouloude-were—were expelled from a school in Mulhouse, Alsace, for refusing to remove

---

[14] United States General Accounting Office, http://www.gao.gov/archive/1997/og97016.pdf

their traditional headscarves. The expulsion was the result of the newly enacted "French law on secularity and conspicuous religious symbols in schools," which took effect on September 2, 2004. The law is an amendment to the French Code of Education and is supposed to expand upon the principles of the separation of state and religious activities by prohibiting students from "the wearing of signs or behaviours by which the pupils express openly a religious membership."[15]

Although the law has received significant support from the majority of the French population, it has been highly controversial, particularly among French Muslims. Many Muslims believeve that the law infringes upon France's constitutional provision for freedom of opinion and conscience, in addition to discriminating against Muslims.

There are several reasons in support of the law. Many cite gender equality as a primary reason, claiming that many Muslim females are pressured into wearing the headscarf and do not freely choose to wear it. In addition, the law further enforces the separation of state and religion. Finally, although not explicitly stated, many point to the rise in Muslim extremism as a primary reason for the creation of the law. If this is the case, then the law has more to do with political order than freedom of conscience.

For Khouloudewere, the expulsion order "destroyed [her] life."[16] For her, wearing a headscarf was a free choice and an expression of faith protected by the French constitution. In response to the law, she was quoted as saying, "What they want is to see us in tight pants like all the girls."[17] The law placed her in the position where she was forced to choose between two things she believed to be important: her education and her faith.

Is the law morally justified? Should the value of political order be placed above one's freedom of conscience? Was the expulsion order morally justified? Were Khouloudewere's and Dounia's refusal to obey the law morally justified?

Case 28: Right to Health Care Provision vs. the Right to Refuse

In recent years, some pharmacists have refused to fill prescriptions for contraceptives for unmarried women or for the so-called "morning after" pill. Their refusals have been based on their desire not to support or promote either sex between unmarried partners or, in the case of the "morning after" pilll, something they believe tantamount to abortion. These refusals have been reported from states such as Texas, Missouri, California, and New Hampshire. Such incidents

---

[15] Law 2004-228 of March 15, 2004, http://translate.google.com/translate?u=http%3A%2F%2F www.legifrance.gouv.fr%2FWAspad%2FUnTexteDeJorf%3Fnumjo%3DMENX0400001L&langpair=fr%7Cen&hl=en&safe=off&c2coff=1&ie=UTF-8&oe=UTF-8&prev=%2Flanguage_tools

[16] Elaine Ganley, "France Expelling Students Who Defy Law Banning Religious Signs," Associated Press, October 22, 2004.

[17] Ibid.

have been highly controversial, pitting the personal morality of pharmacists against their professional obligation to serve the public.

Conflicts between the personal morality of professionals and their professional obligations to the public arise in other professions as well. Physicians may not want to perform abortions or to prescribe contraceptives for unmarried women or participate in physician-assisted suicide where it is legal. Attorneys may have personal moral objections to defending some clients. The situation is especially acute when no other professional is available to serve the client or when time is at a premium, as in the "morning after" pill, which must be taken very soon aftaer a possible conception. In addition, contraceptives are sometimes needed for reasons other than escaping the consequences of extramarital intercourse. Thus, a pharmacist's judgment may be misguided.

Recently several states have become involved in the controversy. Several state legislatures are considering bills that protect the rights of pharmacists to refuse to fill prescriptions, while others are considering bills that would mandate that pharmacists fill any valid prescription without question. Are pharmacists morally justified in refusing medical care for personal moral reasons?

Case 29: Stem Cell Research

On August 11, 2001, President George W. Bush announced that federal funding for stem cell research would be restricted to research on existing lines of stem cells, thereby eliminating funding for the creation of new lines of cells. Since that announcement, the President and the U.S. Congress have been in a struggle to determine where the line should be drawn with regard to public support for stem cell research. In April 2004, 206 members of Congress—including some Republicans—signed a letter asking the president to relax restrictions on stem cell research. In May 2005, despite the president's threat to veto the legislation, the House of Representatives voted 238–194 to permit the use of surplus embryos from in-vitro fertilization clinics to be used in stem cell research with donor permission. One major reason for Congress' support of stem cell research is the promise of treating over 100 diseases by using stem cells, including blindness, diabetes, Parkinson's disease, and sickle cell anemia.

The major source of debate derives from the need to destroy the blastocyst (5–7-day-old embryo) in order to "harvest" stem cells for research purposes. Stem cells are undifferentiated cells that have the capacity to differentiate into other cell types. This enables stem cells to be used to replenish other cells so long as the body is alive, as well as repair specific tissue or grow organs. Stem cells can be derived from undifferentiated cells in adult tissue; however, these stem cells do not have the same regenerative potential as embryonic stem cells. Stem cells are extracted from the blastocyst when the cluster of stem cells numbers 100–150.

Many who oppose stem cell research equate the procedure with abortion, believing the blastocyst is a human and thereby a holder of human rights. According to this line of argument, the destruction of the blastocyst violates its right to life. In addition, some are opposed to the creation of blastocysts in the laboratory for the express purpose of harvesting stem cells, arguing that this reduces genetically human entities to the status of means to an end rather than ends in themselves. This argument appeals to the deeply held belief of some citizens in the right to life.

The counterargument lies in pointing out that, biologically speaking, blastocysts are not individual persons. At five days old, blastocysts are still at a stage when they can divide to become identical twins or converge to become a chimera, i.e., an individual with two different genetic makeups. Further, blastocysts have no functional systems of any kind, whether they be respiratory, circulatory, or nervous. In fact, blastocysts have nothing but undifferentiated cell tissue. Certainly they are neither conscious nor self-aware.

Even if blastocysts are held to possess rights, proponents of stem cell research point to the amount of human suffering that could be alleviated as a result of the research. Thus, the stem cell research debate places the rights of the blastocysts (if any) in conflict with the right to life and the right to health care of living persons who suffer from diseases that might be successfully treated by stem cell treatment.

Can stem cell research be morally justified?

Case 30: *The Morality of Preventive War*

On March 20, 2003, the United States launched Operation Iraqi Freedom, invading Iraq without direct or explicit military provocation and without the explicit approval of the United Nations Security Council. To justify the invasion, Bush administration officials called it a preemptive strike. Its purpose was to respond to the possibility of an Iraqi attack upon American interests. The stated reasons for the invasion were several: to collect information on and eliminate weapons of mass destruction (WMD) programs and terrorist groups in Iraq; to end the UN sanctions on Iraq and deliver humanitarian aid to Iraqis; to end the Saddam Hussein regime and aid Iraq in the transition to democracy; and to make secure Iraq's oil fields as well as other resources.

"Preemptive" is a legal term applied to military initiatives aimed at averting an imminent military threat. In this case, Operation Iraqi Freedom was aimed at averting the possibility of an Iraqi military threat. At the time of invasion, U.S. officials conceded that Iraq posed no direct and impending military threat to American interests. Rather, they stated that Iraq posed a possible threat in three ways: (1) Iraqi missiles were positioned to threaten the United States, in violation of the cease-fire agreement signed after the 1991 Gulf War; (2) Iraqi biological and chemical weapons were ready for use and could possibly be given to terrorist groups who threatened the United States; and (3) Iraq might one day develop nuclear weapons. U.S. authorities believed that the potentially disastrous consequences of failing to address these possibilities was sufficient to warrant the use of military force against Iraq. In light of these considerations, many believe that "preventive war" is a more appropriate term than "preemptive war" to describe the U.S. invasion of Iraq.

While preventive war has the advantage of possibly providing greater security from potentially dangerous military threats, it also has many regrettable aspects. First, many argue it is illegal under international law. Article 2, number 4 of the UN Charter (a charter ratified by the United States) states that member states must refrain from any use of force other than for self-defense; any force used for purposes other than self-defense is considered aggression. Any use of aggressive force requires explicit approval of the UN Security Council under Article 42 of the Charter. Accordingly, preventive war is plausibly classified as a war of aggression under international law. Second, preventive war sets a dangerous precedent for future military ventures. If deemed acceptable, it extends the scope of permissible force to include wars initiated based solely upon suspicion of a threat, since "possible threat" can be interpreted quite broadly. This would allow a nation to use military force against states that refuse to cooperate with or endorse its interests, justifying the use of force as "preventive" in nature. Finally, if preventive war becomes accepted practice, it may prompt nations to use force as more than a last resort in international relations and potentially cause an escalation in armed conflict.

Was the United States morally justified in invading Iraq in March 2003? Can preventive war in general be morally justified?

Case 31: *Torture and Intelligence*

In response to the attacks on the United States on September 11, 2001, President George W. Bush initiated a campaign to end global terrorism. Bush called the campaign the "War on Terror," declaring that "[i]t will not end until every terrorist group of global reach has been found, stopped and defeated."[18] Since this declaration (as of July 2005), the United States has invaded Afghanistan (October 2001) and Iraq (March 2003) in an effort to accomplish this objective.

To further this objective, the United States has taken captive many people suspected to be involved in terrorist activities. A majority of those detained by the United States are being held in military prisons at Guantanamo Bay, Cuba, and at Abu Ghraib in Iraq. One important reason for detaining suspects is to obtain information that may be helpful in preventing future terrorist acts and eradicating terrorist groups. Since terrorist acts are most often carried out by highly secretive groups, the most helpful information is likely to be obtained from those who are associated with terrorist groups. Such information may prevent thousands of innocent deaths caused by terrorist attacks.

However, it is unlikely that detained suspects will simply volunteer the information they hold. Thus, the United States must resort to interrogation tactics to extract the intelligence from the detainees. In an article dated April 30, 2004, Seymour Hersh reported to the public that the interrogation tactics used at the Abu Ghraib military prison were abusive and that detainees were tortured to

---

[18] http://www.whitehouse.gov/news/releases/2001/09/20010920-8.html

extract information.[19] Hersh's report was corroborated by eyewitness testimony from prison guards. In addition, reports alleging abuse at Guantanamo Bay were filed in August 2004 by detainees released to Britain. These reports were supported by the findings of an investigation by the International Committee of the Red Cross which were printed in July 2004. Some of the interrogation tactics reported to be used at Abu Ghraib and Guantanamo Bay include physical beatings, intimidation by dogs, prolonged use of stress positions, sexual and cultural humiliation, and forced injections. All of these tactics are prohibited under international law.

Can torture of a few be morally justified if it helps prevent future terrorist attacks on many others? Can the human rights of individuals be violated to protect the rights of others? Do the ends justify the means in cases such as this one?

Case 32: Ward Churchill and Academic Freedom

In an essay entitled, "Some People Push Back: On the Justice of Roosting Chickens," University of Colorado professor Ward Churchill argued that many who worked in the World Trade Center were part of "a technocratic corps at the very heart of America's global financial empire" and were the equivalent of "little Eichmanns."[20] In January 2005, Bill O'Reilly, host of the FOX News show *The O'Reilly Factor*, quoted parts of Churchill's essay and suggested that his viewers email Hamilton College in New York, asking the college to cancel Churchill's invitation to lecture there. Subsequent to the segment, Churchill became the center of a nationwide controversy and many labeled him an "anti-American" and a "terrorist-supporter."

The controversy brought the issue of academic freedom into the nation's attention once again. Churchill's detractors argued that he had "gone to far," that his writings were "treasonous," and that students shouldn't have to be exposed to his teachings. Colorado, Governor Bill Owens called for Churchill's dismissal from the University of Colorado and the University's Board of Regents initiated an investigation into his work. However, the University of Colorado does have policies protecting the academic freedom of its faculty. According to these policies, "The faculty member is entitled to freedom in the classroom in discussion [of] the subject, but should be careful not to introduce into teaching controversial matter that has no relation to the subject," and further, "When speaking or writing as citizens, [faculty] should be free from university censorship or discipline."[21] Many have argued that the content of Churchill's essay is clearly within the bounds of his expertise—ethnic studies. If this is the case, then the essay would

---

[19] http://www.newyorker.com/fact/content/?040510fa_fact

[20] Ward Churchill, "Some People Push Back: On the Justice of Roosting Chickens," http://www.kers plebedeb.com/mystuff/s11/churchill.html

[21] Richard T. DeGeorge, "Academic Freedom Under Attack," *The Bryan-College Station Eagle*, May 20, 2005.

be protected under the university's academic freedom policies. Further, the University of Colorado's Standing Committee on Research Committee found that Churchill's remarks were protected by the First Amendment of the U.S. Constitution.

Are the attempts to remove Churchill from his academic post morally justified? Is it morally justifiable to limit academic freedom? Are there moral reasons to protect academic freedom?

Case 33: Women in Combat

The matter of women in combat has been controversial for a number of years, but since at least 2003, it has gained particular prominence in American public debate due to two issues, among others: the capture and rescue of Jessica Lynch in April 2003 and the decline in American military recruitment.

Opponents of placing women in a combat situation tend to argue their case from a utilitarian perspective, citing a number of considerations meant to demonstrate that women in combat detracts from the greater good of society. Opponents note that women will be particularly vulnerable to rape on the battlefield, especially if captured by the enemy. Also, women are likely to be a sexual distraction for male soldiers, perhaps even becoming victims of sexual harassment, thereby inhibiting the performance of a largely male military and jeopardizing the accomplishment of the military's objective. Further, it is argued that male soldiers might take foolish risks to defend or rescue women soldiers, thus unnecessarily endangering their own lives. Finally, opponents argue that women generally have less upper body strength than men, making them a potential liability on the battlefield. (Of course, these arguments are subject to scrutiny, and many of them may be inaccurate in their portrayal of the risks posed by women in combat.)

Proponents of women in combat tend to argue that excluding women from combat infringes upon their civil rights. To begin with, some argue that excluding women from combat inhibits them from pursuing their desired career and that employment discrimination based on gender is prohibited by the 14th Amendment. Further, some claim that the principle of gender equality entails that women should have equal opportunity to contribute to the defense and security of their country. Finally, it is argued that resistance to women in combat is likely to further entrench sexist attitudes among a large segment of the American population, thereby implicitly creating a gender-biased environment.

Is it morally justifiable to subordinate women's rights to the "greater good," which is, according to some, better served by excluding women from combat status?

Index